Biography – Dr. M A Ramphele

D R. MAMPHELA ALETTA RAMPHELE has been a student activist, a medical doctor, a community development activist, a researcher, a university executive, a global public servant and is now an active citizen in both the public and private sectors.

Following the Soweto uprising in 1976, she was detained without trial, released after five months and soon afterwards served with an apartheid banning order. She studied Medicine at the then University of Natal, has a B.Comm degree, a Diploma in Tropical Hygiene, a Diploma in Public Health and a PhD in Social Anthropology. She went on to become Vice-Chancellor of UCT, then one of four managing directors of the World Bank, based in Washington, DC.

Dr Ramphele is the author of several books and publications on socio-economic issues in South Africa. She has received numerous national and international awards acknowledging her scholarship and leading role in spearheading projects for disadvantaged people in South Africa and elsewhere.

Dr Ramphele has served as chairperson of Gold Fields, Circle Capital Ventures (Pty) Limited, Technology Innovation Agency (TIA), as a director of Medi-Clinic Corporation Limited and Remgro Limited and is currently a trustee of the Nelson Mandela Foundation. She was founder of the Open Society Foundation for South Africa and the Citizens Movement.

In January 2013, Dr. Ramphele became the leader of Agang SA, a party for all South Africans which won two seats in the national elections held in May 2014. Post elections, Dr Ramphele retired from party politics to return to her role as an active citizen.

MAMPHELA RAMPHELE
My Life
A Passion for FREEDOM

I.B. TAURIS

LONDON · NEW YORK

To my late parents, my sons
and my grandchildren

Published in 2014 by I.B.Tauris & Co. Ltd
6 Salem Road, London W2 4BU
175 Fifth Avenue, New York NY 10010
www.ibtauris.com

Distributed in the United States and Canada exclusively by
Palgrave Macmillan, 175 Fifth Avenue, New York NY 10010

Published by agreement with NB Publishers, a division of Media24 Boeke (Pty) Ltd.
Originally published by Tafelberg, an imprint of NB Publishers, Cape Town,
South Africa in 2013.

ISBN: 978 1 78453 042 6
eISBN: 978 0 85773 779 3

A full CIP record for this book is available from the British Library
A full CIP record is available from the Library of Congress
Library of Congress catalog card: available

Printed and bound in Great Britain by Page Bros, Norwich.

Contents

Preface 7

1 One hot afternoon in December 11
2 Moeng etla ka gešo, re je ka wena 21
3 The notion of home 32
4 boSofasonke 46
5 School, the institution 52
6 Matriculation is not a mattress 66
7 The death of my father 72
8 Initiation into activism 79
9 Frank Talk and Black Consciousness 86
10 Personal relationships 102
11 '. . . ours is to accept and bear the pain' 115
12 Community life in King 127
13 A huge historical burden 143
14 Detention 152
15 'Well, Dr Ramphele, goodbye, you bitch!' 162
16 A brief interlude 167
17 That fateful day – 12 September 1977 177
18 A matter of survival 193
19 Forging an independent lifestyle 206
20 Cape Town 212
21 As mother and professional 228

22 When the engine stopped   243
23 Smelling the flowers   251
24 The pain of loss   258
25 Stretching across boundaries   263
26 In my wildest dreams   270
27 If you had all the cards on your side   280
28 A woman in a hurry   288
29 The VC years   295
30 Funding the changes   302
31 Moving on   309
32 An exit strategy   316
33 Being an active citizen   323
34 Mobilising against the fear   329
35 Agang   334

By the same author   341

Index   343

Preface

ONE IS ALWAYS AMBIVALENT ABOUT TELLING ONE'S STORY. Critics may charge that one is being self-seeking or ask whether one is as true to one's demons as to one's angels. The issue of selective memory also rears its head: it is so easy to rewrite history for one's own benefit.

Among those who originally inspired me to tell my story was Mrs Albertina Sisulu. She has said: 'We are required to walk our own road – and then stop, assess what we have learned and share it with others. It is only in this way that the next generation can learn from those who have walked before them . . . We can do no more than tell our story. They must do with it what they will.'[1]

Storytelling is a historical imperative. We cannot successfully navigate uncharted waters without some script to guide us. This is particularly so for women, especially black women. Women have to find a script, a narrative to live by, because all other scripts are likely to depict them in roles that fit the conventional stereotypes.

Storytelling is also an urgent project for black women in South Africa where so much forgetfulness is willed upon people. It is much more convenient to forget the past than to recall its ugly face. Today hardly anyone is willing to acknowledge the support once given to the iniquitous system of apartheid, which caused so much pain to so many.

---

1   C. Villa-Vicencio, *The Spirit of Hope* (Johannesburg, 1993), p. 259.

With the formal death of apartheid, its former supporters have disappeared.

All the same, the temerity of writing one's biography still needs to be explained. It is a foolish act by any description. Why should one make oneself so vulnerable? There are mitigating factors for this foolish act. I believe that growing up under apartheid promoted premature ageing. One's childhood, adolescence and young adulthood were knocked out of one very rudely. One either grew up and survived, or was destroyed along the way.

I have other inspirations for my storytelling. The important women in my life have shaped my life through texts that have come my way in the form of praise poetry (some of which is captured in my narrative). They chanted and ululated at occasions where celebration was called for, and also had the courage to sing the praises of fallen heroes. I cannot match their elegance, but in transforming their stories into the written word, I am paying my dues for the rich milk I drank from them.

I have other more pressing reasons to tell my story. It is a story of loss. The many losses I have suffered in my short lifespan have forced me into greater self-reflection. Other people's stories have also aided my own personal growth and made me more conscious of the interconnectedness of pain and human suffering. The loss of country, the loss of innocence, of space for creativity, personal freedom and one's loved ones are important themes in this book. Storytelling is part of the struggle to transcend loss. This struggle for transcendence is a major theme of my narrative, as well as a historical imperative for our deeply wounded society. The past cannot be undone: it has to be transcended.

I must also acknowledge my hope that if I make myself vulnerable in this narrative there will be less reason for women in general to be seen as 'transgressives'. If this story helps to make women feel good about who they are, and turns what is seen as abnormal for women into everyday practice, then I would have managed to intimate another possible female destiny[2] – a destiny worth living and dying for. But greater will be my joy when the sons and daughters of South Africa see this alternative female destiny as mainstream and desirable. Only then shall we be truly free to reach for the sky.

2 C. Heilbrun, *Writing a Woman's Life* (New York, 1988).

RAMPHELE AND MAHLAELA FAMILY TREES

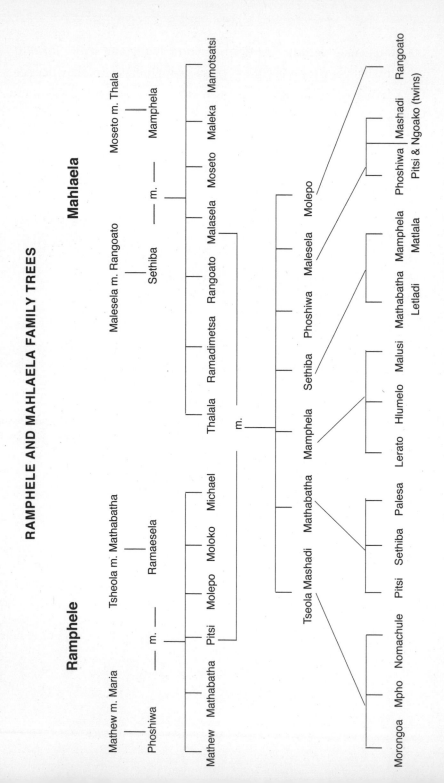

Ramphele

Mahlaela

One hot afternoon in December

HELEN FRANTZ HOSPITAL IN THE BOCHUM DISTRICT OF what was then northern Transvaal – now Limpopo Province – was a desolate set of buildings, most of which are hidden from the lazy gaze of passing motorists by thornbush. A lethargic stream which more often than not struggled to justify its status because of the perennial droughts, trickled across the road under a narrow bridge, a few metres from the hospital. It was here that I was born at two o'clock on the afternoon of 28 December 1947, having inconvenienced my mother in no small measure.

A pregnancy in the summer heat was no small feat. The Bochum district has a harsh climate and only hardy species survive. The vegetation tells the story of repeated long droughts. Sparse thornbush and an abundance of morula trees cover the flat countryside, and villages provide the only relief from the monotony of the landscape, which stretches all the way towards the Botswana border. There is hardly a wild animal that thrives there: only occasionally would one see a frightened hare scurry across the gravel road at night. Temperatures range from the upper thirties at the height of summer to the lower teens in mid-winter. Late December and January present the greatest challenges.

My mother had more than simply the burden of pregnancy to deal with. For a woman to be able to deliver in Helen Frantz Hospital during those days of poor transport and communication, she had to book in as an expectant mother and manage under difficult conditions, catering for herself in the antenatal section for a few weeks until she went into labour. My mother had to forgo Christmas celebrations to ensure the safe delivery in hospital of her third child.

Both my parents were primary school teachers – a position of relative privilege in their social environment at the time, which placed me in a better position to survive and thrive than most of my contemporaries. My mother had no reason to anticipate the problems which lay ahead. The midwife who attended to her at my birth was, according to my mother, most unhelpful. She disparaged any request from my mother for help during labour as the cry of a spoilt schoolteacher seeking special attention. As a result my mother delivered me without any assistance from the midwife. She only came in later to cut the umbilical cord, heaping more scorn as she tidied up. I was to bleed heavily from the improperly tied stump of cord that night and, according to my mother, nearly died over the next few days from a combination of neonatal jaundice and the aftereffects of blood loss.

But my mother was not an ordinary schoolteacher. Born on 19 February 1919, the third in a family of nine, she leaned more towards her own mother in both looks and personality. Her father, Sethiba Michael Mahlaela, born in 1885, was a tobacco and corn farmer who was also an evangelist of the Dutch Reformed Church. He was a short, gentle man with soft, keen eyes and a sharp intellect. His wife Matlala Aletta, born Masekela in 1887, was a remarkable woman, tall and beautiful with an incredible intellect. She was better known by her praise name, Mamphela.[3]

Mamphela was a teacher before her marriage. Her extraordinary memory was an asset to the largely illiterate people among whom she lived, for in those days births and deaths were not registered by any authority.

---

3 Praise names are important linkages with one's clan and are used both as endearments and as a mark of respect among Sotho-speaking people in Limpopo Province.

She was a mobile archive for the region. She could recall most birth-days, deaths and other important events in the life of the people of her village and surrounding areas. Children born in the locality used to come to her to find out when they were born, before going to register at school. She would enquire who their parents were, where they lived, and would make a connection with some event and say, 'Oh, you are so-and-so's child, you were born on this or that date, because I remember that this or that happened just before you were born.'

Mamphela's talents were numerous: a facility for communication and organisation, traditional healing learned from her mother, and efficient management of the household supported by many practical skills. She mastered the art of roasting pork and preserving it in its own fat for up to three months – a useful skill in an environment where there was no refrigeration. Her own personality balanced the kindness of her husband, whom unscrupulous people often took advantage of. She called him 'kgwebeane', the easy one to cheat. She spoke her mind openly, sometimes to the embarrassment of her kindly husband. She was aware of her capabilities and was full of self-confidence. Her most determined statements were always prefixed by 'Rare Serogole', a reference to her father's praise name (Serogole). She did not suffer fools easily.

My mother, Rangoato Rahab, had fond memories of her childhood on a communal farm in the Moletsi district, about thirty kilometres due west of Pietersburg – now Polokwane. They lived in a seven-roomed house with a corrugated-iron roof, the first in the area. Both her father's and her mother's relatives lived within walking distance, and it was accepted that she could stay in the homes of other family members whenever she wanted to. This multiplicity of abodes came in handy. Whenever she had been naughty at home she could escape punishment by going off somewhere else to avoid repercussions.

Naughty she was indeed. For example, when she was about ten, she climbed a very tall blue-gum tree in search of birds' eggs, a feat which was the preserve of boys who used it to test their climbing skills. My mother was not one to be outdone by anybody, boy or girl. A particularly small bird known in the area as lentshwarelele had made its nest right at the top of the tallest tree. My mother climbed the tree to get to the nest, but lost her nerve once she reached the top and could not summon the courage to climb down. Her younger brother, Malesela Thomas, went to call for help. Her father came and put a long ladder against the tree and gently coaxed her down. Her mother, Koko[4] Mamphela, was not one to let a child get away so easily. As soon as she stepped down, my grandmother went at her with a stick which had been produced during the anxious moments before her descent – a tension-breaking tactic my mother used regularly at our expense as we grew up.

Shortly after this incident, my mother was bitten by a spider while searching for birds' eggs. She had taken her baby brother, Moseto Moses, to be breastfed by their mother, who was doing the family laundry by the river. As she carried the baby home and shepherded Malesela, she saw a bird's nest on the side of the footpath. She sat the baby down on the path and went over to get the eggs. It happened suddenly: a bite and then immediate swelling of the hand, face and every part of the upper body. My mother put Moseto on her back and hurried Malesela along, crying all the way back to their mother at the river. My grandmother rushed her to an old man who was a healer, known as Rakgolo Ngwanamorena (Son of the king) to all the children. He gave her a mixture to drink, incised her swollen blue finger and sprinkled some permanganate of potash, or makgonatsohle (cure for all ailments), onto the wound. She felt rapid relief.

My mother's passion for independence bordered on stubbornness. She recalled an occasion when she was beaten, pinched and abused

---

4 Koko is the Northern Sotho designation for grandmother; and Rakgolo, for grandfather.

verbally by older girls, mostly cousins of hers, with whom she was play-ing kgole. This is a game similar to hockey, but it is played over long distances, hence the name kgole, which means 'far'. The device used as a ball was a rounded, polished piece of wood. On this particular occasion the older girls were using my mother's ball, which one of her male cousins had made for her. She became frustrated at losing repeat-edly, and just before the seniors could score another goal, she grabbed the ball, sat down and held it tightly between her legs, refusing to budge. Her concerned elder sister, Ramadimetsa Salphy, a much gentler soul, pleaded with her, but to no avail. In the end they all gave up, to my mother's delight. She often reminded people that it was not insig-nificant that an extension of her praise name was Nkgakgathu nama moshifa (The tough one who is like the ligament supporting the neck muscles of a beast).

My parents owed their meeting, courtship and eventual marriage to Bethesda Normal College, where they both trained as teachers in the late 1930s. My mother's eyes sparkled as she recalled the time she first set eyes on Pitsi Eliphaz. He was smashingly handsome, tall and strongly built, with well-proportioned facial features. She was envied by all her friends for having captured his attentions. Pitsi was the top student at the college and a crafty soccer player, Columbia being his cheer name. My mother remembered him as a quiet, reserved and shy person at college. Pitsi was born in July 1916 at Stofberg Bible School in the Free State, where his parents, Phoshiwa Nicodemus and Ramaesela Chris-tina Ramphele, were living at the time to enable Phoshiwa to complete his training as an evangelist of the Dutch Reformed Church. Pitsi was his parents' third son in a family of six boys. Coincidentally, I share with both my parents place number three in terms of order of birth – a not insignificant factor in shaping one's life path.

The Ramphele family was supported during the three years of Phoshi-wa's training by Ramaesela's widowed mother, Ramaesela Ruth Tsheola, who had also been married to a Ramphele. After her husband's death she was left to fend for herself and her only daughter. She took up employment as a domestic for a white farmer in the district of Moletsi. She also farmed on her own account and could regularly send corn, beans, dried meat, spinach and other food for the upkeep of her daughter's family while my grandfather trained at Stofberg Bible School.

My great-grandmother was illiterate. In order to send the produce to her daughter, and undaunted by the obstacles placed in her way, she would catch a ride on an ox cart, known as sephumamagapu (breaker of watermelons) because of the bumpiness of the ride, and get to Pietersburg railway station. Here she would request the officials to help her fill in the requisite forms for railage.

She told my mother a story which best demonstrates her resourcefulness. Early one morning she was on her way to work when she came upon a big trunk, which must have fallen from a passing ox-wagon. Having made sure that there was no one in sight, she decided to push it off the road and conceal it under some bushes. She spent an anxious day wondering if her employers would mention that some traveller had made enquiries about lost property, or fearing someone else would come upon her treasure. At the end of the day, she deliberately finished her chores later than the other staff members to secure the privacy she needed for the task ahead. Under cover of darkness she carried the heavy trunk on her head all the way home. Once there, she found that it contained clothes for a whole family. What a gift from the gods for her needy daughter's family! She buried the trunk in her backyard, having satisfied herself that the owners were unlikely to reclaim it, selected some clothing for both her grandchildren and their parents, and sent them off in the usual way. At intervals she returned to the treasure chest, which remained in its hide-out, and sent instalments of clothing to her family until the trunk was empty. By this time she was confident enough to use it for storing her personal effects.

My grandfather completed his training at Stofberg and was posted by the church to Uitkyk as an evangelist. He was a strong leader of his church and was sought after for his wisdom. He established himself as an important member of the local community of peasant farmers, and made a comfortable living for himself and his family.

When my parents married in 1942, my great-grandmother, Koko Tsheola, was assigned as a baby-sitter for my father's children. In 1945 she moved from Uitkyk No. 1, the communal Ramphele home, to join my parents at Kranspoort Mission Station, which nestled comfortably at the foot of the Soutpansberg range of mountains, about fifty kilometres from Louis Trichardt in the then northern Transvaal. The Soutpansberg district stood in stark contrast to Bochum. Besides the beauty of the landscape with its rugged mountains and gentle valleys, the lush vegetation bore witness to the abundant rainfall, and the gurgling streams and rich variety of birdlife sang the praises of mother nature.

My father had been transferred from his home village to this area in 1944 on promotion to become the principal of the Stephanus Hofmeyer School. My great-grandmother looked after all of us except Molepo, the last born, a laatlammetjie, who arrived on 10 October 1961. Koko Tsheola died in 1964, then over a hundred years old, according to the estimates of my maternal grandmother, Koko Mamphela, the mobile archive. The two knew each other well as they were distant cousins. I remember Koko Tsheola as a kindly old woman with a face etched by a pattern of firmly set wrinkles and graced by her kindly soft eyes, which were given to watering. My memory of her dates back to 1953 when she supervised me in my role as caretaker of my younger brother Phoshiwa, born on 25 May 1952, thereby enabling my mother to resume her teaching post at the local school. I was six then. Koko Tsheola carried out a great number of household chores for her age. She walked with a slight shuffle, supported by a walking stick. The shuffle became more pronounced as she got older. She meticulously swept the mud floor of our three-bedroomed house and its surroundings, and washed dishes and pots. My responsibility was to mind the baby and to play with my toddler brother, Sethiba. I carried Phoshiwa on my back to encourage him to sleep, which then freed me to play.

Koko Tsheola spoiled us rotten as children. She was the embodiment of a fairy godmother, though with limited means to cater for our childhood fantasies. She divided up among us most of her old-age pension, which amounted then to a little less than £5 per quarter, starting with my eldest sister, Mashadi Ramaesela Ruth, born on 27 March 1943. Mashadi, who was named after her, was her favourite great-grandchild. The next allocation would go to my elder brother, Mathabatha Alfred, born on 6 February 1945. 1 was the third in line and would get an allocation to suit my status. Next would be my younger brother, Sethiba Michael, born on 28 March 1950. We used our spoils to buy sweets at a local store run by an Indian man, known as Makana, who had a large family living on the property. The only unpleasant memory I have of my great-grandmother was of the pinching she once gave me because I had not responded to her repeated calls to go on an errand for her. She told us stories about her childhood as well as many riddles and folktales in the warmth of our kitchen, in which stood my mother's efficient black coal-stove with the proud label 'Welcome Dover'.

—◈◈◈—

There is more to names in our family tree than a casual observer might notice. Naming of children among the North Sotho people, where my roots lie, is a major part of the process of incorporating new arrivals into the extended family. The name you are given also signifies your position within the lineage, which has major implications for access to scarce resources. Your namesake often looks after your interests in vital ways. Women play an important role in this system as partners to their brothers, who are the heirs in the family. Women partners are regarded as female husbands (borakgadi) and without them important rituals in their partner brothers' families cannot be carried out successfully.

Central to these rituals is the naming ceremony, which takes place at the end of a wedding feast. The bride is introduced to the ancestors by the presiding female husband as Ma-So-and-so (Mother of So-and-so), according to the line of succession. For example, the wife of the first-born son is given the responsibility of perpetuating the name of her father-in-law, and therefore receives a title with his praise name attached, such as Matlou, Matshwene or Mangwoatshipa. Her own first-born son will then be known by the father-in-law's name but, given the reverence attached to it, women are only allowed to use the praise name. If the first-born child is a girl, she is named after the mother of the man, unless special arrangements are made by the woman's family to 'ask for a name' (go kgopela leina). Such an 'asked-for name' was customarily that of the woman's mother.

Sons other than first-borns name their own first-born sons after their immediate elder brothers. If the first-born is a girl, she is named after the partner female husband unless the latter indicates otherwise, as when another family name is in danger of becoming extinct, because of a couple's infertility or some other unforeseen circumstance. The next son has to keep his immediate elder brother's name alive, and so on down the line. If there are more than two children, then alternate children are named after members of the maternal family, starting with the mother's parents, then her siblings and other important relatives.

The names of children in an extended family within this system are not only predictable, but also pregnant with meaning and pulsate with the tensions embedded within each patrilineage. With knowledge of the naming system one can deduce the family tree from a set of names. Children born out of wedlock can also be easily identified by their names, which are out of kilter with the system, unless some agreement is reached between the two families to ritually adopt the child 'who has come with his mother'. In most cases such children are adopted by their mothers' brothers and brought up in their households to avoid the conflicts which often occur in families with children 'who came with their mothers'.

My mother was Matlou, thus my elder brother's praise name was Tlou, as he was named after my father's immediate elder brother Mathabatha, with the same praise name. My sister, Mashadi Ramaesela Ruth, being the eldest daughter, was named after an important female in the Ramphele lineage. Because he had no sisters my father had greater freedom in naming her, so he chose his grandmother's name, Ramaesela. Mashadi, her first name, was given to her by my maternal grandmother, Koko Mamphela, in honour of the German woman who was the founder and matron of Helen Frantz Hospital at the time of her birth. Helen Frantz was given the name Mashadi by the locals, because she could not pronounce the Sotho word for 'women' (basadi), referring to them instead as mashadi.

The European names which occur in my family deserve comment. They embody the legacy of the missionaries, who saw it as their duty to give Africans 'Christian' names as part of the sacrament of baptism. African names were regarded as heathen and unacceptable to God. Considerations of convenience were thus turned into a theodicy – for most whites did not, and still are unwilling to, learn African names, some of which are tongue twisters for foreigners. The ease with which most whites shrug off attempts to pronounce African names is a logical consequence of the low status accorded Africans historically: there were no incentives to learn to pronounce their names properly nor sanctions in the event of failure. Thus even those Africans who were not baptised were given 'slave names' by white employers for their convenience.

Chapter 2

Moeng etla ka gešo, re je ka wena

NEGOTIATING EXTENDED FAMILY RELATIONS CAN BE A tricky process. The fifty kilometres which separated Uitkyk No. 1, my father's parents' home, and our own home in Kranspoort in the Mara district did not pose any threat to the closely knit extended family network, and yet gave our nuclear family sufficient distance to develop its distinctive lifestyle. My mother's parents were also within reach in their home in Krantzplaas, twenty kilometres due west of Uitkyk, where they had moved in December 1942.

Family ties were strengthened by regular school-holiday visits to my father's home in Uitkyk. These trips were great occasions for all. There was never any need for my father to announce our intended arrival: there was mutual understanding that specificities such as dates were unimportant in the flow of communication within the extended family. People did not have to keep diaries – there was always time for everything, and no need to be uptight about schedules. Everyone relaxed in the knowledge that the visits would happen during the course of the school vacations.

My recollection of these visits dates back to the beginning of December 1953. Our mode of transport – the envy of the locals at the time – was a mule wagon. My father owned a span of six mules, which were a source of much family pride. Mules combine the elegance and beauty of horses with the sedateness of donkeys. My father's mules were handsome animals; all but Japie had shiny black-haired skins. The journey to

Uitkyk was an exciting day-long trip. We set off early in the morning laden with provisions. My cousin Oupa Phoshiwa, my father's eldest brother's son, whom he adopted after his own father had died in a car accident, took great delight in being in charge of the mule wagon. He loved speed and would ensure that we arrived at our destination early in the afternoon.

My brothers and sister and I enjoyed playing a game of spotting interesting things on the way, particularly the infrequent cars which passed us on the gravel road, throwing up clouds of dust. As we drew nearer to Uitkyk, we vied with each other in identifying members of our family as they milled around the homestead oblivious of our impending arrival.

The welcome opened with loud praise-singing by my grandmother who sang the family praise song as well as our individual praises. This was high-class theatre with my paternal grandmother as the lead actor generating a pulsating emotional atmosphere. She would emerge from the nearby fields, and occupy the centre stage, elegantly strutting about as she shrilly proclaimed:

Ke bana ba sebešo segolo sa Bashita-Meetse, Bakwena, ba gaModubu wa mela nokeng dikala tša okama madiba, bana ba kgomo e tšhweu Mathabatha. Ke Phjatla-dihlaka-tsetsepa tša mogatša' Moganwa wa gaBosega. Lena methepa le yang mashemong le ntlele nyoba ya nkgopo le a mpona ke Letladi ke kgopame.

Ke bana ba Phoshiwa Madumetša rangwane wa Sekgopetšane, Matšhoša, ba ga Mahlo-mahwibidu a gaMathabatha a hwibila a etšwa go Ramphele, Mohlaloga. Phoshiwa ka mekgolodi ya marumo. Ke Matšhoša-dibata, Ramathiba-tsebe wa bo Mafepeng o ntše leweng la nkwe o ntše a shitisa nkwe go bopa. Mokgoši wa gabo Mmaselaelo o hlabja o lebana le Mmatšhwaana. Ke batho wa ga boMafoša ntsikitsiki kua moseo le kua monyako.

Ke bana ba Pitsi ya boMmatlala a bo Noko. Ke phoofolo ya maba-labala, Mamongwangwai wa mabaka, mesela ke metshanyelo, melomo ke metloutlo. Ke Lesetša Rabotse o tšwa badimong. Ke Motšhishi ga-toga dinose dilo tša botse ga di gatiwe otla roba mamapo. Ke papago Lehlaba o thopa di ile go fula Moeketsi, ya sakeng a thopela kgosi ke mang? Nna ke thopile gaManyoba-Tsokotlana kgomo yešu e sa retiwa Moletši'a Raphuti. Ke Seya-nokeng-ka-legata Lesetša, a be a pega ka seatla sa monna wa kua gaManangana. Ke motho wa gabo Molepo ke Matshwana' Boshega, Tlou-setumula megala. Ke ditlogolo tša Kgetsi ya go rwala bana ba Lesetša e subela nabo Mmedike ga gabo Letlatša.

Ke ba gaNhloma-Marumo, ba gaRamphele wa Tswetla, Mohlaloga, batho ba tšwang Bodupe ba gaMmathepe-a-Polokwane. Bodupe wee-ba-gaMmangwako-a-Molobe!!

The rules of equity demanded that she incorporate the praise song of the Mahlaelas, her son's in-laws, as an acknowledgement of their part in perpetuating the Ramphele lineage through the gift of their fertile daughter:

Ke ditlogolo tša Mahlaela-a-Mmutele'ntotoma. Ba gaRamotse wa kgang ga o dulwe e ka motse wa mashoboro. Ke ba gaSekata-ka-pitsi wa ga boSefagwana sa boMatsiri. Ke bana ba Sethiba-dipata-tša-makgowa, Sethiba a hlabiwa mogolo batho ba dikobo ba tletše gona a be a lamo-lela Moloto kua Madikoti, thaba ya maaka, thaba e phaswa ka morago. Ke Phatola-motagwana. Ke phatela kua Maribišeng. Maribišeng go hlomilwe folaga ya go iletša ditoro. Ditoro di na le bjala ba bogale ba go taga boMatshere a boDinonyana.

Ke motho wa ga boMakgatša-ka-patla wa ga boRaisibe. Ba re o rile o kgatša ka patla wa ekiša mang le mogwera wa gago o saka wa mo tseba. Ke Lefalaolo la gaPhahla-nkgori, le le rileng kgomo, la re motho. Ke batho ba tšwang Dikgabong. Ke Matebele Makwankwane a hloka kgomo a ja motho. Ke Ditlou, phoofolo tše dikgolo. Ke batho ba tšwang Kgobadi, gaNyedimane-a-Tlokwa.

Ke bana ba Rangoato wa ga boMalesela, sa naga sa lešoka. Ke motho wa ga boMoseto, Setlogolo sa Mmankwana-a-modumo le bo Malekola a sena tšhemo Moroko wa jwala wa boMautšana. Ke ditlogolo tša bo-Masekela-a-Molobare, Bakwena Baroka-meetse-a-pula. Ke tše dithlaba-tša-gaMabolesa, bare ga dia ripelwa bokwala, direpetšwe go hlaba tše dingwe. Ke bana ba Mamphela wa gabo dikgoši, monnyana wa ga-Ramothopo, kgaetšedi wa boSefadima sa boMontsho-ke-fifetše. Ke ditlogolo tša Raisibe, Thalala-a-tsoku, wa top a yena o humile le dinala. Ke ditlogolo tša boMaleka a dutse, Moraswi Letebele, batho ba ga bo-Sanaga sa lešoka.

Never one known for false modesty, my grandmother always ended the praise-singing by acknowledging her own central role in the extended family, as a 'jack' that lifted all implements, large and small:

Ke batlogolo ba Jack, tshipi ya go rwala tše dingwe. Shate-shatee!! Wo a sareng moshate o llela dilo, ore nkabe ele tša gabo! Bodupe wee--!! BaMmangwako![5]

The electric atmosphere thus generated was enhanced by the ululating and dancing which went with every phrase, even the neighbours coming to join in. As Harold Scheub has correctly observed, African oral tradition in this form is able to distil the essence of the human experience and offer it in memorable form to help shape future relations and action.[6]

---

5 Praise songs are difficult, if not impossible, to translate. The substance of my grandmother's words is given in the following pages.
6 H. Scheub, *The Xhosa Ntsomi* (Oxford, 1975), p. 1.

My grandmother was a true artist, adept at recasting family narratives into poetic language. The heroes of my family were for the most part predictably identified as the males in both my paternal and maternal family lines. The namesakes of Phoshiwa (my paternal grandfather), Pitsi (my father) and Sethiba (my maternal grandfather) were singled out as brave men who took on challenges in spite of the considerable odds against them. Phoshiwa's bravery silenced even tigers (o dutše leweng la nkwe ontše a shitiša nkzue go bopa). Pitsi was the warrior who went to capture enemy livestock and carried home with him trophies in the form of a human skull, which he used as a water container, and a human hand as a balancing mechanism within the skull to prevent spillage as he carried the water home (seya nokeng to legata la motho a be a pega ka seatla sa monna wa kua gaManangana). Sethiba, on the other hand, was a handsome only child, a leader and warrior who blocked the white settlers' way, and was killed in the process, while ugly cowards stood by (Sethiba dipata tša makgowa, Sethiba a hlabiwa mogolo batho ba dikobo ba tletse).

But some significant women received honourable mention as important sisters of the heroes, or as co-actors: Thalala, Mamphela, Kgetsi, Rangoato, and Jack (my paternal grandmother's nickname). She had great admiration for her own mother, who saved her from an unwanted marriage at puberty to a local chief in their village. Her beauty had attracted the elders of the village. Koko Tsheola, realising that the net was closing in, had to flee and went to live in a different area where her daughter was safe.

My family's heroes moved to the boundaries of their communities. Both my paternal and maternal grandfathers took the risk to part with traditional lifestyles and elected to become evangelists of the Dutch Reformed Church. My maternal grandfather, Sethiba, had the advantage that his own father had converted to Christianity whereas my paternal grandfather, Phoshiwa, was a pioneer in his family. It came as no surprise that my father would move even farther outwards – taking up a teaching position and physically moving to the Soutpansberg district (Mmedike a boLetlatsa). My paternal grandmother's creativity is demonstrated by her extension of the family praise song to incorporate new images etched by transitions into new historical realities. She expanded her text by transforming old tales, and infused them with contemporary imagery and themes.

Elaborate formal greetings of each relative, young and old, followed the emotional praise-singing, and cooled the air. These formal greetings were confusing for us children. Some adults insisted on being kissed, while others expected us to clap our hands and hold them in a clasped position for them to be kissed by the adult through the mediation of their own hands in a style intended to show deference towards adults. You were never sure what to expect.

The offloading of the provisions provided the next exciting moment for the welcoming party. The fresh fruit and vegetables which we brought from the better-endowed Soutpansberg district were a treat for the residents of Uitkyk. Young and old would tuck into the fruit as they carried the provisions from the wagon into one of the many huts around the homestead.

My father's natal homestead was a large one consisting of a corrugated-iron-roofed house together with several rondavels situated round an enclosed courtyard, or lapa. There were other buildings on the periphery: two rondavels, one the private room of my grandparents and the other for Koko Tsheola, and a three-roomed thatched mud house which belonged to one of my father's brothers. A one-roomed flat on one wing of the central house belonged to my father, and this we used during our visits. The size of the homestead signified my grandfather's success as a patriarch, blessed as he was with sons and grandchildren, and with the material means to sustain a coherent extended family.

My grandfather was a tall, strikingly handsome man, strongly built with a well-proportioned body. He was generally a stern man with strong views on many matters. His face would, however, light up when he was in a good mood. He was fond of telling us stories of his youth heavily peppered with jokes, which he told at his own or other people's expense. As he told them he would literally roll around in fits of laughter on a goatskin under a large shady tree. This served as a gathering place for the family's midday meals and afternoon rest away from the blistering summer heat.

Like most of his contemporaries, my grandfather was an authoritarian patriarch. He ruled his family with a firm hand. To underline his control over his descendants, he issued an edict that all his grandchildren were to refer to him as Papa and his wife as Mma, whereas their own parents were to be called Brother and Sister. This was a major symbolic statement about the lines of authority within the family. But my mother would have none of it. As a compromise, my father suggested the use of Daddy and Mommy – an interesting way of diverting patriarchal tensions through flight into another language. But my mother stood her ground. We thus grew up calling my grandfather Papa, my grandmother Mma-o-mogolo (Big mother), and my father Daddy. Having been successfully challenged by my mother, the edict was sufficiently weakened to allow my father's younger brothers flexibility in their own family relations.

My mother fought many battles within this patriarchal family system. She walked a tightrope as she carved out space for herself to live with dignity within the extended family She established a delicate balance between challenging those aspects of the many rigid rules about gender roles, lines of authority and the conduct of relations that violated her dignity, and avoiding actions that would undermine the system and create anxiety and instability. She faithfully fulfilled her responsibilities as a ngwetsi and a lethari (newly married and young woman in the village) – no mean feat – but she would not be bullied by anyone.

Young married women were often reminded that mosadi ke tšhwene o lewa mabogo, a woman's only real value lies in the fruits of her labour, including her reproductive labour.

Newly married women had to establish their credentials as hard workers from the very first day after their wedding. The luxuries of a honeymoon were not for them. But even an authoritarian system as tough as this patriarchy recognised the limits of human endurance – a wise step in ensuring its perpetuation. It was customary for the newly married woman to go back to her natal home after two weeks, go tsholla bongwetši (literally, to pour out one's newly married status). This was an opportunity for her to have a break from the hard work, to share experiences with her old friends and relatives, and to get useful advice about how to tackle some of the challenges of her new life. You could look at it as a retreat of sorts.

Upon her return to her in-laws, the bride was expected to fit into the routine of her new family, and demonstrate her capacity to produce goods and services for her new family, as well as to reproduce. Any undue delay in falling pregnant set tongues wagging about possible infertility. Given the level of physical exertion, one wonders how the newlyweds ever managed to make love, let alone conceive. Most women did.

My mother survived the punishing schedule of a young married woman through a combination of creativity, hard work and courage in standing up for her rights. She established boundaries beyond which she would not allow anyone to go. She tackled her brothers-in-law on many levels to let them know that she was not at their beck and call, but should be treated with respect if they expected respect from her. They were quick to blame her attitude on her professional status, for none of them had married a professional woman.

A major bone of contention was the holy of holies – slaughtering of animals, from which women were excluded because their potential for pollution was thought to pose a threat to the generative capacity of livestock. When a beast was slaughtered, the men were in the habit of delaying the process – keeping women waiting being part of the whole exercise of power by men over women. Slaughtering after sunset was quite common. This caused enormous frustration among the women, who had to wait for the meat which was to be prepared for supper. The men had little incentive to change this practice. They chose certain tender parts such as the liver, heart and spleen to cook for themselves on a makeshift fireplace, thus ensuring that their needs were catered for. They had scant concern for the children falling asleep before food was ready – it was the women's responsibility to feed the children.

On one occasion my mother decided that the critical boundary had been crossed. She calmly walked up to the men's fireplace and carried away the pot containing the meat with tender portions which was ready for consumption. She dished it out together with the porridge which the women had prepared. My father was placed in an invidious position – he was torn between loyalty to his brothers and the compelling logic of his wife's actions. In the end he decided to stay out of it. His brothers were stunned! No woman had ever dared to touch a pot cooked by men. The other women, including my grandmother, were jubilant that the spell had been broken. From then on there was greater cooperation between men and women with the slaughtering. The men were still allowed to roast some liver over open coals, but gave the women more control over the rest of the meat. My mother's transgressive act had liberated both men and women in the extended family from an archaic custom.

My mother also challenged the iniquitous practice of compelling daughters-in-law to return to domestic chores three days after delivery of their babies. After delivering her second child, she simply told her mother-in-law that she was going to stay put in her bedroom for the next ten days. My grandmother was appalled by the prospect of being laughed at by her friends in the village, who would notice that she was fetching water, cooking and doing other domestic chores, while her daughter-in-law enjoyed the luxury of postnatal recuperation. Grudgingly, the older woman came to terms with it and even defended her daughter-in-law's position in the village.

My mother was a survivor. She endeared herself to everyone through her hard work, skilled housekeeping and, above all, her delicious cooking. Her father-in-law was particularly proud of her in this regard, denigrating other daughters-in-law who were less competent. The way into my grandfather's heart was through special attention to his palate – a truism my mother always kept in mind. My grandfather's favourite treats were freshly baked bread, vetkoek (deep-fried cakes) and piping hot tea, or mafisa-molomo (burner of lips). He would sing my mother's praises as he drank one cup after another and munched the accompaniments. Because of her special culinary skills my mother was spared the discomfort of working in the fields.

Our visits to Uitkyk were mixed blessings. While we enjoyed catching up with family and the novelty of visiting the area, we found the extended family arrangements very taxing. The rigid boundaries between male and female separated me from my younger brothers during our vacations. I missed them terribly, and they in turn missed the warmth of the nuclear family.

Water had to be carried from a windmill about a kilometre away by female members of the household for all domestic purposes. This was hard water, which took some getting accustomed to for those of us used to fresh water from sparkling mountain streams. My mother spent most of her time with the other women in the household cooking and feeding the multitudes, including villagers who took advantage of our presence as visitors to share in the windfall. There is a saying in Northern Sotho, Moeng etla ka gešo, re je ka wena (Visitor, come to our home so that we can eat through you). And how! It was not unusual for my mother to feed up to twenty-five people at each meal. We found the custom of feeding men first, elderly women next and children last, very frustrating, because sometimes food would run out. We were also not used to eating out of a communal dish with so many other children, who were quite adept at tucking the food away quickly.

Children were also sent around a lot. It seemed that some adults could not bear the sight of children playing happily – it was seen as idleness, which called for action. My father's youngest brother was the worst offender on this score. He made us pick up gravel stones in the hot December sun and stash them along the fence around the large homestead. You were not expected to argue or question such instructions. After all, children were regarded as part of the family estate – property to be handled as you pleased. It did not take long for all of us to long for our own home.

The nuclear family home stood in sharp contrast to that of my extended family. My memory of my childhood goes back to a rainy day at the beginning of 1953 when we were moving house from one end of Kranspoort to another. We used a mule-drawn cart to transport the household furniture and personal effects. It was a confusing day for me as a little girl who could contribute nothing to the process, though I was made to understand very clearly that I had to keep out of the way of the busy adults. It was strange to sleep in a new house, which was to become my home for the next twelve years.

Chapter 3

The notion of home

T HE NOTION OF HOME AS MORE THAN THE PHYSICAL structure one inhabits took on a special meaning for me as a little girl. Our new home was a mud-brick house with a mud floor which had to be smeared with cow dung at least once a fortnight by my mother. The floor itself had to be strengthened and smoothed over with specially prepared mud mixed with dung (go dila le go ritela) at least once a year. The house had three bedrooms, a kitchen, a pantry, and a living room which served both as a dining and a relaxation area. Children were explicitly discouraged from using the living-room. It was reserved for adult use, and had to be kept in good shape for the entertainment of visitors who dropped by quite often. There was a front stoep (veranda) and an enclosed mud-floored space (lapa) at the back of the house which was used most frequently by the family, particularly in the afternoons when the sun hid its hot rays behind the Soutpansberg. We often sat on floor mats made of goatskin and straw. The few chairs which we had were mainly used by visitors, and women and children deferred to men in this respect.

The house had a large garden with flowers in the front, and vegetables and fruit trees on the rest of the property. A pigsty and fowl run stood at the farthest end of our backyard next to a pit latrine. I can still remember the characteristic smells around our house – a mixture of fresh flowers, dry earth and a whiff of tobacco from my father's pipe.

The village in which we lived was well planned with three main streets,

Bloed, Mahomed and Church streets, as well as two semi-developed ones on the outskirts. Each street had an irrigation furrow which was used by residents to water their gardens in turn. There was one tap for the hundred or so households. Refuse removal was the responsibility of individual householders, as was the cleanliness of streets. Most households used the open veld on the other side of the gravel main road as a public toilet. This patch of veld (phomoshene, derived from the word 'permission') was polluted beyond description by human excreta, but it was strategically hidden away by thornbush.

Kranspoort was a tidy village. Villagers were proud owners of flower and vegetable gardens and numerous fruit trees. Great effort went into maintaining their houses. There were only two families other than the dominee's with cement houses. One belonged to a well-to-do builder[7] and the other to a teacher who headed a school in the Soekmekaar area. The teacher's wife, Mrs Pauline Moshakga, was my mother's great friend.

The laundry was done at the river every week. Huge bundles of laundry were carried on women's heads to the river. Washing clothes provided an occasion for village women to meet and share the latest news and concerns. I picked up a lot from the unrestrained talk of the women, who treated us children as part of the open environment and spoke their minds quite frankly on many issues including troubled marriages, family feuds and general village politics.

I had hoped to start school in 1953, having turned five in December 1952. I found staying at home very boring. But I was given no choice by my parents, as I had to look after my younger brother, Phoshiwa, then seven months old. My great-grandmother was getting on in years and could not cope alone with a baby. I cried bitterly on the day school opened, but had to come to terms with the finality of the decision adults had made. I subsequently spent many happy days playing with my two

---

7 Our family moved into this house in 1964.

baby brothers, Sethiba and Phoshiwa, in our house and yard, particularly among the fruit trees. I learnt to climb the orange trees which were closest to the house, but was discouraged from this activity by my great-grandmother, who feared for my safety. She also said that it was inappropriate for a girl to be climbing trees. I was later to pay the price of this adventurousness with an injury to the back of my right thigh, which left a permanent linear scar.

Our household in Kranspoort was organised for maximum efficiency by my mother, who had to juggle her roles as wife, mother to seven children and schoolteacher without the benefit of domestic help. She was a tough marshal and expected every one of us to make a contribution to the smooth running of the house. We woke up at set times and had specific tasks allocated to each of us which had to be done before and after school. There was a division of labour between the boys and the girls, but it was not rigid. My brothers had to fetch water from the village tap just as we did, but they had the benefit of using a wheelbarrow, which could carry two twenty-litre containers. They also shared in the making of endless cups of tea for my mother and her occasional guests. They made their own beds, and later when both my sister and I were away at boarding school or working, the younger ones learned to cook, bake, iron and so on. My mother was a pragmatist. Traditional gender roles were cast aside to make room for survival.

My father was a great provider for his family. We were the best-fed children in the area. He often came home unexpectedly with a goat or sheep for slaughter. If none of my brothers were home at the time, he would encourage me to help him slaughter the beast. Those were the most tender of our moments together. He never referred to me by name, except in class where he was my teacher. He always called me Mommy, because I was named after his mother-in-law. We had great fun skinning the beast and opening it up, and finally eating the liver roasted on the coals as a reward.

My father was also a generous man. He believed in sharing with those less fortunate than us. We always had children from needy families in the district living with us, so that they could attend school. Such decisions he would make on the spur of the moment whenever he identified a needy child, much to my mother's frustration. We were not wealthy, but by local standards we were well off. We slept on floor-beds until the 1960s when we began to share beds in the children's rooms. To make our floor-beds we spread either straw mats or goatskins on the mud floor with a blanket placed on top. My mother made soft feather pillows (from carefully selected and preserved chicken feathers) for each of us, and we had enough warm blankets to cover ourselves even during the cold winter months.

My mother was a strict disciplinarian. She was intolerant of any naughtiness on our part, and also ruthless in punishing any misdeed. I received many beatings for breaking things, which made me even more nervous and thus led to further losses. I remember an occasion in 1959 when she had gone to a Mothers' Union church conference in Meadowlands Township in Soweto, and we had been left in the care of my father. It was dusk, and I was wiping the glass cover of our paraffin lamp, from which we derived reflected prestige, when it fell from my hands. What a disaster! I put the pieces together and knelt down and prayed: 'God, nothing is impossible for you. Please put together what has been broken and save me from the inevitable.' Disappointment awaited me when I opened my eyes. I hid the lamp away and lit a candle. My father, who was lying on his bed reading, did not comment on the candle when he came out to have his supper, but after two days, he called me. I burst out crying, expecting the worst. He embraced me, wiped my tears and sent me off to the shop to buy another one. I could not believe his response. I still cherish that touch of softness.

We were nonetheless deeply appreciative of my mother's domestic competence. We enjoyed treats which many children in the village had no idea about: freshly baked bread, dumplings, soup on cold days, pancakes, canned fruit, jam, cakes and puddings. Our greatest regret was that we could never have enough of the treats, particularly pancakes, which were my father's favourite and of which he was given the lion's share. I learnt to cook and bake quite early, because I enjoyed being near my mother and watching what she was doing. I promised myself that when I was old enough I would make myself a plateful of pancakes and eat them to my heart's content – a promise I kept years later, in 1974, when I was expecting my first child.

My father stayed aloof from many family concerns. He kept to his room in his favourite position – horizontal – with a book in his hand. We longed to get to know him better, but were not rewarded much. We would delight in taking tea to him, and in doing whatever would give an opportunity for direct contact. When occasionally he came into the kitchen, where most of the family spent their time, it would be like Christmas! We would giggle at each one of his jokes and hang on to whatever he had to say. But these were brief and rare occasions.

When my father became angry or grumpy, we would be quite scared. When drinking, he would fly into a rage over a mistake one of us had made some days before, which we would have forgotten about by then. Perhaps one of my brothers had been careless with tools or livestock, or had not performed his domestic chores properly. On other occasions it would be complaints about the way my mother and we girls ran the household, which did not meet his high standards. Those were painful days, and unless Koko Tsheola intervened timeously, we would end up being beaten. I can only surmise that he bore grudges, and that he was inhibited by his shyness from expressing his feelings. Alcohol released him from these inhibitions.

His role as both father and teacher to his children was also not uncomplicated. So too his relationship with his wife, who had to negotiate the tensions of collegiality at work and a marriage partnership. He was always punctual and could not tolerate anything less from others. This was infuriating for my mother, who had to attend to his domestic needs and still be on time at school. He was a wonderful teacher who enthused his pupils with the joy of learning. Although he was supposed to teach us through the medium of Northern Sotho, as was required by Bantu Education at the time, he quietly insisted on teaching us in English during the course of the year, and would only drill us in Northern Sotho for examination purposes. I still remember some of the ridiculous words such as okosijeni (oxygen) which we had to learn in science. He also departed from the official syllabus, which had a heavy ideological content, though he would caution us to produce what was required for the external examination at the end of Standard 6.

I was a naughty pupil, easily bored in class, and rarely challenged intellectually. My father tried to keep me disciplined by seating me next to boys, in the vain hope that I would be shy and quieten down. I soon found a way of amusing myself, in most cases at the expense of the boy beside me. One such boy used to be so frightened when asked questions in class that he would wet himself as soon as his name was called out. I would draw the attention of the whole class to this poor boy's pants by turning around to gaze at the wet patch.

I had problems reconciling my father's role as my teacher and parent. He would appear to treat me so indifferently in class that I was saddened. Although I was his best student, few if any words of praise would come my way. He expected me to do well, and would show disappointment if I got anything wrong. He also seemed to be much stricter on me than on other children. Any mistake would unleash severe punishment. I had to be perfect.

My father had a sizeable library to feed his love of books. I had access to the full range of Shakespeare's plays, the *Encyclopaedia Britannica* and many English novels and books of general interest to my father's generation, which I read through as soon as I could. I remember many conversations between adults in my presence, to which I was not supposed to be privy, but which I perfectly understood.

My childhood social world was complex in its own way. Our neighbours across the street were the family of a widowed woman who worked as a domestic in Louis Trichardt, fifty kilometres away, leaving her children in the care of her kindly mother-in-law, Koko Sanie Seko. The second-oldest girl, Rebecca, was a very aggressive person, a street fighter known for her toughness. On the few occasions we played with them, we ended up with a disagreement or even a fight. We thus tended to play on our own and avoided the street.

These neighbours resented our position of relative comfort. My mother's generosity in sharing leftover food with those less fortunate did not placate them. Their mother also became sulky and moody towards my mother on the few occasions she was home over weekends or on leave. It became so bad that we stopped having anything to do with them. The last straw was when one of my mother's large black pigs, fattened for the next winter slaughter, was found dead. A postmortem revealed that someone had pierced it with a piece of wire, which was left in situ – a more agonising death the poor pig could not have experienced. The carcass, which had signs of sepsis, was not fit for human consumption and was used to make soap for the household. Rumours abounded about who could have been responsible, but we never got to know the truth.

There were other neighbours who were part of my childhood world. Koko Mma-Abinere Tau (Mother of Abner) was a large woman whose property adjoined the back of ours. She liked sitting on the veranda of her house and surveying all passers-by. She got the latest news from casual conversations with those who cared to stop for a chat across the fence. Her house was dark, poorly ventilated and untidy. She also liked eating meat that was off, which she claimed was tastier than fresh meat. Her house had an unpleasant odour. She came in handy whenever my mother needed to dispose of unwanted meat which had gone off. She was a stingy woman, known as the Jew, because people in this village perceived Jews as particularly stingy. A story was often told of her putting a steaming hot teapot between her legs to conceal it from passers-by who she feared would be tempted to drop in for a cup of tea – a not unfounded fear, given the practice of the time. She demanded being greeted by children passing by and would clear her throat audibly to attract attention. If this failed, she would resort to scolding those she labelled as disrespectful.

Showing respect for adults was an important attribute sought and nurtured in children. I remember being reduced to tears by a cruel comment from a woman, known as Setlotlo, who lived in our street. I had greeted her and her guests in the customary way, Realotša! (Greetings!), but she was engaged in a conversation with other adults on her veranda and did not hear me. Those who heard me responded in a loving way, but she turned and scolded me fiercely for being disrespectful and not greeting. I was rescued from this verbal abuse by the others, but even then she did not apologise. Children's feelings were frequently hurt in this manner.

Koko Mma-Abinere had redeeming features too. She had a beautiful soprano voice, which she put to good use as a church choir member and Sunday school teacher. She also had a good sense of humour and an ability to laugh at herself. Her husband had deserted her and was rumoured to be having an affair with Setlotlo, who had at one stage burned her severely by pouring boiling water with caustic soda over her back. She spent many months at Elim Hospital. She often joked about the fact that her beauty transcended the scars occasioned by that traumatic experience.

Kranspoort had a friendly village atmosphere where personal safety was not at risk. We grew up with a deep sense of physical security. There were tight social networks in this closely knit community. The residents felt bound together by the common identity of being believers (Christians) in contrast to 'the heathens' (non-believers), also referred to as ba gaLosta (lost ones), who lived on surrounding farms and who were regarded as inferior. The term 'heathen' was used quite unconsciously in conversations and was also a rebuke for residents failing to behave 'properly'. It was partly this 'insider' versus 'outsider' approach which led to the break-up of the mission station in 1956 over a dispute to bury an 'outsider', the mother of one of the residents, as I shall detail later.

Social networks revolved around kith and kin. Many households had extended family members living in different parts of the village and, because of its small size, most kept in almost daily contact with one another. There were also close friendships which involved parents and children from particular households. These friendships evolved into reciprocal relationships which approximated kinships. It was the custom in this village to address others respectfully using the same terms normally reserved for relatives, such as 'uncle', 'aunt', 'sister', 'brother', 'granny' and so on. It was thus sometimes difficult to distinguish between kinships and friendships, unless one knew the family histories of those involved.

Support flowed along the contours of social networks. Those well connected were protected from the harsh realities of poverty and the disruptive effects of migrant labour, which were a common experience of most households. Households shared and borrowed necessities from one another as part of life. Food was the most common item of such exchanges, though the natural fertility of the area and the bountiful fruit and vegetables also ensured that few people ever went hungry.

Emotional and other forms of social support were also an important aspect of village life. Many women had to raise their children alone because their men were migrant workers. Most of the affected households functioned reasonably well, aided by regular remittances and annual visits from the migrants. That the experience of absent husbands was common reduced the pain of separation. Similarly affected women rallied together for mutual support.

There were also a few women migrants, such as our neighbour who I have referred to, who were single parents or widows and had to leave their children in the care of others while they sought employment to support their households. Some children ended up living at home without any adult present, but relying on neighbours for adult support in times of need.

I developed some understanding of the remittance patterns of several households because my father handled the village mail as one of his responsibilities as school principal. The mail arrived twice a week on the railway bus, which passed through Kranspoort on its way to and from Alldays, farther west along the foot of the Soutpansberg. The mailbag had to be fetched at about 10.30 a.m. by one of the schoolboys and brought to the school for sorting. The post was then distributed at the end of the school assembly when names of recipients of letters were called out, and their children or neighbours' children collected and delivered them. Registered letters were treated differently. Once notified, children were asked to alert their parents or neighbours, who had to come personally and sign for their registered items. The same applied to parcels. It was clearly a system based on trust, but sensibly tempered with safeguards.

We often had people come to our home after school to collect their registered mail which my father kept for them. Some came to enquire about possible parcels even if they had not received notification. These were the desperate women whose men were not regular remitters. My mother often gave them food on the quiet as they left our house.

Households which lived on the margins of supportive networks experienced abject poverty. These households tended to be on the outskirts of the village, and were in most cases relatively new arrivals. Their properties were also not as well endowed with fruit trees and were less fertile, providing little opportunity for growing vegetables. The irrigation water which flowed along the street furrows reached them last, and often when it was too late and too dark to water properly.

Pain and joy were shared by residents. People supported one another in times of illness or loss through death. Funerals were communal responsibilities: at these times every member of the community played a supportive role. News of death was spread by word of mouth and people rallied to the bereaved household. A few old women would immediately move into the household to provide support, and remain there until some days after the funeral. Younger women helped with the practicalities of keeping the household clean, fed and comfortable.

Women were also responsible for preparing a meal for all those attending the funeral. A beast, commonly an ox for a grown-up man or a cow for a woman, was often slaughtered the night before the funeral. It was in some cases an expensive affair, but fellow villagers brought food and other goods as well as monetary contributions to help the affected family.

Children were not allowed to go to funerals, except those of close relatives, but we often watched processions as they passed by, and clandestinely listened to the conversations of adults around these issues. Death remained a mystery to us. Our curiosity was not seen as legitimate by adults, so we could not ask direct questions. There was an uneasy silence around death.

My closest encounter with death in my childhood was in 1955 when my mother gave birth to a baby boy on a Saturday afternoon (although I remember the day vividly, I don't remember the date). It was a home birth assisted by the local midwife, Sister Nteta. We were shown the child after it was bathed, and were excited. Birth was another mystery – an area of silence which children had no right to explore. My paternal grandmother had come a few weeks before the birth to help support my mother during this period. Early on the Sunday morning my grand-mother called my sister, elder brother and me, and told us that the baby was no more. The child had died during the course of its first night. I did not understand how this was possible, but from my sister's reaction, I understood that its death was a reality. Her tears were infectious. We were later asked to go to the Sebatis, my mother's relatives, for the day.

I still remember seeing my father, just before we left, digging what must have been the baby's grave, in an enclosure (lapa) on the side of the house. He was assisted by one or two other men. We came home that afternoon to find a freshly smeared mud patch which my great-grand-mother, Koko Tsheola, looked after and to which she repeatedly applied a mixture of cow dung and soil for the next few months until it faded into the rest of the lapa. It was customary for newborn babies and still-borns to be buried within the homestead – they were not regarded as fully developed, independent persons to be interred in the public grave-yard. We were not given the opportunity to share this loss with my mother, who we hardly saw for the next few days, as she was confined to bed. This silence was very confusing to me as a child.

Sharing festivities was also part of life in Kranspoort. The residents knew how to celebrate in style. Weddings were elaborate, as were Christ-mas and New Year celebrations, which were particularly valued as times for family reunions and sharing of treats brought home by the makarapa (returning migrants). Almost all children were bought new clothes, and, for the fortunate few, new shoes were included. Homes were decorated with fresh colourful mud and cow-dung applications, as well as deco-rative paper ribbons and balloons for those who could afford such luxuries. Most people strung strips of colourful leftover material, and hung them on doorways. There were no Christmas trees, nor did any-one expect Father Christmas to come with presents or a stocking full of goodies down non-existent chimneys. People shared food and drink and the joy of life in song and dance.

On Christmas Day children walked in groups from house to house asking for 'Christmas', rather like the 'trick or treat' which American children indulge in on Halloween. Towards late afternoon, groups of children from different street choirs assembled in strategic places for friendly singing competitions. Good dancers displayed their talents. My most embarrassing moments came when I was pressured by my friends to join in the dancing. I was a typical wallflower. I was shy and tended to hide behind others, or bolted when I sensed that the net was closing in. Nonetheless I enjoyed the carnival atmosphere with all the streets brightened with colour, laughter and song.

I was never really a sociable child outside the family setting. I preferred my mother's company to that of children my age. So I took on myself the role of a human pram and made myself useful by carrying my brothers on my back, thus relieving my overworked mother of the task. I also went around visiting with her on Sunday afternoons – the only time off she enjoyed. My presence enabled her to socialise with her friends in the secure knowledge that my baby brothers were in good hands.

In addition to Christmas and New Year, weddings were also wonderful occasions, and preparations for them were elaborate. Food and song were central to successful wedding feasts. There was often fierce competition between the bride's and groom's entourages in capturing the attention of the crowds through song and dance. White weddings were the norm. Wedding dresses were of varying degrees of sophistication depending on the means of the households involved. No expense was spared by parents on such occasions. It was an honour for young girls to be chosen as bridesmaids.

The wedding started with a procession to the church, for the marriage to be solemnised by the dominee. An even more vigorous parade with singing and dancing took place back to the bride's home, where there would be more singing before the main meal was served to all the guests. After the meal the couple changed into another set of clothes, normally smart formal suits, and paraded along the street before retracing their steps back home. After an interval of an hour or two of continuous singing, the couple were seated in full view of the public in the household's lapa where they were given advice about how to make their marriage a success, go laiwa. The parents of the bride or bridegroom, whichever was the case, started off the advice session, each pep talk being accompanied by a gift for the couple. After all the relatives had their turn, the general public joined in for their penny's worth. These sessions often lasted into the late evening, with songs interspersed between the speeches.

The general tone of the advice was that marriage was difficult and that tolerance was the key to success. The woman was the focus for most of the advice. On her shoulders rested enormous responsibilities to create a new home, and to care for her husband and his family – indeed, to immerse herself in his family and to lose her maiden identity. Her child-bearing responsibilities were also stressed: heaven forbid that a woman should shun this duty or be unable to discharge it. It was not surprising that most brides spent the entire session sobbing uncontrollably. But it was also expected that the bride weep to show her sadness at having to leave the natal home, or else she was seen as being too eager for marriage. Such eagerness was regarded as a bad omen for the future of the couple. The groom's family celebrated the marriage in a manner they saw fit, but in general the same ceremony was repeated.

boSofasonke

MY INTRODUCTION TO POLITICS WAS A SILENT ONE. I remember my parents discussing politics in hushed tones, particularly after my aunt Ramadimetsa's husband had been detained under the 90-days detention clause which the Nationalist government introduced to deal with rebellion against their authoritarian rule. At this time the anti-pass campaign organised by the Pan Africanist Congress (PAC), and later strengthened by the involvement of the African National Congress (ANC), was gaining momentum on the Witwatersrand and farther afield. My uncle Solly Mogomotsi was a member of the ANC and had been a member of the South African Communist Party (SACP) before it was banned in 1950. The SACP affiliation could be traced back to his active union membership in the boiler-making industry. My aunt spent many anxious weeks searching for her husband while he was detained, with no assistance from the authorities.

My own elder sister, Mashadi, was expelled from high school in her matriculation year because she had participated in a demonstration against the celebrations of South Africa's becoming a republic in 1961. All schoolchildren were handed miniature South African flags, which we carried high as we paraded around the school under the watchful eyes of our teachers. I remember the day vividly, though we did not know what the occasion was about. I wonder how much of the symbolic weight of that day impinged on the teachers, and how much, if any, discussion took place about the significance of the day's events.

My sister and her classmates refused to celebrate what they understood to be a worsening situation of oppression for black South Africans.
They were summarily expelled, and put on homebound trains with the
help of police. It was a bitter disappointment for my father, who was a
strong believer in education as an essential part of a child's development and an escape route out of poverty. He was, however, wise enough
not to make my sister feel too guilty about her stance. He took it in his
stride and expected everybody else to do so. It was not a matter for discussion with us children. We understood that we were not to ask any
questions about it.

My sister's expulsion was not an uncomplicated event for my father
as principal of Stephanus Hofmeyer School, which was also part of
Afrikaner hegemony. My father was expected to be an active member
of the local Dutch Reformed Church: conducting Sunday school, being
a church warden, the church choirmaster, as well as interpreter for the
local dominee. The Reverend Lukas van der Merwe was certainly not an
easy person to work with. He was a bully, a racist, a chauvinist of the
worst kind. It is difficult to remember a redeeming feature in him. His
wife was a gentle woman who endured many abuses, some of them
public, from her ill-tempered husband. She was a kindly woman who
was a source of great comfort and assistance to many local women,
especially in matters of health. She saved many lives in a place far from
medical facilities and with poor means of transport. According to my
mother, I owe my own life to her. I contracted severe whooping cough
at the age of three months. It was the advice given by Mrs Van der
Merwe, together with the remedies she brought from Louis Trichardt to
dampen the cough, which my mother is convinced saved my life.

As pupils from the local school, one of our responsibilities was to
keep the dominee's house and yard clean. This entailed sweeping the
open spaces between the fruit trees around his house with makeshift
brooms fashioned from local bushes. We were not allowed to touch

any of the delicious-looking fruit on the trees. It took extraordinary discipline for children our age to do so, but the alternative was too ghastly to contemplate. The dominee was a merciless man.

He ruled his congregation at the Kranspoort Mission Station like a farmer presiding over his property. He took over the communal mission fruit farm, employed his parishioners at starvation wages and denigrated them in the most racist way. He had a peculiar sense of morality which he applied to blacks under his charge. They were not to drink alcohol of any kind, on pain of expulsion from the mission, or suspension from the church sacraments for three months. This prohibition was a puritanical version of the liquor laws of the time, which prohibited Africans from buying and consuming 'European' alcohol. He also decreed that any unmarried woman who became pregnant faced immediate expulsion from the mission – being given a trekpas (dismissal) as the practice was referred to, no different from the sanctions racist farmers used against 'stubborn natives'. He was himself not a teetotaller, nor did we know enough about his morality to be convinced that he was the puritan he insisted others should be.

A particularly painful memory I have is of a classmate who fell pregnant during her first year at boarding school at the age of about fourteen. She had one of those 'one-night affairs' with an older boy from the village whose father was a trusted assistant to the dominee as the chief koster (church bell-ringer and usher). She came from one of the poorest families. Her mother had been abandoned by her father, who married another woman and left her without any means of support except charity from locals. The girl was cast out in her pathetic pregnant state. After giving birth to a sickly child, she was not allowed to come home to whatever emotional support her mother could have provided. The death of her miserable child almost a year later released her from her agony. She came back to the village and was assisted by her elder sister to return to high school, and later qualified as a primary school teacher.

My father negotiated a fine line between obedience to and defiance of this racist tyrant. He understood that he was in the belly of the beast, but was not prepared to sacrifice his human dignity in the process of surviving. He enjoyed his beer and other alcoholic beverages with a 'coloured' friend of his, Mr Philip Bekker, who lived in a neighbouring 'coloured' village. The dominee knew all about this aspect of my father's life, but never raised it. He probably sensed the limits which my father had set in their relations.

I remember my mother proudly relating to her friends how much the dominee respected my father, in spite of his racism. She said that whenever my father accompanied the dominee on district parish visits, they would be invited by his Afrikaner friends for lunch. They would set a separate table for my father in the same diningroom! That was an honour in the 1960s in rural racist South Africa.

The high-handedness of this man eventually led to a mass expulsion of two-thirds of the mission villagers between 1955 and 1956. The events were the product of local and national grievances coinciding and igniting into open rebellion. It was a significant development involving people who had been compliant and docile. Most of the men in the village were migrant workers, a significant proportion of whom were working as labourers on the Witwatersrand. The Defiance Campaign of the 1950s, the Kliptown Congress of the People of 1955, and the anti-pass campaign triggered by the extension of the pass laws to women, kindled a rebellious spirit in many of these migrants, who in turn influenced their relatives in Kranspoort. It required only a small spark to set the mission village alight. This spark was provided by the dominee when he refused to allow an old woman, the mother of a resident of the village, to be buried in the mission graveyard, because she was a 'heathen' (someone who had not converted to Christianity). This old woman used to live on a farm in the mountains above the mission village and had been brought to her daughter's home for nursing in the twilight of her life.

The battle for the right to have her buried was a fierce and sad one. I have only a vague recollection of it, because I was then only seven years old. I must rely on my mother's recollection of the events. The village was divided between those who supported the dominee's ruling, referred to as boDaza, and those defying it, the boSofasonke (We will die together). It is noteworthy that in the 1950s there was a strong following of the Sofasonke party in the poorest parts of Soweto, and some of the migrant workers may have brought the name back with them for this local struggle. The old woman was defiantly buried in the mission graveyard with the church bells rung by the rebels, who physically took control of the church grounds, Police were called in to protect the dominee. He was beside himself with anger after being humiliated by the public defiance, which included some militant women poking their fingers at his face and calling him 'Lukas' (his first name) instead of the usual respectful Moruti (Preacher).

The conflict raged for months after that episode. The rebellious residents were arrested under various excuses by security policemen and beaten. But they would not give in. A massive removal was then executed with the support of the police. People known to be part of the Sofasonke were given short notice to pack and go. There was no compensation for the property they lost. Many also lost household effects and personal clothing in the rush to leave before the deadline. They left their houses standing, some with furniture, which was later stolen or destroyed by the elements. Only about a third of the village residents remained. These were largely families of civil servants or other people who kept out of the conflict for fear of repercussions. There were bitter feuds between the two groups, and physical and other forms of violence were traded between them regularly.

My father in his usual quiet way successfully walked the tightrope between remaining a loyal civil servant and not antagonising those who were up in arms against the dominee. It was not easy. He took advan-

tage of my mother's eighth pregnancy to send the vulnerable members of his family away at the beginning of 1956 to his natal home in
Uitkyk. My mother and my younger brother, Phoshiwa, went to live
at my mother's family home in Krantzplaas, where she could receive
prenatal care from a nearby clinic. There were no clinics in Uitkyk at
the time.

Sethiba, my younger brother, and I were left in the care of my paternal grandparents. My elder sister, Mashadi, was placed in the care of my
mother's cousin's family, the Mahapas, while my elder brother, Mathabatha, remained at Kranspoort with my father. It was the first family
separation, and it was not easy for us at all. The only reason I can now
think of why all the children did not go with my mother was that my
paternal grandparents would not have approved of 'their grandchildren'
being looked after at my mother's natal home. We were naturally not
consulted in the matter. The separation from both parents for the sake
of keeping the peace between the Rampheles and the Mahlaelas was
traumatic for us. We resented it and cried a lot over it.

Sethiba was then in Sub A, and attended a nearby local school which
catered for only Sub A and B. I had to go to G. H. Frantz Secondary
School, some three kilometres from my grandparents' home. Fortunately an older cousin of mine, Mbatha, attended secondary school
there and could give me a lift on his bicycle. But I had to walk home
from school on those occasions when he had afternoon activities. I
found that hard, not only because of the long distance for my eight-year-
old frame, but particularly because hunger was a constant companion.
There was no lunch packed for me nor was I given pocket money to buy
snacks from the village shop. I was regularly rescued by my mother's
cousin, who was teaching at the same school and living near by. She
would give me food during the school break.

Breakfast in my grandparents' household was mainly tea and dry
stale bread bought from the local store. There was often no food wait-

ing for us when we got home after school. We would then have to make do with whatever leftovers were available from the previous day's supper. Sethiba was even more miserable. He was expected to herd my grandfather's sheep and goats after school, often without any food in his stomach. He also bore the full brunt of my grandfather's authoritarianism and harsh approach to child-rearing. His six-year-old body was subjected to hunger and hard work for most of the nine months of our stay there. I was protected by the relative gentleness with which both my grandparents treated me. My tears, which flowed very readily each time I was hurt or miserable, were a useful lever for obtaining greater and gentler care. In contrast, Sethiba was under pressure to respond to my father's edict that moshimane ke draad, ga a lle ge a e kwa bohloko (a boy is like a piece of wire and should not cry).

I saw my parents only once during the entire nine-month period. Given the distances involved, my father could only afford to come and see us during the June school holidays, and later took us to visit my mother. We had to be torn away from her at the end of the visit. Release came one Sunday morning in September while we were waiting with my grandmother to depart on a church trip to another parish twenty kilometres away. Someone came to tell my grandmother that my mother had just arrived with her new baby. I jumped for joy and ran all the way home. Sethiba could hardly recognise his mother. As she got off the donkey cart that brought her, he thought to himself: That woman with the baby looks like my mother. But he was not sure until my mother called out to him and hugged him. The joy of reunion was indescribable for the two of us. We giggled and danced to the music within our deprived hearts. Our family was finally reunited.

❖❖❖

We moved back to Kranspoort where things had calmed down. The innocence of my childhood was brought to an abrupt end one Wednesday evening late in 1960 just before I went to the weekly evening prayer service. I was twelve years old. I ran to the toilet to relieve myself, only to be confronted by a bloody panty. I had no idea what was happening to me. I quickly changed and ran to church. My special prayer was for the Lord to make the blood go back to where it came from. It was one of my many unsuccessful pleas for God to intervene directly in my life. The blood continued to flow for four or five days.

Fortunately, Miriam Mokgadi Kutumela, one of the many young people who used to stay with us, noticed my bewilderment and offered advice and practical suggestions about appropriate hygienic measures. She also explained what it meant in terms of the development of my sexuality, pregnancy and matters relating to childbirth. She had got to know all these 'facts of life' from the initiation she underwent at puberty in her village. Ironically, the embracing of 'Christian ways' deprived us of such an exposure, while not creating other mechanisms to provide information about human development for young people. One had the worst of all worlds in this regard.

It never occurred to me to tell my mother even though I was close to her in many other ways. The silence which existed between children and adults around sexuality was absolute. I sensed that this was not a matter to raise with her. It took my mother almost a year before she found out that I had reached puberty. Even then she did not talk to me directly about it. She asked her best friend, Mrs Moshakga, to speak to me. Mrs Moshakga was in turn very indirect in her explanation of what puberty was about and said very little which satisfied my curiosity. She simply said, 'This monthly flow of blood signals that you are now a woman. You should not sleep with boys, because you will then have a baby.' But how could I be a woman at the age of twelve? What did sleeping with boys mean? And what was the connection between that and babies? I had to rely on Miriam to respond in detail to my questions, and to interpret some of the innuendoes. My father's encyclopaedias

also came in handy: I could read and follow the biological explanations with the aid of the diagrams.

It is interesting how little the discourse of sexuality between parents
and their children has changed over the years, particularly among
working-class people. In my work with adolescents in the Western
Cape townships I came across the same silences, and the unwillingness
of parents to be open to their children about sexuality and their growing bodies. Many young people still have to rely on friends for information about this vital area of life. It is a measure of how deeply entrenched are the mystique of the human body and the ambivalences
we seem to have about sexuality. Some researchers have suggested that
the incest taboo may have something to do with this silence. Talking
about sex may itself be regarded as a sexual activity.

Chapter 5

School, the institution

I DO NOT REMEMBER PLAYING THE FANTASY GAMES OF 'WHEN I grow up I will be this, that or the other'. Nor do I remember being asked by adults in their usual condescending way what I thought I would become later in life. It may well be that my distance from my peers had a lot to do with my unconcern about a career. But it may also have had to do with the assumption in the village that you automatically became a teacher or nurse if you did well at school, or a policeman or labourer if you did not. Given my academic abilities and the fact that my parents could afford to educate me, my choice of career didn't invite questions from curious adults. I was destined to become a teacher.

Charles Dickens could well have set his bleaker social novels in South Africa and, specifically, in one of the most important secondary educational institutions in the then northern Transvaal. Bethesda was a teacher training college which was started by Dutch Reformed Church missionaries in the 1930s. It was situated about fifty kilometres west of Pietersburg – now Polokwane – in a mission station known as Rita, which nestles under a beautiful, sharply defined koppie whose name it shares. It had an enrolment of about three hundred students, most of whom were in the secondary school section. There were about three boys to each girl, and the boys' and girls' residences lay on either side of the school's teaching and administrative blocks.

Like many of my contemporaries, I arrived with great expectations in January 1962 at what I anticipated would be a place of higher learning.

It was a major step in our lives. Childhood was finally behind us (even though I was only fourteen years old). We were on the road to preparing ourselves for the world of work. But on arrival I was taken aback at the state of the institution.

I was never asked my views of Bethesda, but when our English teacher asked us to write a letter to a friend, telling her about our school and encouraging her to apply for admission, I took off.

Bethesda Normal School

P.O. Kalkbank

Pietersburg

3/4/1964

Dear Friend,

I heard from a mutual friend that you intend to come to this school for your secondary level education. I feel it is only fair that I should give you a sense of what you would be letting yourself in for.

It has been a remarkable last two and a quarter years for me. My romantic vision of boarding school has been dented severely by my experiences here. I shall only focus on a few areas to illustrate my point. First, the dormitories we are housed in are in an appalling state of disrepair. There are bedbugs everywhere, particularly in the hot summer months. The authorities order fumigations only after repeated complaints, and even then the problem gets merely contained for a few months, only to resurface with greater vengeance.

The second major problem area, probably the most important one for young growing bodies such as ours, is the quality of the food. I cannot understand how any responsible adult can expect young people to live on a diet which consists of mainly carbohydrates, occasional meat (often rotten), and little fresh fruit and vegetables. The unchanging and unappetising weekly menu is as follows:

Breakfast – Soft porridge, cooked the night before, often served cold, without any milk, except on Sunday mornings when a quarter loaf of bread with a spoon of jam is served in addition.

Lunch – Hard porridge served with either boiled potato or over-cooked cabbage, and twice a week with meat (often off in the hot summer months due to a lack of refrigerating facilities).

Supper – Hard porridge served with a cup of cocoa with no milk added to it. A quarter loaf of dry bread is served only on Saturday evenings.

It is hardly surprising that the majority of the students, particularly the girls, end up with severe pellagra (a vitamin B complex deficiency). What is even more infuriating, though, is the attitude of the matron. She blames the skin manifestation of the vitamin deficiency disease on the girls themselves. She emphatically denies that it has anything to do with the quality of the food, but claims that it results from the use of skin-lightening creams. Her assertions fly in the face of the diagnosis of the visiting general practitioner, Dr Makunyane, whose opinions she completely ignores.

The quality of education itself is not bad. Most of the teachers are keenly interested in the success of their students. I particularly like my arithmetic and biology teachers, who encourage me to excel. The latter two subjects are my favourites.

Social relations between the students and most of the teachers are a problem area. All our teachers, except those teaching Northern Sotho, are white people, all Afrikaans speaking except our Standard 6 and 7 English teacher. The latter is a kindly old man in his late sixties, Mr Erckels, who lives on his farm, less than ten kilometres from the school. He refers to Serolong[8] as his mother tongue, because he grew up in

---

8 Serolong is a dialect of Setswana, spoken in the northwestern part of the country.

the western Transvaal. We are often taken aback when he says with perfect intonation: Ka se haheso re re ke lengoele (In my language we say it is a knee). Mr Erckels is an exceptionally caring teacher.

The majority of the teachers maintain a 'them and us' attitude. This is manifested in a variety of ways: no handshakes, separate entrances even in the local church which we are compelled to attend every Sunday, racist comments particularly from the spouses of the teachers. There is an invisible wall between students and teachers which is very disturbing, particularly from those teachers whom I really like, and whom I would like to learn to know a bit more.

You have to make your own decision in the end, but I would discourage you from coming to this school. Explore other possibilities. I am planning to go to Setotolwane High School next year for my matriculation years, and am already impatient with the slow passage of time. I will certainly not miss this place.

I wish you all the best.

Yours sincerely,
Aletta[9] Ramphele

Mr Le Roux, our Standard 8 English teacher, was appalled. How could I misuse a class assignment to complain about school conditions? An interesting question which begs the issue: Would he have complained if I had used the assignment to praise the school? He gave me fifty per cent for it, a marked departure from my average in other assignments and tests of eighty per cent and above. The message was clear. But I was not perturbed in the least, because I had given a true account of life at the school as I experienced it. I was also confident that my

9 I used Aletta as my first name until my third year at Medical School when the Black Consciousness Movement challenged us to revert to our indigenous names.

exceptionally good academic standing would protect me against further repercussions. It was good to know that the school could not afford to expel me.

The social distance between students and teachers was exacerbated by the system of huiswerk (Afrikaans for 'housework'), which was a form of forced labour intended to remind students that education was not an escape route from the inferior position blacks were 'destined' to occupy. Each student was allocated to a staff member one afternoon a week for about two hours. Most were asked to do the menial domestic chores, such as sweeping the ground around the house, washing pots, scrubbing floors and ironing – a peculiar way to promote good relations between staff and students.

Some of the staff were more pleasant to work for than others. So too they differed in generosity. While several gave food at the end of the afternoon, others remained quite indifferent to the hunger that was a constant companion of the boarders. The principal's wife, Mrs Grütter, who was also our music teacher, was the most unpleasant of all. She often reminded those students who seemed to her unenthusiastic in their tasks: 'You were born to work for us.' But there was a positive side even to this racist. It is to Mrs Grütter that I owe my interest in classical music. She was a pianist who taught music with great enthusiasm.

But how is one to explain that my parents, who had trained at Bethesda in the late 1930s, and had endured the same experiences, let me follow in their footsteps? My mother's recollection of their life as students at this school differed only marginally from my own experience: the dormitories infested with bedbugs, the poor-quality food, the attitudes of 'them and us'. The whole ambience of the place did not seem to have undergone much change over the intervening decades. Why then did she not discourage me from making this choice?

Part of the explanation lies in the limited choices available to Africans: there were few boarding schools of quality at the time. There was also a strong conservative ethos which constrained my parents from exploring even the few alternatives open to us. I could have gone to Setotolwane High School from the very beginning of secondary school, but that would have been trail-blazing for a little girl and my parents would have found it difficult to accept. Setotolwane was formerly known as Diocesan College, having been founded by missionaries of the Anglican Church, and its religious ethos reflected its origins. With their conservative Dutch Reformed background my parents would have found it hard to send me there. On top of that, the authoritarian Dominee Van der Merwe at Kranspoort would not have made their lives any easier for letting their daughter 'go astray' and be lost to another denomination. It was assumed that children from Dutch Reformed missions would retain their denominational allegiances and go to Bethesda Normal College or Emmarentia High School, a course both my elder sister and brother followed. So the question of a different choice of school did not even arise.

The first few weeks of the 1962 school year were traumatic for me. Initiation was still alive and well at Bèthesda in the 1960s, and we were humiliated in every possible way, as part of the ritual. The intimidating atmosphere became evident from the time we got onto the steam train at Mara Station where we joined students from Messina. We were assaulted with shouts of mesela (tails), to indicate that we were the last to come into the institution. It was also my first train ride. I had occasionally seen the passenger train pull off from Mara Station on its way to or from Pietersburg, but had never been on it until January 1962. The novelty of the experiences unfolding around me proved overwhelming. My heart was pounding in my tiny chest all the way. What an introduction to leaving home!

The same insecurity and sense of impending doom pervaded our arrival at Bethesda. No effort was made by either the school or fellow students to put us at ease, and make us feel welcome. Any senior student could order a mosela to run errands or engage in demeaning acts at any time. This 'treatment' lasted for about one and a half weeks, ending on the night of a belated welcome concert given by the school in the main hall. The last lap on this gruelling initiation track was running as fast as our frightened legs could carry us to our room immediately after the concert. Here we were at last free. That week and a half were the longest in my adolescent life. I cried myself to sleep during those first nights.

Mathabatha, my elder brother, who attended the same school at the time, was my only source of support and continuity with the protective family life I had left behind. He took the risk of breaking the rules during my first week at boarding school to check on me and to reassure me – an offence punishable by expulsion. He came to stand outside our classroom window before the classes started, and caught the attention of a fellow student, who then called me to the window. The minute I saw him I burst out crying. I had never felt so far from my family before, and I was miserable. He just stood there and comforted me.

Networks of support were critical in this environment. Homegirls were the most important people, particularly in the first few months of boarding school life, before one had made friends with girls from other parts of the country. Homegirls protected one from gross abuse during initiation, even though they could not completely shield one from the humiliation of the entire process. One of my homegirls was assigned to keep watch over me and to intervene where appropriate. Sometimes serious fights broke out between seniors about the reasonableness of the 'treatment' meted out to a particular mosela. Those unfortunate enough to be outside this protective network were often grossly abused.

Networks of support were also vital in enabling you to survive the inadequacy of even the few essentials that were supplied. The school provided an iron spring bed with a coir mattress for each student. There were dormitories ranging from four beds each for seniors, to ones with twenty beds or so. There were neither lockers nor desks. You had to bring your own blankets, pillows and linen. Our personal effects were held in locked tin trunks kept in the locker room adjacent to each dormitory, and supervised by a prefect.

We had to rely heavily on our own resources to supplement the inadequate food supplied in the boarding school. From home at the beginning of term we brought scones, chicken, rusks, tinned food, dried meat and vegetables, biscuits, and a variety of preserved food. The resourcefulness of your family was severely tested. Homegirl groups, varying in size from two to ten, often shared their provisions, as well as the occasional food parcel sent from home. In addition we bought provisions from the store at Kalkbank once a week.

My brother and I had to learn to make do with one pound ten shillings each per quarter, which our father sent us as pocket money. It was barely enough to cover basic necessities, including toiletries. Mashadi, my elder sister, who was then working as an assistant in a fish and chips shop in Soweto, played an important part in rescuing me from total despair. I used to jump for joy each time I received a parcel from her, because I knew that there would be treats: biscuits, sweets, tinned beef and fish, toiletries and, occasionally, a pair of stockings or a handkerchief. You really learned to appreciate such small tokens of love from your family.

The custom of sharing had its drawbacks. There were wide differences among students in the quality of provisions brought from home, the regularity and amount of pocket money, and the number of parcels sent from home during term. Tensions also developed around the amount of communal food each devoured. Small eaters were at a decided disadvantage. There was also difficulty in catering for different tastes. Some people with less delicate palates ate whatever came their way, and thus paid little attention to the needs of others in preparing food.

Survival is a stronger force than the fear of offending others. After the first year of sharing with about eight homegirls, I took the plunge. I felt that having complete control over my supplies would enable me to budget better, and spread my resources over a longer period. I had also learned to bake biscuits, and my mother loaded me with provisions, which used to last me until just before the end of term. My severe weight loss during the first year also prompted more regular pocket money and food parcels from home.

I had suffered a lot during the first year from near-starvation. As I could not bring myself to eat what I considered food unfit for human consumption, I often had to survive from Monday to Friday drinking only cocoa at supper time, with sugar water during the day. My small frame took severe punishment, but my will not to be reduced to an animal kept me going. So when I decided to eat alone, homegirls were dismayed but let me go. Thereafter I occasionally shared some food with them, but it stopped being an obligation.

Bethesda Normal College was like an island of Protestant morality in the Bushveld. The location of boarding schools in remote rural areas had its benefits and drawbacks. The isolated and barren rural setting offered few cultural, intellectual and leisure opportunities. Some adults, however, felt that it was an appropriate environment for taming restless adolescents. The fewer the 'distractions' from the learning process, or so it was felt, the better the outcome. The majority of these schools also obliged by laying down rigid rules enforced by autocratic matrons or boarding masters. Bethesda was no exception.

Most of the male students spent their weekends loitering near the school and in the village of Rita. Some of the younger ones were responsible for looking after the herd of cattle which the school relied upon for its meat supply. Fridays and Mondays were slaughter days. The beasts were usually shot by one of the teachers, and the older male students were responsible for skinning, cutting up the meat, and storing it away. The meat was kept in large bath tubs for a day or two without any refrigeration – with predictable consequences in summer.

Female students were under stricter rules. You could only go to the Kalkbank shopping centre if you had permission from the head prefect, who had to be given a list of potential shoppers by midweek for the Saturday morning outing. Numbers were strictly controlled – not more than twenty at a time were allowed. A prefect had to accompany the shoppers. The four-kilometre walk was quite hard for younger, frailer persons like me, but it was fun and a welcome change from the dull surroundings of the boarding house.

Sundays were strictly observed as days of compulsory worship. A morning service was held at the local Dutch Reformed church conducted in Afrikaans with Northern Sotho interpretation for the local villagers. Racial segregation was entrenched in both the entrance points and the seating – after all, it was God's law to keep blacks and whites apart, and one had to be even stricter in His house in this regard. Men and women also sat separately, presumably to reduce the temptation of being attracted to someone of the opposite sex. We had to be protected from ourselves.

Activities organised by the Student Christian Movement (SCM) and Mokgatlo wa Ba Bacha (MBB) dominated Sunday afternoons and evenings. Varying degrees of charismatic religiosity were in evidence particularly among female students. These tendencies were encouraged by the school authorities, who saw religion as the cornerstone of good behaviour. I found some solace in the various religious activities, particularly the singing, which was a major part of them, and I became a full member of the MBB.

In spite of this gloomy picture, the school had its warm and enjoyable sides too. We developed close friendships among ourselves. I became friendly with a group of three girls in my class: Moloko Laka (a homegirl) with a tall beautiful body, dry wit and a stutter, Mphika

Molokoane (from Musina, then still Messina) who was the shortest of the foursome, with a perfect baby face, gentle nature and softly spoken manner, and Greta Mogooane (from Natalspruit, on the East Rand), to whom I was closest. Greta's attributes stood out as gentleness, neatness and generosity of spirit. She was also physically attractive and petite. She did not keep the unwritten rule that prevailed among urban students not to befriend country bumpkins like myself.

Students from rural areas also kept to themselves. Any association with those from urban areas was viewed as potentially destabilising and polluting, as there was a widely held belief at the time that cities had a corrupting influence on young people. Bana be South ba tla go lahletša (Children from the South – a metaphor for the Witwatersrand area – will lead you astray) were the words of caution uttered by senior home-girls. Boundaries between town and country were evident, and reinforced in social relations at the school.

As a foursome, we operated on the margins of all conventions. We enjoyed sitting next to one another in class, sharing jokes and gossip, helping one another with school work, and occasionally sharing treats, which were few and far between. We were all very different personalities, but enjoyed each other's company, and complemented each other's strengths. We referred to one another as 'Penkop' or 'Pennie', from an Afrikaans set book we were reading at the time. This was the story of a group of mischievous young people who were given the same nickname.

It was hard to part from my friends at the end of our Standard 8 year, when I moved to Setotlwane High School for my matriculation. The class farewell party we organised at the end of 1964 was a great success. Food was in abundance, a rare event indeed. We celebrated our years together, and shared the hope of new beginnings. I was not sad about leaving Bethesda; my only regret was having to leave my friends behind. We kept up a brisk flow of correspondence for the rest of our school days, but lost contact later.

Chapter 6

Matriculation is not a mattress

G ENDER STEREOTYPING IN CAREER CHOICES WAS DEEPLY entrenched in those years. All but one of my female classmates chose to proceed to teacher training. Some saw teacher training as a strategy for securing a career before attempting matriculation, while others saw teaching as their final career choice. There was a widely held view that only bright pupils should attempt matric. 'Matriculation is not a mattress' was the popular saying, a reminder that only hard work would ensure success. I was one of only two girls among a handful of boys in my class who opted for matric. The other exceptional girl was Hester Motau from Belfast in the then eastern Transvaal, now Mpumalanga. She was older than me and came from a family of teachers that had high expectations of their daughter.

Not only were the three years at Bethesda difficult socially, but I felt intellectually under-stimulated most of the time. Although I came top of my class in every subject, I did not have to exert myself at all. On the contrary, I was bored most of the time, and tended to make careless mistakes. My arithmetic teacher, Mr Henning, used to be frustrated by these mistakes, because he was convinced that 'I could easily not drop any marks at all' in his subject if I put my mind to it. With hindsight, I think he should have attempted to teach me mathematics instead of the mechanical arithmetic I found so boring, but Bethesda was not concerned with teaching blacks mathematics. They took very seriously Dr Verwoerd's words which he had used in motivating the introduction of the Bantu Education Act of 1953: 'Bantu' children should not be shown green pastures where they would never be allowed to graze.

Career guidance was non-existent during our school days. Your horizons were not widened beyond the known. The few positive role models for us were confined to the traditional professions of teaching and nursing. There was almost a sense of inevitability about replicating the known from one generation to the next.

Yet I had never entertained the thought of becoming a teacher. I just knew that I had to do something else. I was strongly attracted to science and the world of numbers, but could see no career prospect in science short of becoming a high-school science teacher. I had seen the discrimination against black teachers even at a higher level. I also knew from my mother's experience that female teachers had even greater barriers to overcome. I would not become a teacher.

What about nursing? My sister Mashadi started training as a nurse at Baragwanath Hospital in 1964. I did not like what I heard from her. The authoritarian rule of seniors over juniors, and the role of both as handmaidens of the doctors, did not appeal to me. The little I had heard about doctors suggested that medicine could offer me the greatest professional freedom and satisfaction. It was not the desire to serve which influenced my career choice, but the passion for freedom to be my own mistress in a society in which being black and female defined the boundaries within which you could legitimately operate.

My career choice was not easily accepted by others. My father had good reason to dissuade me. He was, unbeknown to me then, suffering from a fatal illness, cancer of the oesophagus, and knew that he would not be able to support my ambitious choice. His suggestion was that I choose teaching as a quick route to earning an income in order that I might help my mother support the rest of my siblings. I argued that if I were to follow my own chosen career, I would in the long run be of greater assistance to my mother. But where was the money to come from? he asked. 'The Lord will provide,' I said, with childish confidence. He looked at me sadly, and gave me his blessing.

It was customary at Kranspoort for all the boarding-school students to present themselves to the dominee at the end of the school holidays, and bid him goodbye – an odd custom, given the lack of interest he had shown in us. It was more a means of symbolising the feudal relationship which existed between him and the community, a subtle mechanism of control which enabled him to keep tabs on his 'flock'. It was not for you to question, but to obey.

In January 1965 I accordingly went to pay my respects before departing for Setotolwane High School. Dominee Van der Merwe was appalled when he heard what my plans were. He dismissed them as a pipe dream. How could I – a woman, a black person and poor at that – ever expect to become a medical doctor? He told me that his own daughter had given up a similar ambition and settled for being a nurse. What hope did I have? He must have read defiance in my face, so he delivered the final blow: 'Your father is dying of cancer. Who is going to finance your education anyway?' Although I was aware that my father was seriously ill, I had up to then kept hoping he would be cured. It was cruel for a teenager to be told this painful news with such insensitivity. I was devastated.

Although I wept on my way home, I did not tell my mother about the dominee's remarks. I didn't want to add to her intolerable burden of pain, anxiety and fear of her impending loss. I decided that the best way forward would be to prove the dominee wrong. But the path to a medical career had a number of major hurdles.

My easy pass through Standard 8 with a distinction, and topping the whole group of black students of 1964, was soured by my lack of training in mathematics. I spent the first two weeks in Standard 9 trying anxiously to understand how one could add and subtract alphabetical letters, let alone divide and multiply them. Fortunately, the principal of our new school had been my biology teacher at Bethesda, and I felt confident enough to approach him with my problem. Special extra classes were arranged for about five of us. Our mathematics teacher was an elderly retired person from the white education system. He was a dedicated teacher who patiently took us through the basic principles of mathematics. At the end of the first term I was more confident, but it was a struggle to work out all the configurations.

In contrast, I fell in love with physical science, and understood the principles with ease. I was challenged by Mr Gouws, our science teacher, who promised me a prize of R50 if I gained a distinction in physical science in my matric examinations. That R50 turned out to be the only cash I had at the beginning of my university career in 1967. I bought myself a pretty pink dress which fitted me perfectly. It was to be my only fancy dress for many years.

The generosity of Mr Gouws and his friend Mr Bowman, the English teacher, sustained me throughout my matric years. Mr Bowman considered me too thin, and insisted that I should take multivitamins, which he personally supplied. The political affiliations of both these teachers did not stop them from liking me as a person. Mr Bowman even adorned me with a National Party badge in one of his enthusiastic moments. My political naïveté at the time prevented me from taking in the full symbolic significance of such an adornment.

It was the lack of access to information – the embodiment of the powerlessness of most poor rural communities – that nearly cost me my medical career. I had no idea that to gain entrance to a university you had to apply near the beginning of the second term for the following academic year. By the time I applied to Natal University, the only medical school at the time which took African students without seeking permission from government, it was too late for the 1967 academic year. Mr Gouws advised me to go to the University of the North to do my premedical courses, and then to proceed to Natal in 1968.

I did not have a bursary, nor did I know how to apply for financial assistance. I decided to present myself as I was – penniless. At the University of the North I was advised by the admission officers to fill in forms for a state loan of R100, which was sufficient to cover most of the tuition fees, and permitted me to be registered. I had no money for stationery or set books. I borrowed from friends, and was fortunate enough to have a generous boyfriend, Dick Mmabane, who supported me financially and emotionally during those difficult years. I lived on the hope that somehow the money problem would be resolved even though I did not have the faintest clue how.

A bigger challenge to my plans lay ahead. To qualify for admission to the second year of study at Natal Medical School the following year, I had to pass all four subjects: chemistry, physics, botany and zoology. I had no difficulties with the last three, but chemistry proved to be a problem. Professor De Villiers, then head of the Department of Chemistry, made it plain to our first-year class at the beginning of term that we were going to have a hard time. He made no bones about his displeasure at the size of our class. He told us that it was not possible for 73 'Bantus' to pass Chemistry 1. There was no doubt in his mind that 'Bantus' could not master chemistry, and he made it his mission to prove this.

He would breeze into the classroom – his cold blue eyes not making contact with anyone, but emitting sparks of hatred whenever one attracted his attention and dared to ask a question. In his own section of the work, organic chemistry, he made learning almost impossible. He lectured from scraps of notes which were visibly yellowing with age. He wrote some of the difficult formulae on the board, with a duster in one hand, and as soon as he got to the end of a long formula, he would begin to erase what he had written last, relishing the anxiety he read on our faces. He prescribed no textbook, nor suggested any reference works. We relied on notes from senior students who had in turn pieced them together from their seniors' disjointed notebooks.

A greater anti-educationist you could not find. He was the talk of the university and a law unto himself. There were many students in our class who were attempting Chemistry 1 for the third or fourth time, because it was a compulsory minor for a BSc. He held the key to the successful completion of a university education for all students who wanted to make science a career – a powerful position, which he savoured openly.

I was fortunate to scrape through with a D symbol, the only one with a D among the handful of people who passed the final-year examination at the first attempt in 1967. I was horrified by this first D symbol in my academic career, but was grateful for small mercies, because failure would have endangered my admission to Natal Medical School. In contrast, I got a B aggregate for the other courses. My good performance in the other three subjects during the first half of the year prompted the Dean of Science to review my matriculation results, and to offer me a full-cost bursary, which solved my financial problems for 1967.

The death of my father

THE DEATH OF MY FATHER ON 21 MAY 1967 INTRODUCED me to the reality of the pain of loss. The fact that he had been ill since 1963 with cancer of the oesophagus, and that he showed all the signs of suffering from an incurable illness, did not prevent me from praying for a miracle to heal him. I could not see why an omnipotent and loving God could refuse me. It was to be my third major disappointment with God.

Because my father had been a distant parent for most of my childhood, every intimate moment we shared was very special. Our last moment of closeness took place during the Easter holidays of 1967, a few weeks before his death, when I went to visit him at Baragwanath Hospital where he lay dying. My sister was one of the nurses in his ward, which made her pain worse in some ways, but gave her more time with him during his last days. I trimmed his fingernails as we chatted. I listened to him as he talked about his disappointment with his eldest son, Mathabatha, the apple of his eye, who had not once come to see him in hospital. But he still managed to retain his dry sense of humour. He listened with interest to my impressions of the University of the North. I also introduced him to my first serious boyfriend, Dick Mmabane, who was later to become my husband.

Dick was a gentle, stockily built man with a keen sense of humour and great generosity of spirit. He could not be described as handsome in the ordinary sense of the word, but his attractive personality made up for what he lacked in physical looks. He had been my classmate at Setotlwane High School, but our relationship had only developed at the tail end of our matric year. He became a great source of support during the difficult months ahead.

The sense of loss I felt when I heard the news of my father's death from Mr Renoster, the Chief Warden of Residences at the University of the North, was immense. The train trip from Pietersburg to Mara later that night, the bus ride to Kranspoort the following day, and the sadness of having to deal with anxious questions about the meaning of death from my nine-year-old brother Thomas, who had been put by my mother in the care of a kind neighbour, all left me drained.

Dick generously sent me money by telegraph which I had to cash at the nearest post office, Mara, some fifteen kilometres away. The only form of transport available at the time was my father's Raleigh bicycle. A young man from the local primary school gave me a ride on its frame to and from Mara. The physical discomfort was nowhere near the emotional pain at the death of my father. If anything, the fact that I had to rely on this primitive means of transport underlined what it meant to lose a provider.

The journey later that week to my father's natal home in Uitkyk, where he was to be buried, was arranged by his old friend Mr Philip Bekker, who gave Thomas and me a lift in his van on Saturday morning – the day of the funeral. The sight of my grieving mother as she sat with other female relatives near my father's coffin was a confirmation of the reality of the loss and the finality of death. My father was unreachable – he lay motionless in the coffin. My mother was also unreachable as a nurturing figure to share my grief – she was nursing her own wound and could not comfort even her own children. We had to deal with our pain in our own individual ways. Tears were an inadequate answer; I felt numb in between the streams of tears.

My mother had arrived on Friday evening in the hearse accompanied by a busload of relatives from Johannesburg. The evening service had been held in the large family courtyard, and many locals kept an all-night vigil with singing and preaching. An ox was slaughtered in accordance with custom, to signify the death of a male head of household, as well as to provide meat for the meal after the burial the following day.

The final farewell to my father took place in the local church, where we filed past his open coffin during the funeral service. Dominee Van der Merwe came from Kranspoort to conduct the funeral service – an uncharacteristically generous act much appreciated by my family. My father looked so emaciated from the long-drawn-out illness. His handsome face was but a shadow of its old self. My mother looked frail and was supported by my father's aunt, Rakgadi Maria, and all seven children stood together. Molepo, the last born, then only six years old, was bewildered. He had travelled with my mother on the many visits to my father in hospital. Morongwa, my sister's two-year-old daughter, who my mother was looking after at the time, was also confused by the funeral activities.

The material deprivation my mother suffered as a result of my father's death greatly increased the sense of loss in our family. Her black mourning clothes, a mark of ritual pollution, signified her vulnerability. Her own mother, Koko Mamphela, went to live with her for three months in Kranspoort after the funeral to lend support and companionship. But the gap was too wide to be bridged even by maternal love.

The vulnerability of a widow often takes on concrete forms, which act as further insults to the wounded soul. At the beginning of 1968 my mother had to move out of the comfortable brick house allocated to my father as principal teacher of the local school. She then moved into a mud house on the edge of the village; this served only to increase her sense of marginalisation. She had to cope with not only emotional and material loss, but also the loss of status which she had derived from her spouse. All these she found too much to bear.

In 1969 she decided to return to Uitkyk in search of a better job and greater support from being closer to her family. She took up a teaching post at Ngoanamago School, which offered her a principalship, and thus a slightly higher income. This was the beginning of her wanderings from post to post seeking better prospects. She ended her teaching career at Maupje in February 1979 when she finally retired at the age of sixty.

At the end of 1967, the year of my father's death, I spent the summer vacation in Johannesburg with Dick Mmabane. During my stay at the house of my mother's elder sister, Mamogolo Ramadimetsa, which had been my base during that holiday, I was rudely interrupted by a telegraphic message from Natal Medical School:

YOU HAVE BEEN ADMITTED STOP PLEASE REPORT TO MRS WHITBY AT THE REGISTRATION OFFICE NOT LATER THAN 11TH JANUARY 1968 STOP

I was dismayed. I could not make head or tail of it. It was my first encounter with a telegram. My anxiety about my admission to the medical school led me to read the STOPs as directives for me to stop entertaining the hope of being admitted to the school. I burst into tears. Fortunately Mamogolo Ramadimetsa was there to calm me down and reassure me. It was a rude initiation for a country bumpkin into the world of telegraphic language.

The level of material deprivation which I endured in the late 1960s and 1970s seems unbelievable even to me today, looking back. Train fare for a second-class return ticket was simply beyond the means of my family. My mother, the only breadwinner, was earning R86 per month as a teacher. I had to appeal to Mamogolo Ramadimetsa to lend me R55, which enabled me to buy a ticket from Johannesburg to Durban, shop for some provisions, and have a bit of pocket money to see me to the medical school doors. Dick Mmabane gave me some money as well, which helped. I had to take each challenge as it came. I refused to think about where the next block of money would come from.

I sat nervously in the train compartment, before being joined by Khoadi Molaba, from Alexandra township in Johannesburg, and later by Patrick Jwili and his mother, who joined us at Balfour Station. Mrs Jwili was clearly very proud of her son, who had earned a master's degree from an American university after having completed his BSc at Fort Hare University in the Cape. She had misgivings about my intention of being in the same class as her son and Khoadi Molaba, who also had a Fort Hare BSc. She mercilessly set out to whittle away any remnant of self-confidence I had. How could I, a female and lacking as well the head start of a degree which the other two possessed, hope to make my way at medical school? Another vote of no confidence.

Patrick Jwili turned out to be a very amusing character who had acquired a fair number of Americanisms and unfortunately did not in the end make a success of his medical studies. He was excluded in third year. As things transpired, Mrs Jwili was partly right. My squeamish nature made my life very difficult. One of the compulsory experiments in physiology involved pithing a live frog (destroying the spinal cord by inserting a sharp needle into the spinal column), dissecting out its calf muscle, and running a series of tests to measure muscle function under different conditions. There were various stories at medical school of people whose careers had been frustrated by this particular experiment. One such person, Matsapola, was reported to have stabbed the frog in frustration and left it pinned to the experimental table, walking away never to be seen again at the medical school. The experiment acquired the nickname 'Matsapola' from this unfortunate incident.

Our physiology teacher tried in vain to desensitise me by encouraging me to play around with my hand in a bucket full of frogs. I simply could not stand the slimy creatures. In the final exam, by the time I eventually mustered enough courage to hold on to the frog (half an hour into experimental time), I was desperate. I squeezed all life out of the poor devil, and was so confused that I connected gas for use on the burner, instead of oxygen, to the muscle chamber, which killed off any prospect of muscle reaction. I was devastated. I sat down after wiping off tears of frustration and wrote about the theory behind the experiment in a desperate attempt to redeem myself. I was relieved to pass physiology in the end – never mind the third-class pass obtained.

Anatomy, another major second-year course, was much more interesting and better taught under the leadership of Professor Keen. Our first day in the dissecting room was marked by anxiety and fear of the unknown cadavers. How were you to overcome your sensibilities, and not only handle dead bodies but dissect them as well? Necessity triumphs over many barriers. The initial fear of the cadaver gradually gave way and with less than reverence some of the students started playing with body parts. It may well be that the unspoken and unacknowledged guilt about breaking an important taboo compelled you to be outrageous so as to be able to make light of the moment and live with yourself. We often had to be called to order by Professor Keen, who insisted on decorum in the dissecting room.

The blind faith of my high-school years, which urged me on to make the difficult career decision, paid off handsomely. My good matriculation grades and above-average performance in my premedical courses at the University of the North attracted the attention of the Medical School administrators. In addition to the full-cost grant from the Department of Bantu Education worth R450, which was then available to every African student, I won the 1968 South African Jewish Women's Association Scholarship worth about R200 and the Sir Ernest Oppenheimer Bursary worth R150 annually for the rest of my medical school years.

For the first time in my life I was in the lap of luxury. I could not bear the thought of spending this considerable sum of money on myself alone, as many of my contemporaries did. They bought clothes, music systems, and sometimes even cars. I led a modest life and sent my mother about R50 every so many months. That support was crucial for my mother to educate my younger brothers.

The rest of my medical subjects became less and less interesting to me as extracurricular activities began to take centre stage. Mediocrity became the hallmark of my performance. I scraped through the remaining years at medical school, gaining second-class passes as the best grades. So low was my interest in my medical career that I did not even celebrate my final-year success or attend graduation. A career so hard fought for became less and less attractive the closer I came to attaining my goal.

Chapter 8

Initiation into activism

THE COMPANY YOU KEEP OFTEN SHAPES YOUR LIFE IN significant ways. My friendship with Vuyelwa Mashalaba, a class-mate who I met in the first few days at medical school in January 1968, played a major role in shaping my future interests. Vuyelwa was a strik-ingly beautiful woman with sharp features, a smooth olive complexion, and a strong, well-proportioned body. She exuded self-confidence and spoke with a distinctive, polished English accent. She came from a family of strong, high-achieving sisters, headed by their widowed mother, who lived in Maclear, in the Eastern Cape.

Vuyelwa played tennis and loved classical music. She also had a large record collection of Miriam Makeba's music. She rekindled my love for classical music and tried to teach me tennis. Her enthusiasm failed to compensate for my lack of talent in sports, and we agreed to abandon what was clearly a road to nowhere.

Vuyelwa soon introduced me to her circle of friends, which included Steve Biko, Charles Sibisi, Chapman Palweni and Goolam Abram and, later, to Ben Mgulwa, Aubrey Mokoape, Ben Ngubane and many others who were student leaders at the time. We all attended student body meetings regularly from the middle of 1968. It was a completely new world for me. I listened quietly but with great interest to the debates on student politics of the day, which were dominated by criticism of the white liberal politics of the National Union of South African Students (NUSAS). I had to strain to follow the quick exchanges peppered as they were with acronyms, which were like Greek to me. I also marvelled at the self-confidence of student activists and the facility most of them had in using English to communicate.

Steve Biko was the main critic of white liberal politics, having been active as a NUSAS official and a member of the Students' Representative Council (SRC) at Natal. The thrust of his criticism was that white liberals' opposition to racial discrimination was ineffectual and unlikely to lead to any fundamental change in South Africa because it lacked a coherent critique of racism and its socioeconomic manifestations. He contended that few white liberals were themselves committed to non-racialism and social justice to the extent of being prepared to sacrifice their privileged position in society in the quest for greater equity. He cited the ease with which former NUSAS leaders and other activists settled into privileged positions once they graduated from university as evidence that white liberal politics was viewed as a pastime that one pursued so long as it did not interfere with the 'real' world of white privilege.

Steve also spoke out against the paternalism of white liberals who tended to dominate opposition politics in the 1960s. He felt that their paternalism in part stemmed from their deep-seated feelings of superiority towards black people. He criticised their definition of multi-racialism, which assumed the superiority of Western culture and the automatic assimilation of blacks into its fold. He was critical of the reliance blacks placed on white leadership. He charged blacks with lack of faith in themselves and of having internalised an inferiority complex: such self-inflicted psychological oppression ensured their continued physical and political oppression. He urged black students to see themselves as black first and foremost, and to commit themselves to the total liberation of all black people in South Africa.

Steve's conclusion was that the only way to effect fundamental change in South Africa would be for the oppressed people themselves to take the initiative and to work for their own liberation. He drew on the experiences and the approaches of the Black Power movement in the United States for inspiration, as well as on the Négritude writers such as Frantz Fanon and Aimé Césaire who he quoted extensively in his speeches and later in his writings.

Ben Ngubane was Steve Biko's main opponent in the debates. Ben's view was that the forces of apartheid were powerful and evil and should be denied the pleasure of seeing disunity among the anti-apartheid ranks. He conceded the points Steve was making in his critique, but disagreed with the suggestion that black politics be consolidated away from the white liberal fold.

Ben defended NUSAS on the medical school campus to the very last, when the student body finally voted narrowly in favour of Steve's motion of central disaffiliation from NUSAS. This paved the way for the black South African Students' Organisation (SASO)[10] to operate on a par with NUSAS, using a campus branch affiliation system. Ben argued that NUSAS had stood firm in the face of harassment by the apartheid state and thus deserved the loyalty of all freedom-loving students. He was an eloquent speaker, but was no match for the younger and more passionate Biko. Ben often lost his temper, and became more cynical and disillusioned, finally fading out of the political arena, only to re-emerge in the 1980s as an Inkatha official – a not insignificant political move, crowned with a cabinet post in the first Government of National Unity in 1994.

The tentacles of apartheid spread everywhere in South Africa in the 1960s. The section of Natal University which catered for black students was known as the University of Natal Non-European Section.

---

10 SASO was founded in July 1969, with Steve Biko as its first president.

(This became known as the University of Natal Black Section (UNB) after SASO requested that the name be officially changed in 1970.) Professor Owen Horwood was principal of the university at the time. He later became Minister of Finance, and was revealed to have been party to the Information Scandal which rocked the National Party government of John Vorster, and finally forced Vorster to resign. Horwood shamelessly asserted that he had taken particular care, as Minister of Finance charged with responsibility for government expenditure, not to read the documents he had signed to authorise the expenditure of vast sums of public money to promote apartheid. The irony of history lies in the fact that the same man unknowingly promoted the emergence of radical black student politics in South Africa. For it was Horwood who authorised the financing of a seminar at Mariannhill which led to the formation of SASO. Perhaps he would also have pleaded not guilty had he been confronted. How could anyone have expected him to care about black student politics at the time? After all, he was only a vice-chancellor, not a keeper of his students.

Historical accidents do give rise to major tides which sweep the unwary aside or redirect them into paths that they could not have anticipated. The formation of SASO and the subsequent maturation of the Black Consciousness Movement into a political force to be reckoned with became the main focus of Steve Biko's life. One could not help admiring this tall, handsome, eloquent and totally dedicated activist.

Natal Medical School did not only provide me with medical training, but it offered an environment for the transformation of my life from an innocent rural girl to a person who became alive to the vast possibilities which life has to offer. I took time to absorb the vibrancy around me. I was keenly interested in the discussions, which were a political education for me. I learned about the true history of my country, the struggle to resist conquest, and later the struggle for equal rights with those who had conquered us, the stories of the heroes of the struggle (no women were included in these narratives at the time), and the role students could and should play to take the struggle forward. I began to understand and to interpret my own personal experiences of racism and oppression in the light of the discussions going on around me. Given my rural background and lack of access to news media and political discussions till then, I had not fully grasped the relation between the personal and the political.

The University of the North had not presented me with any opportunities for exposure to student activism during 1967. The university authorities were rigidly part of the apartheid system and ensured that the university fulfilled its mission of training blacks for subservient roles in society, discouraging any public debate on political issues. The then registrar used to boast, 'My vel is my graad' (My skin is my degree), an acknowledgement that he held this senior position simply because of the colour of his skin. The SRC at the University of the North was no more than an efficient organiser of entertainment activities, posing no challenge to authority at the institution. I did not once attend a student meeting or hold a political discussion at the University of the North. Social life revolved around entertainment events such as ballroom dancing, sports, picnics and parties. A fine preparation for life as a petit bourgeois on the margins of society and power.

<hr />

At the University of Natal the circle of friends centred on Steve Biko coalesced into a tight-knit community as the activism intensified. I was drawn closer into this circle and began to adopt some of the behaviour of the group. I shed the wig I used to wear whenever I felt I needed to look more 'respectable' than my short boyish hair suggested. The 'black is beautiful' slogan of the time had its desired impact on all of us. Some of us switched over to the use of our African names instead of the 'slave names' we had hitherto used. I also became more daring in my outfits, taking advantage of my figure and the fashion trends of the time, which were affordable even to me with my shoestring budget: hot pants became my speciality. Hot pants were exceedingly short pants which fitted snugly around one's body, hovering tantalisingly around the limits of modesty.

Once tested, the boundaries of conventional behaviour began to fall. I started experimenting with smoking cigarettes by offering to light for those needing a smoke. I would comment that it was unlikely I could smoke, but continued to take a puff or two until I got hooked and started buying cigarettes myself. I chose the mild blend Vuyelwa smoked. I also started drinking beer and other alcoholic beverages shared by the group. I slowly but surely embraced the student culture of the 1960s.

We lived at the Alan Taylor Residence, which was a segregated residence for black students at Natal University. An old army barrack situated next to the Mobil Oil Refinery in Austerville, not far from Durban Airport, it had been used during the Second World War to house troops and was then renovated to serve as a student residence when the medical school was established in 1951. We commuted daily by bus to and from medical school in Umbilo Road, some five kilometres away, to attend classes and participate in university activities. Only preliminary[11] and first-year students attended classes at the Alan Taylor premises. The level of pollution from the oil refinery was such that you could see traces of soot when you blew your nose, and the bed linen would be covered with a black layer of dust if you left a window open on a windy day. We justified our cigarette smoking by pointing to the inevitability of inhaling carcinogens in the environment in which we were forced to live. A lame excuse for engaging in risk-taking behaviour, but it sounded very smart at the time.

---

11 Preliminary year (popularly called Prelim) was used as an academic support year for those students who did not have satisfactory matriculation mathematics and science grades to be admitted directly into first year.

We used to have parties on weekends at which we drank beer and sat around in the smoke-filled room of one of the members of the group, talking politics, listening to Malcolm X's speeches on tape, as well as those of Martin Luther King Jr, discussing banned books which were secretly circulated among friends, sharing jokes, and also singing and dancing. Our weekends were carefree and full of fun. We became welded together into a sharing and caring community. At the beginning of each year younger people who were new students joined the community – Malusi Mpumlwana, Keith Mokoape and Seolo Solombela were the most notable additions to our group.

Frank Talk and Black Consciousness

T HE YEAR 1970 MARKED THE REAL TURNING POINT IN THE
maturation of the Black Consciousness Movement. Steve Biko and
Barney Pityana were participants in a seminar of student leaders of all
colours and political persuasions, held at the Abe Bailey Institute (now
the Centre for Conflict Resolution) at the University of Cape Town
(UCT) during the 1969 December holidays. In the preparation for their
presentation a lot of their own thoughts were clarified, and their papers
reflected a growing sense of confidence in the importance of their mission as student leaders and the role they were to play as liberators of
their own people.[12]

Maturation brought about a growing sense of the need for self-
definition. Common terms of the time such as 'non-white' and 'non-
European' exemplified the extent to which both blacks and whites in
South Africa had accepted European 'whiteness' as the gold standard
against which all else was to be measured. Steve articulated his thoughts
on this issue in the regular feature he contributed in the SASO *News-
letter* with the title 'I Write What I Like', under the pseudonym of Frank
Talk, both defiant symbolic statements by the author. The term 'black'
was adopted and defined as referring to 'those who are politically, socially and economically discriminated against, and identified themselves

---

12 The conference proceedings were later published by David Philip under the title
Student Perspectives on South Africa (Cape Town, 1972).

as such'. It was thus possible for one to remain a 'non-white' by virtue of failure to identify with the struggle for liberation – a rather interesting twist of logic which shows up the ridiculousness of race definitions and exposes their perilous political foundations. But the 1970s was the decade when blacks of necessity had to redefine race politics as a first step away from their entrapment and disempowerment by centuries of racism. The demands of philosophical precision were not allowed to interfere with this self-definition.

I spent many late nights helping Steve meet deadlines for his articles. He was notoriously poor at managing time. I would write down his thoughts as a stream of consciousness which he would dictate to me, and later I would read the text back to him as he typed with two fingers until it was done – not uncommonly in the early hours of the morning of the deadline.

Aubrey Mokoape, Keith's elder brother, used to engage Steve in serious all-night discussions. Aubrey's sympathies lay with the Pan Africanist Congress, with which he had cut his political teeth as a high-school student. Steve enjoyed the debates with Aubrey. He found Aubrey challenging and intellectually stimulating, forcing him to clarify his own thoughts on a number of questions in his espousal of the Black Consciousness philosophy. Aubrey argued from his Africanist perspective against the inclusion of 'coloureds' and Indians in the Black Consciousness Movement. As he became more and more liberated by increasing levels of alcohol, he would argue that Indians should be reminded that there was a ship leaving Durban harbour every Thursday for India which they should be encouraged to make use of. And what about the 'coloureds'? someone would ask good-naturedly. He would respond good-humouredly in the style of some of the 1960s Pan Africanist demagogues: 'The coloureds – eh – the – eh – coloureds – underground!'

A number of African students shared this view and expressed their reservations about sharing a political programme with Indians. For example, Klaas Mogotlane summed up his feelings by stating that he would hate to see Steve dying for the liberation of Indians! Langa Duba, a final-year student in 1969, would occasionally stagger into Steve's room after his regular weekend binges, and express his dismay at the company Steve was keeping: 'Biko, you are going down, my friend. Your room is full of curry! You are going down, my friend!'

Goolam Abram (Gees), himself classified Indian, used to laugh at this anti-Indian rhetoric, particularly that coming from the Langa Dubas of those days. He was also Aubrey Mokoape's friend and would listen to the invitation to take the ship to India as an 'honorary African' and be able to laugh off this brand of Africanist fantasy. Gees understood the depth of Africans' anger towards Indians and the reasons for their mistrust. The rise of Idi Amin as the leader of Uganda and his expulsion of Asians simply fuelled the fires of hatred and mistrust. Strini Moodley, the SASO Director of Publications at the time, devoted an entire address to warning Indian students that they would face the same fate unless they dedicated themselves to the struggle for liberation and justice for all.

◇◇◇

Barney Pityana became more and more part of the community of activists at UNB from 1970 onwards. He had fallen victim to the mass expulsions from Fort Hare in 1969. He was elected the new Permanent Secretary of SASO after the annual General Student Council in June 1970. Steve managed to negotiate with the Alan Taylor authorities for the use of space at the residence as premises for the national head office of the fledgling organisation. Barney's presence injected a measure of greater discipline into the running of SASO. His methodical approach to tasks and his organisational skills boosted SASO's image considerably and transformed it into a more professional national student organisation. Steve used to concede that Barney was a better organiser and writer because he was more disciplined. Barney and Steve complemented each other's strengths as well as mitigated each other's weaknesses.

The location of the SASO head office at UNB made political sense in the light of the central role played by the Natal Medical School community in the leadership of the nascent Black Consciousness Movement. In the first place, Natal University was the most liberal of the campuses with a significant black student population, in stark contrast to the oppressive political climate at the other universities set aside for exclusive use by black students. One could with advantage exploit the professed non-racialism of Natal University. In the second place, medical students had a sense of leadership and mission in relation to their less fortunate counterparts in the so-called bush colleges[13] where political activities were more constrained. SASO was thus able to function in a supportive environment which allowed open access to all.

From 1970 onwards I became increasingly drawn into activism as a friend of Steve and Barney and as a member of the SASO local committee, whose chairperson (or chairman, in the language of the time) I later became. We organised many discussion sessions on campus, canvassed for active membership, and got involved in work camps as part of our commitment to active engagement in the problems which plagued oppressed communities. Medical students ran a clinic at the Alan Taylor Residence for poor people, named Happy Valley Clinic, after the ironic name of the surrounding district where desperately poor communities lived. We participated in the weekend sessions at this clinic. The Happy Valley Clinic was a shoestring affair which was enthusiastically used by the local people – more a commentary on their desperate circumstances than a reflection of the quality of the service it offered.

We also established contact with another poor community in New

---

13 The university colleges established by the National Party government for the exclusive use of black people in line with the policy of separate development.

Farm, near the Gandhi Centre in Phoenix. Mewa Ramgobin, then married to Ela Gandhi, a grand-daughter of the Mahatma, was an enthusiastic supporter of the new student politics and assisted our work in the area. We soon opened a clinic at the Gandhi Centre which served the poor people in that area. Our knowledge of community development was dangerous, but our enthusiasm compensated for many potentially devastating errors of judgement in our dealings with the local people.

An added complication to community development at New Farm was the entry of predominantly white students led by Dr Rick Turner, a political science lecturer at the University of Natal known for his socialist views. Rick used to visit the Alan Taylor Residence and became friendly with all of us. He argued at length with Steve about the analytical limitations of Black Consciousness, which a socialist perspective could remedy by adding a class analysis to address some of the complexities of power relations in South Africa. Steve in turn pointed out to Rick that an economic class analysis which ignored the racist nature of capitalist exploitation in South Africa, and in many other parts of the globe, was itself inadequate. White workers identified more with white owners of capital than with black workers, Steve would conclude. The debate would drift into a discussion of the false consciousness of white workers, ending with Steve challenging Rick to go out and conscientise white workers to prove that his approach would work in apartheid South Africa. Steve's often-quoted remark in this regard was: 'Go and talk to Van Tonder [a stereotypical conservative Afrikaner worker] about solidarity with black workers, and see what his response would be.'

Both viewpoints were part of the reality of social relations in our society, but each lay emphasis on one aspect of the South African problem without due consideration of the complexities. The further development of Black Consciousness depended at that time on its greater recognition of the importance of divisions within the black community along lines of class, gender, age and geographic location. So, too, Marxists in South Africa, as elsewhere, needed to recognise the importance of racial categories as a determinant of a person's place in a racist society, as well as developing a better-integrated analysis of gender, age and geographic place.[14]

Few white activists saw the conscientisation of whites as an attractive proposition. It was not surprising that Rick Turner took his disciples to the New Farm area to work in the same community where we had been engaged. It was the height of insensitivity on his part, and engendered a lot of anger from black students, who saw it as a demonstration of white arrogance and a direct challenge. If ever there was a case of Black Consciousness needing to stand up to white people, one couldn't have written a better script than this one. The dispute was finally resolved through discussions in which Steve participated in a mediatory role, but it left a nasty taste in the mouth.

The greatest challenge to my nascent leadership qualities came in December 1971. 1 was assigned by the SASO head office to lead a student work camp in December 1971 to Winterveld, a huge squatter area near Pretoria, which continues to present a problem to local authorities and development workers. We were accommodated by Sister Doris, who ran her own private clinic in Mabopane, a nearby township, and were co-hosted by the local Catholic church run by two priests, one of whom I still remember, Fr Clement Mokoka. It was not an easy assignment. We were far from prepared for the tasks we were to undertake, namely, assessing the needs of the local community and identifying a project we could undertake effectively in the limited time we had over the December holiday period. Only youthful enthusiasm could explain our courage in tackling such a complex task without the requisite training.

---

14 A more elaborate critique of this aspect of the Black Consciousness Movement in South Africa is to be found in my contribution to *Bounds of Possibility*, edited by Barney Pityana, Mamphela Ramphele, Malusi Mpumlwana and Lindy Wilson (Cape Town and London, 1991).

Problems surfaced at a number of levels. Firstly, our hosts were not as supportive as had been expected when we made the original arrangement. The Catholic priests were quarrelling among themselves and wanted us to take sides in their conflicts. Sister Doris was a temperamental woman whose real focus did not seem to have been nursing care. She was often away from her clinic, commuting to her home in the Pretoria township of Mamelodi, leaving us to run the clinic without supervision – a scary experience especially with deliveries of babies, which came unexpectedly.

Then again, communication with the SASO head office and guidance from its staff were not what they should have been. Harry Nengwekhulu, the Permanent Organiser, who was directly responsible for project direction, was often not accessible, as he maintained an extensive travel schedule to keep in touch with all the SASO branches in the country. Whenever I finally tracked him down, his attitude was dismissive. He urged us to be patient with the teething problems we were experiencing. I doubt that he could have offered more support anyway, given the pioneering nature of the work we were doing at the time. We operated on a shoestring budget which left little fat for our basic living needs – a recipe for discontent in the ranks.

Our group of students consisted of about ten activists from different campuses around the country. Welding such a group into a team was a task too daunting for an inexperienced twenty-four-year-old to accomplish without assistance. There was a particularly difficult woman who became increasingly hostile towards me as her frustration grew along with her disillusionment. She threw tantrums and made herself thoroughly unpleasant.

We all became increasingly disillusioned when the local population failed to respond to our attempts to conscientise them. Their sense of powerlessness seemed to be complete. The reality of the powerlessness of the very poorest people threatened the foundations of our idealism.

It became difficult to see how these same people were ever going to rise up against their oppressors and liberate themselves. Not only were they exploited by their white employers, but they also seemed to offer little resistance to black moneymakers who preyed on them, posing as healers, moneylenders and landowners. They seemed so resigned to their fate that one questioned the wisdom of our attempts to engage them in trying to change their circumstances.

I was particularly horrified by the extent to which some medical professionals were acting as sponsors for quacks who posed as healers. One particular case involved a 'Doctor' Mohlala who ran a private clinic which included a maternity section. A prominent general practitioner acted as his sponsor, no doubt for a significant consideration. 'Dr' Mohlala claimed to have done his training in obstetrics at the University of the North – an impossibility, because that university had no medical school. The quest for healing often makes people most vulnerable to exploitation and manipulation by unscrupulous people. The end of the work camp came not a moment too soon. I had learned a few lessons about the real world of community development – the complexities of a culture of survival were to become clearer much later.

———◆◇◆———

My years as a student activist were a time of immense personal growth. As a SASO local chair, I participated in leadership development seminars, which were then referred to as formation schools. I benefited enormously from them. As a result I was able to transcend the naked anger which comes from waking up to the realisation of having been cheated out of a common heritage in your own society. It was painful to realise how you had been systematically disadvantaged simply because of the colour of your skin, an irrelevant attribute. But it was essential knowing this if you were to become more focused on defeating the ends of the oppressors. It was not an easy transition. To live with the knowledge of having been cheated and yet not to seek personal retribution takes a lot of energy and maturity.

I remember Barney threatening to leave us to our own devices because some of us would not accept that some white people could be part of the resource group at one of the leadership development seminars in the early 1970s. The younger, more radical element felt that there was no scope for collaboration with whites in view of their acquiescent racism. Grudgingly, we had to accept that there were truly good white people who were as passionately committed to liberation as we were. Anne Hope, a member of a lay Catholic sisterhood, was a case in point. She was one of the most important resource people in leadership training seminars for young black activists. She used Paulo Freire's methods to help SASO develop a sound methodology for its conscientisation programme. She trained eight of the top leaders, who later trained us.

The confusion which reigned among new converts like me was both a reflection of the proverbial over-eagerness of the converted and an indicator of the danger of political analyses which by their very nature have to operate at the level of generalities to make sense. Distinguishing between white racism as a system to be fought and individual white people who may be innocent bystanders in a racist society was a nuance too complex for many young enthusiasts to grasp. The danger of fundamentalism looms large under such circumstances. Our respect for Barney's integrity and our confidence in his leadership made it possible for us to accept his judgement grudgingly.

I became increasingly self-confident and vocal in student meetings and in national student forums. I had begun to understand the culture of public speaking and the idiom of political discourse. Mastery of the art of using the standing rules of conduct in meetings to neutralise and subdue political opponents in debates was an essential part of the culture. I became quite an aggressive debater and was known for not suffering fools gladly. Moreover, I intimidated men who did not expect aggression from women. Soon a group of similarly inclined women, Vuyelwa Mashalaba, Nomsisi Kraai, Deborah Matshoba and Thenjiwe Mtintso, became a force to be reckoned with at annual SASO meetings. Ours was not a feminist cause at that time – feminism was a later development in my political consciousness – but an insistence on being taken seriously as activists in our own right among our peers.

Our political activism stretched beyond campus engagements. Protest meetings against the continuing imprisonment of black political leaders on Robben Island, commemoration services for those killed in detention, and solidarity meetings with struggles elsewhere in the world were part of the menu of political activism. There was not a dull moment. We linked up with off-campus organisations such as the Natal Indian Congress and other cultural groups which used culture as a safe haven for restricted political expression.

───◇◇◇───

Steve's energy became increasingly focused on his political activism at the expense of his medical studies. It became difficult for him to maintain a balance between his personal development and national service – a common problem of many student activists. It came as no surprise that he was finally excluded from Natal Medical School in the middle of 1971, after failing a supplementary examination for his second-year courses which he was repeating. He was naturally disappointed, but he was not given to brooding over a problem for too long. His attention turned to securing a base from which to pursue his activism. SPROCAS 2,[15] a joint project of the Christian Institute headed by Dr Beyers Naudé and the South African Council of Churches (SACC) headed by Mr John Rees, presented him with an appropriate base. The project had just presented its report of a study coordinated by Rick

---

15 SPROCAS 2, The Study Project on Christianity in Apartheid Society.

Turner which challenged the churches to devise an active programme to promote justice and peace.

The outcome of deliberations on the SPROCAS report was a decision to establish the Black Community Programmes (BCP) as a way of responding to the need for development necessitated by decades of injustice. A parallel white consciousness programme was to have been started to create awareness among whites of the evil of apartheid and the need for repentance. Bennie Khoapa, a social worker who was then working for the Young Men's Christian Association (YMCA), was chosen as the Director of the Black Community Programmes. Bennie had been a supportive admirer of the young student activists of the day. He used to organise an end-of-year party for all of us on the lawn of his house in Umlazi township, where we sat sipping beer and enjoying a braai. He was only too pleased to have Steve as his assistant in the new venture. As it turned out, Steve had thought through some of the issues more than Bennie had, and was enormously helpful to Bennie in negotiating with the Christian Institute and the SACC for a proper supportive relationship that would not stifle the new venture.

Steve had identified the need for documenting the lives of black South Africans as vital to encouraging them to become agents of their own liberation. One had to write history to make history. Documentation and research among blacks were, and remain, under-developed for a variety of reasons. The oral tradition which is strong among Africans did not lay a firm foundation for respect for the written word. Then again, the deliberate under-development of blacks by means of Bantu Education discouraged the emergence of a love for the written word and good record-keeping. Moreover, the instability of the life of the poor and marginal, subject to forced removals and the vicissitudes of inadequate shelter, led to the loss of many important historical and other documents. Finally, the scarcity of black researchers and social scientists made blacks vulnerable to becoming the objects of other people's studies, with all the risks of limited insight inherent in that form of scholarship.

The annual reports of the Institute of Race Relations in the 1960s and early 1970s were a case in point. They were chronicles of the victimisation of blacks at the hands of the apartheid regime. Blacks were denied any active role in the chronicle. Nothing positive about what blacks did was reported with any prominence. It was as if such positive reporting would reduce the impact of the reports on the oppression blacks suffered. Blacks were depicted as the ultimate victims, completely lacking in agency.

Necessity and passion are powerful motivators, overcoming the lack of social science and formal research training. Single-handedly Steve designed the first edition of the *Black Review*, a comprehensive report of what went on in the black community: the good, the bad and the ugly. The areas covered included political developments, education, housing, worker issues, arts and sports. The data were derived from newspaper cuttings, visits to newspaper libraries, and Hansard reports on parliamentary proceedings. Malusi Mpumlwana (who had also been excluded from Natal Medical School at the end of 1970) and Tomeka Mafole and Welile Nhlapo (both of whom had been expelled from Fort Hare earlier for political reasons) became Steve's temporary assistants in the enormous task of putting together the first edition of *Black Review* during the second half of 1971 and the whole of 1972. Ironically, Steve's pioneering work could not be publicly acknowledged without jeopardising the publication of the report: the banning order which was served on him at the beginning of 1973 prohibited him from participating in any publication – part of the state's attempt to limit the spread of ideas of political activists in apartheid South Africa. To protect the baby he had given birth to, other people had to claim credit for it. The first issue of *Black Review* consequently bore the name of Bennie Khoapa as editor.

The success of new ventures often rests on sound administrative capacity – a factor which many radical movements ignore at their peril. Ms Hester Fortune, a beautiful and self-confident woman who was executive secretary of the Black Community Programmes, was the pivot around which the organisation revolved. She kept a measure of sanity in the office of the Black Community Programmes at 86 Beatrice Street in Durban, which became a hive of activity, attracting welcome and unwelcome visitors who wanted a piece of the action. Hester had the sophistication to keep a necessary balance in the office, avoiding complete openness and lack of discipline, while creating a welcoming, supportive environment where serious work was possible.

I spent more time during 1972 at 86 Beatrice Street than I did at medical school, even though it was my final year of study. I helped Steve with his new tasks and became completely absorbed in them. The pursuit of an academic degree was no match for the excitement of being part of a process that was shaping history. Strong personal bonds with fellow activists contributed to the commitment to the cause and the desire for active participation. Bennie remained a restraining yet supportive influence on youthful over-enthusiasm. He was a true elder statesman of the kind of society we were yearning to establish.

Activist life was not without its frustrating moments. The biggest tension arose between the demands of my body for long hours of sleep (eight hours minimum a night) and the culture of late nights which was an integral part of activist life at the time. I could not keep pace with the rest of the activist community. Irritability was an early warning sign for me as the nights became too long for my body to bear. A second problem was my body's need for regular meals. I remember one particularly unpleasant experience of a train journey to Johannesburg with Steve. We had been doing the usual last-minute rushing around when we realised that we had to leave immediately to catch the train, which left Durban at lunch time. We travelled third class, so our carriage stopped quite far from the shops at Pietermaritzburg Station. Steve, who was not particularly agile and was also very tired, could not make it to the café to get us some food before the train pulled out of the station. I felt like screaming from my hunger pangs, which were compounded by the knowledge that the next meal would only be the following day in Johannesburg.

Steve knew what was coming, so he quietly positioned himself on the uncomfortable bunk and fell asleep. I could have killed him! I eventually also fell asleep. We were met at Park Station by Bokwe Mafuna, who took us to his one-roomed house in Alexandra where it took time to prepare brunch. We finally ate at about ten o'clock. My hunger pangs were by then tamed. The frail body had a lot to learn to incorporate the emerging activist in me.

⬥⬥⬥

My increasing activism made me more and more defiant towards authority figures at the medical school. The patronising ways of some of the teachers particularly irked me. The Dean, Professor E. B. Adams, who was also the head of the Department of Medicine, had an unfortunate manner in this regard. He saw no problem in probing the political views of students in his tutorial group. He completely ignored any body language from us indicating our discomfort with his inquisitions. He was particularly preoccupied with developments in what was then Rhodesia, and would open the tutorial discussions with 'Ms Ramphele, what do you think of the situation in Rhodesia?' I would respond by shrugging my shoulders, because I really did not think that I could hold any sensible political discussion with a conservative English-speaking white South African like him.

I was also critical of his bedside manner. He seemed to me patronising in his treatment of African patients, who would be referred to as 'the old boy' or 'old John' or whatever was the first name of the patient.

He was undoubtedly a good medical specialist, but my antipathy towards him overshadowed my respect for his professional competence. Our relationship became increasingly difficult. After a while I stopped attending his tutorials.

But he would not let his authority be challenged. He called me to his office in the Dean's suite and demanded an explanation. I went over the top in my defiance. I lit a cigarette and refused to put it out when he told me to do so. I told him that when he stopped talking politics in his tutorials he should let me know, so that I could then attend, because we had nothing in common to discuss politically. He was appalled. He reminded me that he had the power to report me to the Medical and Dental Council for my bad behaviour and that my medical career would be at risk. There was no retreat for me. I dared him to act as he pleased. He dismissed me from his office in a rage.

When I completed my final exams at the end of that year, he made it known to his colleagues that he would not have me in his firm in Ward D at King Edward VIII Hospital. Those who knew me assured him that he need not worry about that prospect, as the feeling of antipathy was mutual. I remember seeing him at the international departure hall at the Johannesburg airport – then known as Jan Smuts Airport – a decade later, and not being able to bring myself to greet him. Whether he recognised me or not, I shall never know.

The end of final-year medical examinations was a great relief. The day after results were known we had to take the Hippocratic oath at Howard College on the main university campus. We were given use of graduation gowns, which we signed for and had to return afterwards. The auspiciousness of the occasion and its symbolic significance escaped me. My mind was on more important things. I had to rush back from the ceremony – I did not even stay for the tea which was part of the celebrations. As far as I was concerned I had to get back to Beatrice Street to complete some or other task which was of greater importance to me. I simply left the borrowed gown in the office at the medical school though there was no one to receive it at the time.

I was shocked several months later when I received a letter of demand from the university to return the gown or else pay for it. I wrote back to explain what had happened and to assure the university that I had returned the gown but had unfortunately not signed it in. The university was insistent: they had lost too many gowns to irresponsible students. I lost my cool. I wrote a not-so-polite letter back stating that I attached no value to academic dress, as demonstrated by my graduation *in absentia* earlier that year even though I was in Durban at the time. That settled that.

Looking back now, I feel ashamed of my behaviour, but in the circumstances of the period I felt good about my defiance. As a woman, an African woman at that, one had to be outrageous to be heard, let alone be taken seriously.

Chapter 10

Personal relationships

FOR MOST MEN A CHOICE OF CAREER IS A SEPARATE EXER-
cise from the important task of identifying a life partner. Their
wives are often people they meet while pursuing the career of their
choice. Social pressures on most women, however, often make them
subordinate their career to the need to become desirable as a prospective marriage partner. Young women almost have to position themselves strategically to enter upon the role of a supporting spouse. My
own naïveté did not alert me to this. In fact, it may partly explain why
I have been reasonably successful at making important decisions in many
areas of my life and yet repeatedly made disastrous choices in my personal relationships.

It may well also have to do with paying very little attention to friendships in my childhood and teenage years. I was quite happy keeping
my own company, particularly with a book in my hand, or simply
sleeping. I preferred the company of adults who ignored me and left
me alone to my thoughts or daydreams. My friends were few and far
between, and I did not feel the need for friendships to become complete as a person. But my poor choices may also have stemmed from my
discomfort with traditional relationships with men which I observed
around me, and which I felt did not suit me.

I do not recall having any of the teenage anguish of struggling for an
identity or being preoccupied with my appearance or my self-image or
with the need to be accepted by my peers. I was at peace with myself

and remained attached to my mother as the most important person in my life. My brothers and sister found me a bit of a pain because of my attachment to my mother and my independence and self-confidence, which they felt was excessive.

Being top of your class is a decided disadvantage for any girl at school. None of my classmates felt comfortable with me because they thought I did not have any reason to respect them, and I appeared self-contained to the point of being aloof. Dick Mmabane, who was my classmate in Standard 9 and 10 at Setotolwane High School in 1965 and 1966, decided to take a chance after a long period of watching and waiting. His interest in me was indicated in a gradual, tentative way – he later confessed that he had expected me to dismiss him at first base.

Although I was nearly nineteen years old, and in Standard 10, I had not till then really been interested in males. There had been one or two teachers who showed an interest in me, but I was not responsive. On the contrary, I was quite appalled by the advances of an elderly married teacher, which I regarded as an insult. In fact, I threatened to report him to the headmaster if he dared to repeat his advances. I lost all respect for him and made a public show of not paying attention to his lessons. I openly read magazines during his periods to indicate my defiance. Mine was a trump card he could ignore only at the risk of losing his job. He was indeed fortunate that this incident happened in the days before sexual harassment was recognised for what it is.

My relationship with Dick started playfully, but became intensified over the following months. The intoxication of being madly in love is the stuff first encounters are made of. I could not help wondering why I had not been interested in this wonderful experience before. It is such an affirming feeling to be loved and adored so openly. My heart leapt into a happy rhythm each time we went out together.

Dick's mother, Machipi Mmabane, was no ordinary woman. She was a strong, self-reliant person who had had to fend for herself and her seven children, working herself up from her rural background in the Warmbaths area (now Bela-Bela) of the then Transvaal, through informal trading, to becoming a successful owner of a fish and chips shop in Zone 4, Diepkloof, in Soweto. Dick's father was a shell of a man, who had seen better days. I got to know him as a somewhat unstable person who spent his days drinking home-brewed beer at the local beer garden.

Dick's mother provided well for her eldest son; one of many children, he was the apple of her eye. He dressed well and was well spoken. It is not surprising that he was chosen to speak on behalf of the final-year class at our farewell matric dance at the end of 1966. It was a memorable occasion for me. My sister Mashadi had sent me a fashionable powder-blue short-sleeved crimplene suit, a pair of black patent-leather high-heeled shoes and stockings. It was my first real occasion to dress up. I felt good and Dick looked approvingly at me when I joined him at the party. The evening just melted away. We bid goodbye to our high school days and moved into the world of adulthood.

I had not bargained on the complications of love relationships. We parted after spending a few days together with some friends in the old township in Pietersburg. The December holidays seemed interminably long because I missed Dick so much. It was a relief to catch up with him at the beginning of the 1967 academic year at the University of the North, where we were both new students.

No sooner had I settled in than I began being harassed by his former girlfriend, a senior student at the university. She made it clear that she would not let a 'fresher' (a newcomer) win a love tussle with her. Even though I loved Dick, I felt I was not going to get involved in fights over boyfriends and made that known to both Dick and his former girlfriend. Although Dick was unambiguous in declaring where his interests lay and that their relationship was over, it took a while before she stopped bothering me, and her dislike for me was visible whenever we met. I did not feel that I was missing anything by not being liked by her.

The social life at the University of the North was rather unimaginative. It revolved around a mixture of old-fashioned formalities and some spontaneous activities particularly among the younger students. The older and more mature students tended to be rather formal in both dress and manner. You were expected to walk to and from classes with your friends, to dress up for dinner, and to be walked by your boyfriend from the dining room to your residence, where lovers stood around and chatted until study time at about 7.30 p.m., when all made for the library to settle down for two or three hours of work. It was also customary for the men to accompany their girlfriends back to the residences after the library sessions and to steal a goodnight kiss. Male residences were out of bounds to female students, and men students could only get as far as the entrance hall of the women's residences.

I got bored with this routine and preferred the company of my female friends with whom I could be completely uninhibited. We would walk together to the local shopping centre after our practical laboratory work was done, buy ourselves snacks, including hot vetkoek, and enjoy ourselves. I did not have many fancy clothes, nor cared to dress up except on special occasions.

The world of science students was somewhat on the margins of campus social life. The Science Faculty lay at the lower end of the campus, hidden away behind trees. Our laboratory work also entailed a different schedule from that of social science and humanities students, who were often free in the afternoons. Dick had registered for a law degree, so our worlds grew apart. I got to see him less and less during the week. Senior science students play a useful role as laboratory demonstrators and often help new students with their studies. My friends and I befriended a senior science student who was a laboratory demonstrator in botany. He had a great sense of humour, which made our meal-times more pleasant than the monotonous menus would ordinarily have permitted.

I did not realise that Dick was becoming jealous of what he saw as a close relationship until it was almost too late. It was customary for us to spend Saturday mornings in Pietersburg window-shopping and seeing a movie at the cinema or visiting friends in the township. I waited in vain one weekend for Dick to walk to town. On the Monday afternoon I ran into him and innocently asked where he had been on the weekend. He dismissed my questions lightly without showing his true feelings. I asked him to walk me to the library, and did not detect the irony in his voice when he suggested that I ask the science student (let's call him Sidney) to accompany me. Unfortunately for me, Sidney was nearby and I put the request to him. Dick was devastated. I remained blissfully unaware of the depth of his anger. One of his friends eventually made me aware of the pain I had caused him. We made up, and I became a little wiser.

My insistence on going to Natal Medical School the following year began to create tensions with Dick. He feared that he might lose me if we parted. In my innocence I saw no reason for his concern. I saw no conflict between my career plans and our continued relationship. In any case I would not have changed my plans for the sake of our relationship – not because I did not care for him, but because I wasn't prepared to give up my career. I did not share his anxiety about what distance could do to a love relationship between young people like us. I was, after all, still very green.

We spent the December holidays together in Soweto and had a good time. I was staying with my aunt, Mamogolo Ramadimetsa, in Orlando West, and he would come and visit or take me out. We spent time with his many friends, saw countless movies, ate out and generally had fun. His mother was clearly very proud of her son as a first-generation university student and indulged him a great deal. She even justified buying a house for him in the same area as her own, Zone 4, Diepkloof, in part because he was the eldest son. We had the use of her pick-up truck and never wanted for anything.

It was sad for us to part at the beginning of 1968, but I assured him of my love and promised to remain faithful. We kept in touch by letter and he sent me money to visit him over the Easter holidays. I focused on my studies and ignored many advances from young men at medical school. I made it known to everyone that I was not available. At the end of 1968 Dick's mother passed away suddenly. I comforted him as best as I could during the December holidays, which we spent together. His sisters urged me to remain faithful. They reminded me of the pain he would suffer from losing the two most important women in his life – his mother and myself. I took their concerns seriously.

The year 1969 brought many changes in my own life. My increasing activism and my deeper involvement in the circle of activists brought with it a greater openness to others around me. That brought along its own complications for my relationship with Dick. Steve Biko had been pursuing me seriously for a while, but I had kept him at bay by reiterating my commitment to Dick, to whom I considered myself virtually engaged. I was safe behind this armour for a while.

In the second half of 1969 it became increasingly difficult to resist Steve's advances. I fell hopelessly in love with him, but would not even admit this to myself. We conducted a semi-platonic friendship which frequently 'degenerated' into passion. I became increasingly distressed at my dilemma. How could I desert Dick after all these years, particularly after his mother's death? I could not bear the thought of hurting him. But what of my passionate love for Steve? I was faced with a serious dilemma.

There was really no one I felt I could turn to for advice, because in a sense I feared that they would advise me to follow my heart. But I could not live with the implications of such a decision for Dick, who had been so good to me over the years. I lived in a daze and enjoyed each day as it unfolded. A fellow student, Victor Mafungu, a gentle person who was like a brother to me, used to come and study in my room, and would watch with concern as I floated on this enormous love affair, which I was refusing to acknowledge.

Some of my homeboys at medical school, particularly Joel Matsipa, who knew Dick well, started expressing their concern about my relationship with Steve. I tried to play things down by emphasising its platonic nature as befitted a relationship between activists, but the intoxication of the love affair was self-evident. Both Dick and Steve started putting some pressure on me. Dick urged me to finalise our tentative marriage plans for the summer of 1969/70. Quick action was of the essence to preserve our long-standing relationship. In contrast, the nascent love affair with Steve needed time to unfold. Consequently Steve urged me to take time to make a final decision about marriage. Any delay would work in favour of my relationship with Steve – a fact of which both contenders were acutely aware. I dared not think of even raising the possibility of postponement because it would simply confirm what Dick was beginning to suspect. But a final decision was too frightening to contemplate. I was stuck.

Steve also had poetic talents which he displayed occasionally when moved emotionally. He told me about the poems that he had written as a pupil at Mariannhill High School and had shared with a Catholic nun he liked and respected. The intensity of our relationship brought him to write a poem entitled 'A Love Supreme'. I hung on its every word. I still wonder what became of the poem over the years. It probably got lost in one of the many police raids.

Parting for the summer vacation was not easy. Steve pleaded with me not to make any final decisions about marriage until the following year. He asked for an address at which he could write to me, and I fatefully gave him Dick's home address where I anticipated spending most of my holidays. Steve was going to be attending a student leadership seminar at the Abe Bailey Institute at UCT and promised to keep in touch.

I spent a week or so with Dick. Our relationship had changed. He disapproved of my smoking, but I refused to give it up. His sisters also disapproved, but I was not prepared to compromise. Perhaps there was some vain hope in me that he would pick a fight over it and put the relationship at risk, thus rescuing me from my dilemma. But he knew the limits and resigned himself to this new me, and even bought me cartons of cigarettes from his family business. I went home to my own family in Kranspoort for the rest of the holidays.

Unbeknown to me, Steve dutifully wrote to me and repeated his plea that I should postpone any marriage plans until I was clearer in my mind about where my real feelings stood with regard to the two men in my life. Dick must have opened the letter, and decided there and then to expedite our marriage plans. He sent me a telegram announcing his intention to visit and finalise arrangements for the wedding. His relatives had been to see my family a few months earlier to ask for my hand in marriage – go kgopela sego sa meetse – literally 'to ask for a water container'. My paternal grandfather did not believe in the custom of lobola (bride wealth) and asked the Mmabanes to give whatever token they felt appropriate to mark their appreciation of the gift of a wife. This amounted to about R200. This family involvement also made any reversal of commitments difficult.

I resigned myself to my fate, and even allowed myself to get excited. Dick would not hear of leaving me behind. We left together in my cousin Mbatha Ramphele's car after a day or two. I went to stay with my aunt in Orlando West while a hasty wedding party was arranged by Dick's relatives. The only people from my family who could participate in the wedding celebration were my sister Mashadi and my cousin Rosemary Mogomotsi. We signed and sealed our marriage in front of a magistrate, and I vowed to make it work.

When I got back to medical school in late January 1970, I was a married woman and proudly showed off my wedding rings and photographs. To my homeboys there was an underlying message of 'I told you so'. But my response to Steve was more complex. I do not know how I could have been so insensitive in showing off the same items to Steve without any regard to the hurt it would cause him. He was devastated. He could not believe that I could have killed my relationship with him without so much as an explanation or some apology. He assumed I had received his letter and ignored his final plea.

All he said was 'I see' to the display of my new status, and walked away deeply hurt. He nonetheless respected the distance I had placed between us. I steeled myself in the determination to remain a faithful wife. Steve and I met in the context of our student activism, and pursued a platonic relationship. When he visited the University of the North later that year as the first President of SASO, Dick was one of the people who hosted him. Dick lent Steve his pyjamas – an interesting symbolic declaration of triumph.

I paid frequent visits to my husband, even during term time, to reduce the yawning gap between us. The fourth year of study was not very demanding in view of its focus on practical training in hospitals. I did not enjoy this aspect of my training at all. I did not like the sight of blood – a common companion of medical practitioners. Moreover, I resented the use of helpless patients as 'interesting cases' for teaching purposes. Many patients with painful conditions that evinced classic signs and symptoms had to endure endless queues of eager medical students who all wanted to feel the lump or enlarged organ and to elicit a wince from the hapless patient. Students would talk about 'a liver in ward such-and-such' which was a must for their colleagues to go and feel. I could not associate myself with such depersonalisation of people, and their reduction to the level of inanimate organs of the body.

King Edward VIII Hospital, where I was stationed, was a real hovel of a place – a typical apartheid institution. It was an old, overcrowded, untidy hospital with a constant shortage of linen and with poor-quality food for patients. Children in the paediatric wards would often be swimming in their own excreta. It was not a pleasant place to work in. I did only the bare minimum to stay in the course and qualify for promotion to the next level of training.

It was inevitable that cracks would appear in our marriage. It was a relationship based on celebrating past ties rather than facing the challenges of the divergences that had grown between us. However much I remained faithful, Dick would not trust me. The physical distance between us did not help, nor were my frequent visits sufficient compensation. Dick started drinking heavily and neglected his studies. At the end of 1970 he still had not made enough progress to complete his degree within the foreseeable future. His elder sister Ellen, who had taken over the running of the family business after their mother's death, expressed her concern about Dick's increasingly irresponsible behaviour. She found it difficult to accept his poor performance at university as well as the demands he was making on her for material support. I unwisely entered the fray and expressed my own concerns. He resented my critical comments and flew into an uncharacteristic rage.

Our December 1970 holidays were not pleasant. He drank more and more heavily as if to spite me. He accused me of being unfaithful, which really hurt because I could have chosen to be unfaithful but had been impeccably faithful to my marriage vows. He also became quarrelsome about my smoking and political activism. I went back to medical school unhappy and worried about the future of our marriage. I buried myself in my activism and took pleasure from my circle of friends.

The crunch came in June 1971 when I got back home from the annual SASO conference at Natal Medical School, which I had attended as the local SASO chair. I found that Dick had turned our house into a shebeen, and that he was in the company of township no-hopers – people who had given up the struggle to make their lives meaningful outside the solace of alcohol. It later turned out that he had dropped out of university and had had an affair with an old girlfriend from his

school days whom he was later to marry. He made it clear that he regarded our relationship as dead. I had given political activism priority
by spending time at the SASO conference instead of coming home at
the end of term. On top of it all he also claimed I had been unfaithful.
I was shocked.

The following morning he arranged for me to be taken to my aunt's
home in Orlando West with all my personal belongings. I took all but
my mother's cookbook – a treasure which she had reluctantly let me
borrow because she appreciated my love of cooking. The loss of that
cookbook is one of the regrets I continue to feel about the break-up of
my relationship with Dick.

My aunt was saddened by the breakdown of my marriage. Her husband insisted that I be taken back to Dick's family home. This was
to ensure that they would not be faulted for failing to follow the custom of first finding out the extent of the breakdown before concluding
that there was no chance of a reconciliation. The encounter at the
Mmabanes was humiliating, to say the least. At the meeting of the two
families, Dick refused to discuss any of the issues which had caused
the tensions in our marriage except to say that I had become too much
for him to handle as a wife. The message was clear – we had grown
apart.

Traditional systems stand powerless in the face of breakdowns which
arise out of the kind of tensions that undermined our marriage. There
was no real remedy for the insecurity which my husband felt in relation to the 'new me'. He had married an ideal which he hoped he could
salvage from the past. In turn I had not been prepared to acknowledge
the depth of the fault lines which had arisen in our relationship. I went
back to medical school at the beginning of the second semester in 1971
emotionally exhausted and bewildered at the turn of events. Marriage
breakdowns represent a vote of no confidence in your own decisions
at a very fundamental level. It is not surprising that many people refuse

to face up to that reality even when presented with compelling evidence. I was no exception.

Steve had in the interim got himself married to Ntsiki Mashalaba (a cousin of Vuyelwa's), who had fallen pregnant with his child. He explained to me that after the hurt I had inflicted on him he had given up on romantic love and wanted to settle down and concentrate on political activism. When I came back from my disastrous holiday I told him my marriage lay in ruins. He listened as a true friend and asked me if I thought I had given it my best, and urged me to find out what could be done to save the marriage. I had my doubts. My letters to Dick remained unanswered, and finally I accepted the obvious.

Steve continued to support me as a friend with great integrity. He did not once say 'I told you so', nor took advantage of my distress to get even. It was only a matter of time, however, before the old fire flared again. The love letter which Steve put into my hand on the way to a party with some members of our activist circle had been long in coming. I knew instinctively what its message would be. I could not wait to confirm this. At the first opportunity I went into the toilet and read it. I came out glowing with utter happiness. But how were we to conduct our love affair in the light of Steve's marriage?

That night was the happiest I had experienced in years. We celebrated our reunion in style. We naïvely vowed not to hurt the innocent party – Steve's wife. Ntsiki was then on maternity leave and later returned to Durban to a post as a nurse at the McCord Hospital. Life became increasingly complex as we tried vainly not to make our relationship a public affair. But it was impossible to stop the tongues wagging. Although our long friendship and common political commitment helped to create some respectable explanation for the inordinate amount of time we spent together, it was not easy.

Over the many years before and after my unsuccessful marriage, I got to know and love Bukelwa Biko, Steve's elder sister, who was a senior nurse at King George V Hospital, a local tuberculosis treatment centre. We became very close. I used to talk to her about the difficulties of our triangular love relationship. Though she was sympathetic, she made it clear to Steve and me that we had made this bed and now had to lie in it. She could not believe both of us could have been so stupid in making decisions about our private lives. She would adopt a matronly tone and say, 'You kids are really silly – you must face the consequences of your foolish decisions.' That was easier said than done. She remained an important pillar of support, financially and emotionally.

My divorce was finalised during 1972. I became free again. But tensions over the triad intensified. Some friends started taking sides. Vuyelwa was, understandably, the most vociferous critic of our relationship. She confronted Steve with the hurt that he was causing her cousin through his infidelity, but was told firmly to mind her own business. Others were more diplomatic in their approaches to Steve, but he told them that he was caught on the horns of a dilemma which history had visited on him.

Chapter 11

'. . . ours is to accept and bear the pain'

STEVE AND BARNEY SET UP A JOINT HOUSE DURING 1972 IN Umlazi township. Both their wives, who were nurses at the McCord Hospital, joined them, and later their children, Nkosinathi and Loyiso, also came to stay. It was a communal home in every sense of the word. Activists used it as their own homes, putting a major strain on limited financial and housekeeping resources. I kept my distance out of respect for Ntsiki, and for fear of causing a scene.

Disaster struck us at the beginning of 1973. I had arranged to do my medical internship at King Edward VIII Hospital in Durban in order to be close to Steve. The Schlebusch Commission, instituted by the government to investigate a number of organisations (including NUSAS and the Christian Institute), reported on its findings and the government promptly slapped banning orders on eight NUSAS student leaders, eight SASO leaders, and a number of people associated with the Black Consciousness Movement.

Steve had been running a leadership training seminar in Port Elizabeth with several Black Consciousness leaders, among them Barney, Harry Nengwekhulu and Bokwe Mafuna, as part of a national youth leadership development programme sponsored jointly by SASO and the Black Community Programmes. They were detained for a while by the security police before being transported to their various places of birth. Steve found himself back in his mother's home in Ginsberg, King Williamstown; Harry was taken to Sibasa, in the then Venda 'homeland' in the northern Transvaal; while Barney was confined to New Brighton township in Port Elizabeth. Banning orders subtly employed traditional controls to discipline errant black political activists by sending them back to their natal homes. Symbolically they can be said to have invoked parental control over political transgressors. In practice they put parents in a difficult position, making them sometimes try to restrain their children from taking too many political risks. The news of the banning orders was deeply troubling. The entire top leadership of the Black Consciousness Movement was immobilised at the stroke of a pen. The banning orders varied in their severity, but were issued by the Minister of Justice under the Suppression of Communism Act of 1950, and centred on the following:

- Those affected were prohibited from participating in specified political activity. The organisations from which they were restricted were listed.
- They were prohibited from attending or addressing political gatherings of any sort.
- They were prohibited from publishing or participating in activities which could lead to the dissemination of any sort of publication. Quoting banned people was a criminal offence.
- They were not allowed to enter any educational institution, or participate in teaching.
- They were prevented from attending any social gathering, defined as a meeting of more than one person other than the restricted person. Exceptions were made for bona fide family gatherings or religious services.
- The area of restriction was circumscribed, and most banned people had to report to a local police station weekly and sign a register as proof of compliance with their restrictions.
- They were prohibited from any contact or communication with other banned people.

■ The local magistrate was empowered in each case to grant permission to relax restrictions, but in practice he did so only with the approval of the local security police.

It is interesting that the thrust of the Schlebusch Commission report was ambivalent about the Black Consciousness Movement (BCM) itself. The National Party government was still unsure whether the BCM had not perhaps bought into its own ideological programme of separate development. It liked the growing distance of the BCM from white liberals, but was cautious about the direction in which the leaders were taking the movement. It decided to be safe rather than sorry. This ambivalence gave Steve the space to continue to work for the Black Community Programmes (BCP) by setting up a regional office in an old Anglican Church building at 15 Leopold Street, King Williamstown. He was greatly assisted by Fr David Russell, then ministering to the poor people who had been forcibly removed from different parts of the Eastern Cape and dumped at Dimbaza, a new township near King.[16]

Steve called me from a public phone as soon as he arrived in Ginsberg township. He sounded depressed and angry. His main message was simple: 'I am not prepared to lose you again; we have to remain closely in touch whatever happens.' That was not a difficult injunction to agree to from my side. Nothing was going to stop our relationship from growing to its full potential. I lived off the warmth of the feelings between us and the wonderful memories of our intimate times together. Calls were few and far between until he installed a phone in his mother's house.

Regular commuting to and from King then started. My first aeroplane trip took place the following weekend, at the end of January 1973. It was a bumpy flight, particularly for those in the tail-end seats, which

---

16 King is the popular name for King Williamstown, also referred to by the locals as eQonce, its Xhosa name.

were customarily reserved for blacks in apartheid days. I was met at East London Airport by Mapetla Mohapi and Malusi Mpumlwana, and taken to Zwelitsha township to Nohle Haya's[17] home. There complicated arrangements were made for my accommodation so that I could spend time with Steve without either falling foul of the law relating to his banning order or offending his wife. This was complex and frustrating. I had to wait till late that evening before setting eyes on him, and much later before we had any privacy. It was the first of many visits.

On my return to King Edward Hospital in Durban I arranged with my fellow interns, Jayshree Moodley and Goolam Abram, for a special dispensation to work irregular hours so that I could accumulate enough credit time for long weekend visits to King. They were very supportive. I also put in an application to transfer my internship in the second half of the year to Livingstone Hospital in Port Elizabeth, to be closer to Steve. I started living from one visit to the next and spent an inordinate amount of money on telephone calls to Steve. Such was the cost of a long-distance triangular relationship.

Conducting a love affair on a migratory basis is difficult at the best of times, but in our case there was more than the physical distance to contend with. Port Elizabeth was an unfamiliar place for me. I had only visited it once for the purpose of attending a conference of ASSECA (the Association for the Educational and Cultural Advancement of Africans), which was modelled on the NAACP among African-Americans. ASSECA was run by conservative middle-class Africans led by Mr M. T. Moerane, editor of the *Bantu World,* a Johannesburg paper for the township African market. Our attempts to infiltrate ASSECA and harness it to the cause of black liberation were soundly defeated by a vigilant Mr Moerane, who used the chair effectively to deny our delegates a voice. I had no good memories of Port Elizabeth.

---

17 Nohle subsequently became Steve Biko's secretary and married Mapetla Mohapi.

Returning to Port Elizabeth as a doctor in training a year later was a different experience. Livingstone Hospital was as unlike King Edward Hospital as chalk from cheese. It was a modern, clean and well-run hospital which was a pleasure to work in. The doctors' quarters where I lived were pleasant and airy, and the food was superior. I was glad about the change from Durban. I also preferred the cooler Port Elizabeth weather to the humid heat of Durban.

My departure from Durban had been hasty. I do not remember any regrets other than that of leaving some of my friends. This was particularly true of fellow interns, who were also former classmates. Xola Pemba, a well-built bear of a man, became particularly close and protective of me. We enjoyed many beers together during weekends when we were not on duty. But internship duties were demanding, and the working hours long. The spirit which had been characteristic of Alan Taylor Residence and 86 Beatrice Street had died. Durban had nothing more to offer me.

If I had found the medical internship at King Edward VIII Hospital tough and demanding, worse awaited me during my surgical internship in Port Elizabeth. Weekend duty started at eight in the morning on Friday and went on until four on Monday afternoon. At the end of the month you would be lucky to get more than a wink of sleep on Friday and Saturday night. The casualty department looked like a battlefield – motor-vehicle accidents; stab wounds on chests, abdomens, even on necks (in one case the knife was still *in situ*); various cases of assault on victims who were invariably drunk. It was a mess.

I had to learn to work fast and to master the technique of inserting intercostal underwater drains into stabbed chests – on one occasion I counted ten intercostal drains in one night. These drains were inserted under local anaesthetic, and could be difficult with restless drunken patients. I relied on the theatre nurses who were highly skilled, and they taught me a lot.

By any standard 96 hours of duty was too long for anyone to do justice to any job, let alone one which involved life-and-death decisions. There was no counting how many fatal errors were made under such circumstances. I rebelled after a few months of this punishing schedule. I refused to wake up for Sunday morning ward rounds and asked the sister in charge of the ward to let my seniors know that I was too tired to join them, and that they should leave all instructions in the patients' folders for my attention later in the day. The head of my firm, Mr McQuaide, a specialist general surgeon, did not seem to mind and did not make an issue of it, although my registrar took a dim view of what he perceived as insubordination. I was pleased years later to see that interns had organised themselves nationally to protest against this inhuman system, which has now been modified, though it is still demanding.

The conditions of service under which we worked as newly qualified doctors were appalling. The remuneration system discriminated between blacks and whites. White people earned significantly more than blacks. There was also different pay for 'Bantus' (as Africans were then called officially), 'coloureds' and Indians. To add insult to injury, women also earned less than men. As an African woman I was at the bottom of the pile in terms of salary. My take-home pay amounted to R240 per month in 1973. I had to clothe and feed myself, travel and entertain on this amount. In addition, my widowed mother relied on me more and more for support to educate my brothers. She was still earning less than R200 per month as principal of a lower primary school. It was a tall order.

From Port Elizabeth the commuting to King continued, and in fact intensified. I became expert at hitchhiking after work on a Friday afternoon. Leaving Livingstone at about 4 p.m., I would invariably arrive in King by 7 p.m. The trip back was made on the late-night railway bus, which ran between Umtata (now Mthatha) and Port Elizabeth via King. Hitchhiking was relatively safe in those days.

The few weekends I did not travel to King, I spent with Steve's younger sister, Nobandile (Bandie) Mvovo, who was married to Mxolisi. They lived in Walmer township. Nobandile had come to Durban in 1971 to do a year's secretarial course, which Steve arranged for her to improve her skills. She came to stay with me in my room at Alan Taylor Residence. Steve and I notified the matron, Nomangesi Radebe, a native of King, who gladly agreed to turn a blind eye to this infringement of residence rules. Bandie was blissfully ignorant of my relationship with Steve. She took me as just a friend. One day she asked me who my boyfriend was. I simply said to her that he lived off campus and that she would meet him one day. That day came when she walked into her brother's room and found me in his bed.

I also saw a lot of Barney and Dimza Pityana, who were living under intolerable conditions. The local security police in Port Elizabeth made their lives a misery. No sooner would someone arrive at Barney's mother's house than the security police would be knocking on the door, insisting on taking down the names of those present and questioning the purpose of their visit. It was blatant harassment. The move into their own house in New Brighton township merely shifted the locus of battle with 'the system'. You could hardly conduct a decent conversation with Barney without the intrusion of these crude men. They were certainly a different breed from most of the King security police.

The migrant love affair bore semi-planned fruit at the end of 1973. I fell pregnant, to my great excitement. Towards the close of one of the many weekend visits, I developed an acute abdominal pain. I was distressed. Steve took it lightly as an exaggerated sense of my unhappiness about having to part from him. I became increasingly uncomfortable on the trip back to Port Elizabeth. On arrival at the doctors' quarters I was so ill that I had to be admitted immediately.

The doctor who saw me insisted on an emergency operation. It could have been any number of problems causing this pain, and he was taking no chances. I was distressed at the thought of losing this love child and at the thought of Steve not being able to be with me in that hour of need. My last plea to the anaesthetist before I went under was for him to spare my baby. It turned out that I had a large degenerating fibroid on the surface of my womb, which had become inflamed. The operation was a success. I was discharged after ten days and had to go home to the Transvaal to await the arrival of my baby at the end of May 1974.

I went home via King, where I spent a week or so with Steve. On my arrival at East London Airport I was searched by security policemen, who probably suspected I was carrying written communications from Barney to Steve. They were disappointed, but had a consolation prize in finding old banned literature from my Natal Medical School days which I'd forgotten was in my safekeeping for Steve. Bandie, who had packed my bags from Port Elizabeth, had simply thrown in all the books she found in my room without checking. I was later to be charged under the Suppression of Communism Act and given a suspended sentence for being in possession of banned literature.

It was not easy to face the prospect of not seeing Steve for the months until the baby was born. We parted on a sad note, but the sense of sharing the creation of a new life made the yawning physical distance ahead of us bearable. The pregnancy was only partly planned. Steve was clearly ambivalent about having a love child in the circumstances, but I desperately needed to have something more tangible from our complex relationship. I was after all twenty-six years old and rather liked the idea of motherhood. The thought of sharing in the act of creation with Steve was exhilarating.

Passionate as our relationship was, it was fundamentally unsatisfactory for me. The constant awareness of sharing one's loved one with someone else hurt. The head and the heart were pulling in different directions. 'You have brought this misery upon yourself; this man was all yours, but you rejected him,' I would remind myself. But my heart ached.

I went to live in Johannesburg with my sister Mashadi, who was then staying with my mother's younger sister, Mamotšatši Mabaso, in Zola township in Soweto. It was an overcrowded four-roomed house, which was difficult to keep clean with the ten children my aunt had. I became the housekeeper and spent many frustrating days battling with ill-disciplined children who messed their knickers before their mother came back from work. My aunt was a happy-go-lucky person who just laughed off my concerns about her children's poor toilet habits.

I kept in touch with Steve through regular letters, but it was hard. There were no phones within easy reach. Weeks passed without my hearing his voice. I felt abandoned, and had many tearful days. The situation was exacerbated by a threatened abortion in the seventh month of pregnancy. I had to spend many weeks at Baragwanath Hospital on strict bed-rest to prevent the loss of the baby. I was relieved when I finally gave birth in May 1974 to Lerato (a Sotho word for 'love') – a beautiful girl who looked just like Steve's younger sister, Nobandile Mvovo. After some further neonatal problems, including jaundice, Lerato was strong enough for me to start enjoying her.

I travelled with my sister and Lerato to Pietersburg in June to stay with my mother in Maupje, where she was teaching at the time. It was not easy to adjust to life in a rural area after all the years away, but we managed to make ourselves comfortable with financial support from Mashadi and Steve. But it was an arrangement which could not be sustained. I missed Steve a lot and also yearned to get back to work after all the months of 'idleness'. I decided to leave Lerato with my mother at the beginning of July, when she was barely six weeks, to return to King, and to find employment to support her and my mother. It was a difficult decision, one I was to regret.

Back in King it was wonderful to see Steve again. I soon found a job as a medical officer at Mt Coke Mission Hospital, a few kilometres from King. It was convenient to be so close to Steve and yet have an independent base so as to avoid stepping on his wife's toes.

Mt Coke Hospital was even then an old facility run largely by Methodist missionaries. There were about six doctors on the staff and a large complement of nurses and general workers. It had about a hundred beds and catered largely for the poor local black population. It had a very busy outpatient section, which provided comprehensive care; a maternity section, which had good antenatal and intranatal care; a paediatric unit; and a medical and surgical section. I was put in charge of the paediatric ward.

I learnt much from my colleagues. Medical school does not prepare one adequately for the real world of primary health care. I learned the proper treatment regimens for common paediatric problems, diagnostic skills with minimum technological aid, tooth extraction and so forth. But I failed to learn any surgical operations. There were regular caesarean sections performed for complications of pregnancy or labour, but I just could not bring myself to do the actual operation. Nor could I successfully act as an anaesthetist: there were none at Mt Coke. The surgeon had to do the operation and at the same time keep an eye on the nurse who observed the anaesthetised patient's condition.

I admire those with the expertise and courage to carry out operations successfully under such conditions. I lacked both. I could be used only as an assistant to the surgeon. But the experience I gained at Mt Coke over the six months I worked there stood me in good stead later in life.

<hr />

In August 1974 Lerato suddenly died of pneumonia at the age of two and a half months, barely a month after my departure. It was a tremendous blow and affected me badly. The loss of your child is a loss of part of yourself. It inflicts an intensely intimate and personal pain, particularly when it happens without warning, and you are not there to share the last moments or, indeed, try to prevent the death. Lerato's death left me feeling cheated, but also guilty at having left her at such a tender age with my mother.

I cannot forget the telegram that carried this news. A colleague at Mt Coke Hospital left it in my room for me to read. No one thought to warn me. I could not believe the telegram, and had to be restrained in my screams of denial. I was taken by Malusi Mpumlwana to Ginsberg to Steve's home to share my grief with him as the father of my child, and to make arrangements to go to Pietersburg for the funeral.

I found little comfort in Steve's company, and felt deeply cheated by fate in losing my first and only child. Although her conception had only partly been planned, I had welcomed it, and she was a source of great joy to me as the embodiment of an intense love affair, as her name indeed signified. My pregnancy had been difficult, and so the sense of appreciation and thanks for a normal, beautiful baby had been immense. The disappointment at so brief an encounter with motherhood was deep.

In my laments I kept repeating to Steve how unbearable and unfair it was to lose the only person who belonged to me in a complete sense. Steve had to remind me in the end that Lerato was his child also and that his pain was all the more unbearable because he had been denied the opportunity to see and know her. Steve's mother offered her comforting words in her own dignified way: 'We cannot fight against what God has let happen; ours is to accept and bear the pain.'

The aeroplane trip to Johannesburg in the company of Steve's elder brother Khaya was difficult. I kept hoping for the impossible – that I would discover it was all a mistake. But being met at the airport by some of my relatives put paid to such fantasies. We travelled together in a minibus with close relatives to Uitkyk for the funeral.

My mother was deeply affected by Lerato's death. She arrived a few hours after us, having been to fetch my daughter's body from the mortuary in Pietersburg. She felt she had failed me, though she did all that was humanly possible when Lerato developed a respiratory infection, but was limited by the poor state of health-care services in rural South Africa. Lerato died from lack of high-level care, ironically at the same hospital where her mother was born in 1947. There was no doctor available at the time of her admission, and the nurses on duty were not trained to handle emergencies such as those presented by severe respiratory illness in babies.

The tiny white coffin which contained her body looked so pure and innocent, but represented a barrier to my urge to cuddle her. I derived little comfort from suggestions from relatives that she was too pure to settle in this sinful world. Her beautiful face looked peaceful, but distant. Steve, being banned at the time, could not share the funeral rites with me, but his brother Khaya was there to represent him. The wound of this loss remains to this day. It is covered by a thin scar, given to bleeding at the slightest scratch. And there have been many excruciating scratches.

Community life in King

STEVE BIKO BECAME THE CENTRAL FOCUS OF A NEW COMmunity of activists in King which gradually grew stronger from the time of his banning order at the beginning of 1973. The community was a product of his qualities as a leader. It was also an essential survival strategy for him to deal with the potentially devastating impact of the banning order, which was expressly intended to isolate activists and consequently render them impotent.

The quality of life of people under banning orders depended on a number of factors. Firstly, the temperament of the local security police was a crucial determinant of the kind of surveillance under which you were placed. The more vindictive and aggressive they were, the more stringent and unpleasant the surveillance, and consequently the worse life would become for the person and their family.

Some areas of the country, notably Port Elizabeth and Johannesburg, were notorious as areas of high surveillance. The security police harassed people and their families in the most outrageous ways. Personal privacy was violated by constant searches often made without search warrants, and general nastiness was the hallmark of these security swoops.

Car registration numbers of visitors were noted down and their owners threatened with arrest if ever seen again visiting the banned person. Telephones were tapped as a matter of routine, and mail was monitored and tampered with, often with serious consequences: witness the letter bombs that killed political activists. The Port Elizabeth security police developed the reputation of being the most extreme persecutors. They made Barney Pityana's life an absolute misery, and eventually drove him and his family into exile in 1978.

Then again, the more you could be gainfully employed, the less likely you were to be isolated and frustrated by your banning order. The space for gainful employment itself depended on your professional skills, the employment prospects in the area of restriction, and the willingness of employers to resist security police pressure not to employ a banned person. The people worst hit were those whose professions involved teaching or depended on government employment, such as nurses and social workers. Mrs Winnie Mandela, banned for many years during the 1960s, and then banished to Brandfort in 1977, endured frustrations in this regard because she could not practise as a social worker. Many teachers left the country in the 1960s and 1970s for want of employment.

The support you derived from the local community was also vital for survival. The success of the security police's surveillance depended to a large extent on their ability to engage an army of informers who would keep watch over your every move. Neighbours were a particularly valuable resource for the police, and many succumbed to enormous pressure to act as informers. When neighbours refused to cooperate, the security policemen had to take turns positioning themselves in the vicinity of the banned person's home, a less effective form of surveillance because of its higher profile.

Without doubt, the personality of the banned person made a lot of difference. The more determined and resourceful the individual, the least likely the security police were to hamper the person from leading a reasonably meaningful life under the circumstances. It was a game of nerves where the will of the banned person was pitted against that of his or her captors. The stress generated by living in a state of low-intensity warfare took its toll on many. From the point of view of the security police the desired outcome was for banned people to become their own gaolers and effectively lead isolated lives for fear of arrest for breaking banning orders. Sadly, many South Africans spent miserable years imprisoned in their own homes.

Steve was able to organise his life in King in a manner which permitted him a reasonable quality of life. All the factors I have mentioned worked in his favour, and he progressively neutralised attempts by the local security police to harass him. Charles Sebe, shot to death in 1991 on the orders of Oupa Gqozo, the military ruler of the Ciskei 'homeland', was a particularly nasty customer in his capacity as security policeman in 1973-4. He was rude and crude, and was used by the local white security policemen as a thorn in Steve's side. Charles Sebe would burst into Steve's mother's house, to which Steve was restricted, at odd hours of the day and night, and search for alleged visitors, even walking into Steve's mother's bedroom, from which he would be forcibly extracted by an angry Steve. On one occasion Sebe drew a firearm in the house and threatened to shoot Steve. In the end Steve warned the local security chief that unless Sebe was withdrawn from these missions, he could not guarantee what would happen under provocation. Fortunately, to everybody's relief, Charles Sebe was withdrawn. But other nasty cops, such as Warrant Officer Hattingh, remained a pain in every way.

------ ◇◆◇ ------

As the community at King grew and developed, the transition was made from student activism to professional development work, which proved challenging for both Steve and me. The Black Community Programmes had been set up as the wing of the Black Consciousness Movement to give practical effect to the philosophy of black self-reliance, self-help, and liberation through development of the whole person. Bennie Khoapa, the BCP Director, gave Steve the intellectual space and institutional support to develop programmes that embodied this thrust.

The Eastern Cape Regional Office of BCP as a consequence became a hive of activity.

I was able to keep in touch with developments from my nearby base at Mt Coke Hospital. I arranged to be picked up whenever it was necessary, and Malusi Mpumlwana, who became Steve's general assistant, would drive over to take me to and fro. I would help around the office and participate in all the social activities, which invariably ended late at night.

There was little evidence of a traditional church atmosphere in the disused Anglican Church building at 15 Leopold Street, where an office took shape. Mapetla Mohapi also set up the regional SASO office in the same premises, further expanding the range of activities conducted from that address, to the great displeasure of the local security police. Student activists from Fort Hare and the Federal Theological Seminary in nearby Alice called regularly to enquire about new developments or to participate in projects.

At this address too an increasing number of international and important national political figures called on Steve. These visits further angered the security police, who we referred to as 'the system' (because for us they represented the system of oppression and repression). 'The system' tried to catch Steve breaking his banning order. But we had developed an efficient early warning system, which frustrated them. In a desperate attempt to disrupt our work, they once broke into our office premises and destroyed files and damaged equipment. But there was no way of stopping us.

One of the international visitors who became interested in our work was Angela Mai, a German citizen of South African origin, who had inherited some money from her relatives. This money was frozen in South Africa. Over the years she used it to support good causes. She was alerted to the work of BCP by Dr Beyers Naudé, the Director of the Christian Institute. She became interested in supporting a proposal to set up a community health centre in one of the villages near King, and agreed to give the R20 000 estimated as the cost of setting up the centre.

I was asked to help establish and head this centre, which was to be built in Zinyoka, ten kilometres outside King. I was absolutely thrilled. Here was an opportunity to work formally in an environment where I could live out my commitment to the process of liberation, and also work with Steve. But I did not bargain on the difficulties ahead of me.

None of us had any knowledge about setting up a community health centre. I did not have the slightest idea where you ordered medical supplies, or what quantities would be required, or what the costs would be. I had to visit medical colleagues who were in private practice in the area to enquire. Some were friendly and helpful, but others possibly saw me as a potential future competitor and were cold.

I became increasingly frustrated by the high expectations my activist colleagues had of me, and their unhelpfulness in crucial areas where I needed assistance, such as having ready transport to important meetings or coping with numerous telephone calls. Steve expressed concern about my growing impatience and urged me to relax a bit more. I did not think that he understood how heavily the responsibility of setting up the centre weighed on me.

My colleagues at Mt Coke also became concerned about my frequent absences from the hospital. I did the barest minimum of work to honour my contractual obligations as a medical officer. I even stopped playing bridge with my colleagues, an activity I had come to enjoy during my employment at Mt Coke. Dr Mzimba, who was the leading light in the bridge club, taught me the game, but in the end I would beat him because of the utter recklessness of my opening bids, which unnerved my opponents. Once I gave up playing I missed the fun, but I had greater challenges to attend to.

The security police must have complained to the Mt Coke superintendent, Dr Adendorf, a gentle old man, about my association with 'bad elements' at 15 Leopold Street. He called me to his office and, in a fatherly tone, urged me to be careful about the company I kept. I thanked him for his concern, but indicated that I knew what I was doing.

◇◈◇

The changed circumstances in the growing community of activists in King, and the stressful conditions under which I worked to get the health centre up and running by the beginning of 1975, put considerable stress on my relationship with Steve. I became increasingly frustrated by his unavailability, and became demanding and irritable. Steve remained fairly inattentive. It was unbearable.

On one occasion, three weeks after I had bought my first car, a maroon VW Beetle, I got so angry at Steve's lack of attention that I decided to drive off from a party in Ginsberg township to Nohle Mohapi's house in Zwelitsha township, where I spent the night. After breakfast the following morning, I drove to Mt Coke Hospital. I must have been driving at about 50 km an hour on a gravel road outside Zwelitsha when I heard a bus behind me. I tried to adjust the rearview mirror but just at that point the car swerved slightly off the road. I panicked and turned the wheel abruptly while slamming on the brakes. That was it. The car overturned. I had to get out through the broken rear windscreen. I could not believe the suddenness of the accident, and the extent of the damage to my new car!

An acquaintance stopped soon afterwards and gave me a lift back to Nohle's and notified Steve. There was no sign of serious injury – I had a few bruises only. After arranging for the car to be towed away I fell asleep. I woke up an hour or two later in absolute agony. I was convinced that I had broken my back and that I was going to be paralysed. I became hysterical. I was then taken to Mt Coke Hospital and admitted. The doctors sedated me, and each time I woke up I would ask about my imminent paralysis.

Steve could not come to visit me because Mt Coke was outside his area of restriction. This increased my distress, particularly as I blamed him for having created in part the circumstances which had led to my accident. I was very angry with him. It took a long discussion afterwards for us to make up. He reassured me of his love. Yet he said that the triangular relationship and his growing national profile were bound to continue to constrain our ability to give full expression to our relationship. There was a side of me which felt that he was not really trying, and that he might well be enjoying the best of all worlds.

The pace of preparation for the health centre increased and I became more and more involved. Mr Flask, a local 'coloured' builder, worked furiously to complete the building before the end of 1974. Malusi suggested the name Zanempilo (Bringer of health) for the centre, a reflection of the idealism behind the project. Mr Flask, a gentle person, obliging in every sense, tried his best to satisfy our expectations, and did so at a very reasonable cost. As soon as some rooms became ready for use, we set them up. The stocking of the dispensary was the most demanding. We had to decant liquid medicine from large containers into 50 ml, 100 ml and 200 ml bottles. We also had to count out tablets into twenties in dispensing envelopes. Without the assistance of the many activists, we could not have managed.

Zanempilo Community Health Centre opened its doors to patients in January 1975. Staffing the centre was arranged before the end of 1974. I poached two of the best nursing sisters I had got to know from Mt Coke Hospital: Mrs Nontobeko Moletsane and Mrs Beauty Nongauza. They in turn recruited two junior nurses during the first few months of 1975 to make up the full complement of nursing staff. Two local women were also engaged, one as cook and the other as cleaner and washerwoman. Soon another woman was employed to help with the increasing load of cleaning work.

Zanempilo was a comprehensive health-care centre built on land owned by the Anglican Church and which it shared with an old parish church building that served the local village community of Zinyoka. The centre had an outpatient section where locals came with minor and major ailments, a maternity section with an antenatal clinic, a labour ward, a nursery, and a lie-in ward for post-delivery care. We also had a panel van which served as both ambulance and mobile clinic for villages beyond walking distance from Zinyoka. The centre was open for emergencies 24 hours a day, 7 days a week and 52 weeks of the year. I was on duty all the time for the first year of operation of Zanempilo: a tall order indeed.

It soon became clear that the staffroom which served as my initial accommodation was inadequate for my needs and those of the staff who had to be available for after-hours duty. Mr Flask agreed to build a staff house for an additional R4 000. This turned out to be a very comfortable base for me. It had three bedrooms, a bathroom, and two living rooms – quite a buy at R4 000. The kitchen continued to be provided by the clinic building until much later when a kitchenette was added to the house. Mziwoxolo Ndzengu, a Ginsberg resident, joined us as an ambulance driver and also came to stay in the staff house. His retiring, reliable and loyal nature made it easy for us to maintain our privacy under the same roof. Much later, in 1976, a nurses' home was added to cater for the needs of nurses on overnight duty as well as of an increasing number of nurses coming from outside King who needed accommodation.

It soon became obvious that there had been a serious underestimation of the cost of running such a service, but it was difficult to find willing sponsors. Most of those approached indicated their preference for funding capital and not running costs – a real dilemma for development workers. What was the point of building structures and not supporting their operations? We had to endure many hardships on this score. My salary was about R600 a month, hardly adequate to support myself and to help my mother. But, to add to the hardships, we were also not always paid in time because of the shortage of funds. It was hard for the nurses, who had even fewer resources to fall back on and had more family commitments.

The South African Council of Churches (SACC) under John Rees became the major channel for development funding. But the Joint Screening Committee of the SACC, established to assess project funding proposals and requests, proved a major stumbling block to new ventures seeking funding. It played the unfortunate role of gatekeeper for international aid. The fact that our project was black-led and black-run did not always sit comfortably with some of the leading figures in the funding world. They expected the project to fail either because of incompetence of the staff or because of repression from 'the system'. But after Bennie Khoapa put pressure on the SACC, Zanempilo secured funding, to the relief of all concerned.

As the work of Zanempilo grew, my incompetence in Xhosa became a major embarrassment. I used to rely on nurses to interpret for me in my consultations. One day after about three months of working in this manner, I decided to take the plunge and launched into the language. It was difficult for me coming from a Sesotho background to master the clicks and nuances of the Xhosa language. But village Xhosa with its hlonipha taboo (the respectful language register women use to avoid saying their male in-laws' names or any syllable appearing in those names) added to the challenge. My activist colleagues were not helpful, because we tended to follow the path of least resistance, speaking English as the common language.

I made my intention to learn Xhosa known to some of the influential old women. I pointed out the advantages of direct communication for all of us. They were delighted that their Mosothokazi (Sotho woman) was going to learn the local language. The process of becoming pupil to village women was mutually beneficial beyond the level of language.

We developed respect for one another as they were put in a position of authority over me, being experts in something in which I was incompetent. The medical expertise I brought into the relationship could then be seen in a less mystified light: doctors do not know everything. I was also drawn into a closer human relationship with the women of Zinyoka. They referred to me as Iramram (the delicate one, a reference to my small physical frame).

Zanempilo became the meeting place for activists in the Eastern Cape. It was also a haven for Steve where he could meet visitors away from the vigilant eyes of 'the system'. It took 'the system' a while to overcome their reverence for the medical profession and the respect they had for a place of healing. Once that ethical boundary was crossed they became quite outrageous in walking around the health centre, and had to be physically restrained in some cases from entering the labour ward with a delivery in process. We had fierce arguments about their lack of respect for the dignity of the patients.

One of the early visitors who came to Zanempilo was Donald Woods. Steve's political instincts led him to ask me to see Donald, then editor of the East London *Daily Dispatch*, with a view to getting Donald to visit him. Steve had in mind exploring a collaborative relationship for the benefit of the Black Consciousness Movement (BCM). Donald Woods was at that time an honorary president of NUSAS and had publicly declared his opposition to what he saw as the separatist politics of the BCM. I drove to East London, having made an appointment to see him. I was shown into his large office where he was seated behind an impressive desk.

Donald was a big man with a penetrating look and a smile which shone from the heart. He welcomed me and asked in his Transkei Xhosa what he could do for me. I told him that we were concerned about the fact that newspapers such as the *Dispatch* gave enormous publicity to homeland leaders like Buthelezi and Matanzima but none to those opposing the system from a radical perspective. He demanded to know who the leaders of this radical movement were. I then told him about Steve and the philosophical approach of the BCM. He showed genuine interest and I invited him to King to meet Steve. He responded positively and promptly.

Later I was rather taken aback when I read Donald's book *Asking for Trouble* and found his recollection of our first meeting to be radically different from mine. His account was of a petite and cheeky young woman who burst into his office demanding to see him, and firing questions about his neglect of leaders such as Steve in favour of the Buthelezis of the day. I can only surmise that he must have been disorientated by the shock of meeting for the first time an African woman doctor who was young and self-confident. He must have anticipated the worst.

Not only did the meetings Donald subsequently had with Steve lead to greater publicity for the BCM, but Steve also began to write a regular column under Mapetla Mohapi's name, to bypass his restriction orders. These columns explored current affairs and offered a perspective which had been lacking in the media until then. Donald also asked Steve to identify young blacks who could be trained as journalists. Thenjiwe Mtintso became employed by the *Daily Dispatch* under this scheme. Our relationship with both the newspaper and the Woods family grew with time.

Donald Woods apart, the flow of visitors to Zanempilo included people who came to experience the novel idea of a comprehensive community centre run by activists. These visits also exposed us to potential funders. The positive aspect of this flow of human traffic for those of us working at Zanempilo was the excitement of sharing ideas away from the demands of attending to the sick and poor. It lifted your spirit and enabled you to keep the perspective of being part of something larger than the daily chores.

We established a routine of monthly regional staff meetings at which all heads of divisions within the Eastern Cape Black Community Programmes reported on their work and received constructive criticism and suggestions. The Eastern Cape region grew rapidly under Steve's leadership. It had a Transkei office in Umtata, headed by Mrs Ndamse, which specialised in the establishment of self-help sewing and knitting groups among rural women. Mrs Ndamse's previous involvement with the Young Women's Christian Association (YWCA) put her in a strong position to head this section of the work.

The King activities included Research and Publication, headed by Malusi Mpumlwana, who worked with Thoko Mbanjwa, later to become his wife. It was responsible for the preparation of all BCP publications, and was closely directed by Steve, whose name could not be openly associated with the publications in view of his banning order. Thus Malusi's operation was legally based in Durban under Bennie Khoapa, but physically and intellectually located in King.

Later Mxolisi Mvovo, Nobandile Biko's husband, came to head the sales division of our rapidly growing home industries. He also took charge of Njwaxa Home Industry, which was started by Fr Timothy Stanton, a Community of the Resurrection priest. He was based in Alice at the Federal Theological Seminary. Fr Stanton had been moved by the extreme poverty of the people in the villages surrounding Alice, and had induced some British parishioners to help finance a home industry producing leather purses and tobacco pouches. This industry grew under the joint direction of Mxolisi and Voti Samela, a qualified leather artisan, producing belts, handbags, horse saddles, nail bags and, later, sandals and shoes. The load of orders became such that some of the women in Zinyoka, who we had identified as needy on the basis of their children's nutritional status, were organised into a piece-job group as part of Njwaxa Home Industry to do the finishing-up tasks.

In 1977 the thriving Njwaxa Home Industry moved from its humble premises in a mud house to a well-constructed and well-equipped corrugated-iron factory, financed by ICCO, a Dutch church group which funded development work. It supplied small and large clients all over the Eastern Cape and farther afield, even as far as Durban.

Our own work at Zanempilo grew from small numbers to a brisk flow of people from the village of Zinyoka as well as from more distant villages where we offered mobile clinic services. The majority had minor problems, but the few with major problems were referred to local hospitals, especially Mt Coke, from which I continued to receive support from my former colleagues. Our ambulance service also became active in meeting the needs of villagers lacking transport to reach medical help. This service was particularly welcomed by expectant mothers and their families. We did most of the normal deliveries at the clinic and referred difficult cases to the hospital.

I remember three particularly traumatic fatalities which resulted from lack of experience and poor judgement on my part. Contrary to conventional views, doctors don't bury their mistakes easily, if at all. They remain with you throughout your life. The first was a neonatal death after a difficult bridge delivery in a teenage mother, Mamoswazi's daughter. She should have been referred to the hospital in the first instance before labour advanced. But I was too inexperienced to know better.

The second was that of a young woman who died of a hypersensitivity reaction to penicillin after receiving oral treatment for tonsillitis. We had omitted to ask her if she was sensitive. There is a risk attached to high-volume primary health work where health workers are under pressure to attend to long queues of people. We learned the hard way not to neglect the basics.

The third case was the worst of all. Bukelwa Biko, Steve's elder sister, then a nurse at Fort Beaufort Mental Hospital, came to see me in August 1975 with what she believed was cardiac pain from coronary problems. She had been having chest pains for a few days which had not responded to simple analgesics. I dismissed her concerns. After all she was an African woman, thirty-three years old with no family history of heart disease. How could she think of such a diagnosis? I reassured her, sedated her, and sent her home to rest at her mother's house in Ginsberg. She collapsed and died the following morning. I could not forgive myself. How could I have ignored her long history of cigarette smoking and use of the contraceptive pill after the birth of her only child in 1963? There was no way of explaining my guilt or of comforting the family in their distress. I felt I had betrayed the trust Bukelwa and her family had placed in me.

But there were also joyous moments. A woman who had failed to conceive after two years of marriage came to seek help. On examination I discovered she was still a virgin. I shyly enquired how she and her husband conducted their intimate relations. She acknowledged she had suspected that all was not well with what they were doing, but feared being critical of her husband. It was left to me to discuss the simple solution with the husband. A few months later, the delighted woman came in to show off the evidence of my successful intervention.

We also became popular with local civil servants and other professionals who preferred our care to the impersonal service they received from many of the local hospitals and general practitioners. We charged fees on a progressive scale, and also benefited from the higher rates we could charge the few who had access to medical aid. Thus there was some redistribution of limited resources within the community.

In addition to my medical responsibilities I had to take over the directorship of BCP in the Eastern Cape from Steve when his banning order was further tightened in the first half of 1976. It was a blow which he took in characteristic style. I was simply told by Bennie and Steve that as the second most senior staff member in the Eastern Cape I would have to run the regional office. There was no formal induction – I just had to learn as I went along.

My dual responsibilities increased my burdens, but also accelerated my growth as a person. I had to develop time-management skills to enable me to balance the many and often conflicting demands placed on me. I spent the mornings at Zanempilo attending to patients and other responsibilities. Afternoons were set aside for administrative duties at 15 Leopold Street and attending to staff members who reported to me. I also made time to visit projects in other parts of the Eastern Cape, a responsibility Steve had not been able to discharge because of his restriction orders. A visit to Umtata in March 1977 was the most memorable. Here, in the first 'independent homeland', I had to deal with Mrs Nobantu Ndamse, whose late husband had been a homeland politician. She was quite favourably disposed to the benefits of 'independence'. This was to be a source of tension between Mrs Ndamse and me later. But it was interesting to see how the elite in Umtata benefited from 'independence' while the lot of the poor at best remained unchanged and in most cases worsened.

As part of my new job I had to set aside time to receive visitors and do some public relations work for BCP. Potential funders had to be entertained, and Steve was enormously supportive in imparting some of the skills of communication appropriate to the task. He sat in on a number of discussions with sponsors and important parties, in spite of the prohibitions of his banning order. He could rely on the elaborate early-warning protective system developed by the community around him.

I was also compelled to be more focused, disciplined and goal-directed in my daily activities in order to accomplish as much as possible in the limited time available – a training which has stood me in good stead since then. I became increasingly adept at scheduling my daily activities and not being distracted until I had completed set tasks. The risk of rigidity and impatience with those otherwise inclined was a constant concern. Malusi, who could never keep time or hurry himself to do anything, was a particularly difficult customer to deal with. He was disarmingly charming, and would soothe my ruffled feathers with an engaging smile.

Chapter 13

A huge historical burden

T HE CLOSELY KNIT COMMUNITY WHICH GRADUALLY EMERGED also provided an outlet for social life. We played card games, particularly casino, drank beer, organised braais, danced, and engaged in ordinary activities which made for a good time. Soon people from the surrounding areas, particularly from Ginsberg township, joined in, with mixed results.

The difficulties were many. Firstly, the already stretched budget of the clinic took strain from the regular demands of feeding uninvited guests. I became upset when some people literally camped out at the centre for an entire weekend, expecting to share breakfast, lunch and supper with those of us living there. Meat and drinks were purchased from people's own pockets, but there were some who were less generous and contributed little. Steve and I shared our frustrations around this problem, but found no solution except the occasional joking remark. Steve tried to shame non-contributors into mending their ways, though this had limited success.

Steve also had bore the brunt of the transformation of his mother's house into 'a people's home'. Everybody and anybody felt free to call at Mamcete's[18] any time of the day, and expected to be fed and, if need be, accommodated. Mamcete cooked samp and beans in a large pot and prepared enough gravy to feed the multitudes. She was a good cook,

---

18 Steve's mother's clan name, by which she was fondly known.

and her bread and scones were legendary. We would descend on them as they came out of the oven until we were stuffed. But that all came at a cost which few visitors bothered about.

Then again, the continual festivities did not make for a healthy life-style. Too many late nights and too much alcohol are not good for any-body, but their impact on those on 24-hour duty like myself was con-siderable. I used to resent the inconsiderate noise from the late-night parties which disturbed my sleep. In some cases I would simply have to join in because my complaints went unheeded.

Steve also suffered from the late nights, but once he got going it be-came difficult to stop him. And as long as he kept going, all the admir-ing activists stayed on. He had difficulty waking up after such punish-ing partying. I remember many frustrating mornings when I would plead, cajole and sometimes cry from utter frustration, trying to get him up for an important appointment. He would open one eye and dis-armingly say, 'Just now, Toto – just now.' ('Toto' was an endearing term he used for those he loved.) 'Just now' often extended to half an hour.

Living in community robs you of the pleasures of privacy. Members of our community and other 'hangers-on' felt free to come and go as they pleased, and to use Zanempilo resources and facilities ad lib. It was most frustrating for me to try and balance my professional responsibil-ities with the expectations of members of the community. Some of them soon regarded me as a difficult person who spoiled their fun. I often yearned for the opportunity to curl up in bed undisturbed for hours on end.

We also hosted many out-of-town activists who came to visit and, occasionally, to relieve me in my onerous tasks. Dr Dubs Msauli, a gen-eral practitioner from Mdantsane township in East London, also a mem-ber of our regional BCP board, was a real help to me. He would come on a Saturday afternoon and be on call for the rest of the weekend, giving me a break from the health centre. In 1976, the burden of work became so intolerable for me that Dr Seolo Solombela joined me as an additional medical officer.

Seolo was a lovely person to work with, but it took him time to fit into the community. He was rather traditional in his views about the place of women in society, and had a hard time coming to terms with my position. I was his boss and I participated in what he regarded as manly activities. For example, he took a dim view of my joining in the eating of the sheep heads after braais. I made it clear he had a choice between sharing with me or distancing himself from this violation of tradition by abstaining and preserving his honour as a man. He followed his best interests.

Community life in King grew more complex with the arrival of new members and the intensification of the activism. There are interesting similarities and differences between religious communities and activist communities such as we established in King. In some ways political activism is a form of religion. For one thing, as in the case of religious conviction, political activists are moved by something larger than themselves. They believe in a future which might be better than the present, want to establish a better order, and have compassion for the underdog. Secondly, they share a sense of fellowship with others who are similarly committed. The need for renewing such fellowship in ritualised meetings – church services or political gatherings of the faithful – is also a common feature. At these ritualised meetings one renews one's commitment to the vows taken earlier. The repetition of political slogans and the singing of liberation songs also serve to cement the bonds of fellowship, much in the same way that the Creed serves to bind together Christians in the re-affirmation of their faith.

Then again, there is a common desire of individual members of such communities to conform to the group. The more fundamentalist the tendency, and the more insecure the community feels, the more likely that conformity will be enforced. The repressive climate created by the security police also put demands on activists to conform to certain behaviour so as to minimise security risks.

Both religious and political activist communities tend to operate on a model of overt leadership, be it a superior, bishop, guru or political leader. The risk of a personality cult developing is extremely high in both cases. The more insecure and fundamentalist the tendency of the community, the higher this risk becomes.

Finally, the willingness of individuals to sacrifice or subordinate their personal ambitions or goals for the sake of the group is also a notable similarity. This tendency is often closely tied to a willingness to engage in communal sacrificial acts, either symbolic or involving actual physical violence. Such sacrificial violence is sometimes justified as an important and necessary act to contain communal violence by focusing it on a sacrificial victim.[19] Some of the most gruesome necklace murders[20] committed by political activists in the 1980s involved the sacrificial death of fellow activists suspected of disloyalty. The symbolic purification of the community by fire has significant psychosocial implications. Religious fundamentalists are also known to engage in sacrificial violence, both directed at the self, as in the Waco case in Texas in 1993, or directed at others, as in the case of 'holy wars' or crusades aimed at settling political scores.

There are, however, some important differences between the two kinds of community. In the first place, religious communities suffer less from the burden of personal responsibility for their own and other people's redemption. The belief in a force superior to humans helps to keep a measure of humility about personal abilities within religious communities. Activists who are non-believers are entirely on their own on this score – a huge historical burden for anybody to carry.

---

19 See René Girard on *Violence and the Sacred* (Baltimore, 1992).
20 Killing a victim by setting alight a motor-car tyre filled with petrol, which is placed around the person's neck.

Also, there is a greater recognition in religious communities of the need for renewal and recharging one's batteries than in activist circles. Most, if not all, religious communities prescribe a time for reflection and formal periods of retreat from daily activities. In most cases you also have a confessor or counsellor to guide your spiritual growth. Activist communities, while recognising the importance of recharging batteries, often feel that they cannot afford to allow individuals sorely needed time out. Burnout is a likely and common outcome.

Burnout becomes an even bigger problem for leaders who often lose perspective on the source and nature of their problems, and become more and more driven to accomplish set goals. It is under such circumstances that tyranny takes root as subordinates are driven beyond their human abilities. A vicious cycle set in motion by the self-sacrificial leader's increasing demands for respect and loyalty, and sustained by the fear or unwillingness of subordinates to question the leader's judgements, often lies behind the tragic degeneration of liberation movements into vehicles of human rights abuses. Fundamentalist religious groups are also vulnerable to these abuses.

Our King community had elements of both the good and the bad. Most of us came from Christian homes and had a religious basis for our political commitment. But few, if any, of us were practising Christians. In fact some of us, myself included, actively distanced ourselves from the church, for we saw it as failing to proclaim the good news to the poor and to fight for the liberation of the oppressed. The church in South Africa was divided into three segments: those supporting apartheid, those passively accepting the established order, and a small segment which opposed apartheid actively. We had to rely mainly on our own resources for personal development.

The best-placed activists in many historical settings seem to be those who combine a spiritual and a political base. They are able to draw on the strengths of the two commitments, which are mutually reinforcing.

You could say that it is not possible to be truly spiritual if you have no real concern for the oppressed and downtrodden people of the world in which you live. Thomas Merton, Martin Luther King Jr, Mother Teresa and Desmond Tutu are a few examples of people whose spiritual growth has been related to their personal responses to the circumstances of their time and place.

There was a healthy custom of vigorous debate within our community which worked against the tendency towards conformity. Mapetla Mohapi often had more radical views on many issues, and would engage Steve and Malusi in long discussions. These discussions intensified after his change of jobs towards the end of 1975 from being a SASO regional organiser to becoming the executive director of the Zimele Trust, which focused on self-help projects for ex-political prisoners. Mapetla's exposure to the despair of ex-political prisoners, the divisions among them, and their inability to work together in groups for the common good, made him less starry-eyed about the notion of black solidarity on which we pinned so much of our hopes for the process of liberation. He also had important points to make about the need for more radical strategies than simply conscientising the oppressed to challenge their oppressors. There had to be a more directed programme of resistance which went beyond individual defiance of 'the system'. Even to discuss such directed resistance, a metaphor for the armed struggle, was of course a high risk in view of the vigilance of 'the system'. Mapetla had a sharp wit and nerves of steel underneath his casual exterior.

Contact with those people working for the Border Council of Churches (BCC), a regional body affiliated to the SACC, kept us alive to the importance of valuing different strategies to address the problems of development in our country. Mr Temba Sibeko, then Director of BCC, was an older man with a very different approach to life. He was none-theless supportive of our work, and resisted security police pressure to inform on us. We often made fun of Mr Sibeko's peculiarities: his driving style (hunched ridiculously right up against the steering wheel), his manner of speaking which would often lead him to laugh at his own jokes though they escaped the rest of us, and his ineffectual leadership. Steve was very sensitive about our mischief-making at Mr Sibeko's expense, and would call us to order.

The openness to internal debates helped to develop leadership among younger members of the community. Steve was a very supportive leader. He enabled people to go beyond the limits they had placed on their own capacity and agency. In fact, in certain cases one could say that some people were promoted beyond their level of competence, simply because with Steve about they had the self-confidence to do things they could not otherwise do. Some of those unfortunate people could not sustain the momentum of action at the same level once the support system came apart.

The risk of a cult of personality developing around the leader of our community remained high. Steve did not seek it, but it was imposed on him by people who needed the security of a visibly strong leader. It would also have taken a superhuman to remain unaffected by the open admiration of friend and foe for the positive impact of his ideas and their successful implementation in practical terms. The nature and scope of Steve's contribution to liberation politics in South Africa are all the more remarkable given the constraints of the banning orders under which he operated. And Steve was not superhuman.

The increasing local, national and international attention he received put him into an ever-brighter limelight. Local activists became more and more conscious of the privilege of basking in this glory. 'The Son of Man' label which was attached to him, though it started off as a joke, assumed an aura imbued with symbolism. He was surrounded by admiring hangers-on, which impacted adversely on his lifestyle. He also became more daring in breaking his banning orders, reassured by a supportive and protective local populace.

Our own personal relationship took a dip and reached an all-time low. I was one of only a few people who challenged him on the recklessness of his lifestyle. He became impatient with my criticism. The stress of the triangular relationship was also taking its toll. I remember one particularly unpleasant confrontation between us in Mdantsane township where we had gone in my car to visit Dubs Msauli. Steve would not hear of us going back to King, even though it was already past midnight. After failing to convince him to come along, I threatened to leave without him, and he dared me. Something in me snapped. I took my keys from him, asked those ready to leave to come along, got into the car and drove away. I was furious. Steve had to phone Thenjiwe in King to pick him up later that morning.

He could not forgive me for carrying out my threat. For weeks afterwards we suspended our love relationship and came together as fellow activists with a job to do – a capacity we perfected over the years in our difficult relationship. We were able to switch the focus of our relationship between collegiality, friendship and a love affair. Its multi-layered and multi-faceted nature ensured its resilience.

Like many popular idealistic leaders in history, Steve did not escape the folly of admiring available women at every turn. After all, even pastors such as Martin Luther King Jr and presidents such as J. F. Kennedy have fallen prey to the comfort of adoring women, as well as the exhilaration of unlimited access to their attentions. It must be a welcome break from the tough political battles these leaders have to contend with. There must also be some need to make good the self-sacrificial life which comes with political commitment, often early on in one's life, robbing one of the carefree pleasures of youth. Steve had affairs with women on the BCP staff, within the broader community of activists, and outside. Most of these were fleeting affairs with women who enjoyed the reflected glory of an important man.

I remained blissfully unaware of these escapades, and was therefore saved the added pain. I felt a mixture of revulsion and empathy for Steve when he confessed to me, at the end of 1976, when we both decided to confront the unsatisfactory state of our relationship. My lack of awareness up to that point was in part due to my extraordinary workload and my lack of enthusiasm for the endless parties where these affairs blossomed. It also had to do with my own overconfidence in the indestructibility of our relationship. This had survived many storms, and had so many dimensions that it could grow at the levels of pure friendship or collegiality even during the most difficult emotional periods when intimacy was impossible for weeks on end. But we both knew we were destined to end up together.

Detention

FOR THEIR PART, THE SECURITY POLICE WERE DETERMINED to break our relationship and destroy the King community. With the outbreak of the Soweto riots in June 1976 and the increasing restlessness of schoolchildren and young activists all over the country, the security forces intensified their repressive measures. Captain Schoeman, a tough vindictive cop based in East London, virtually moved into the King security police offices with a mission to discipline us and break our hold on the region.

Mapetla Mohapi was the first to be detained under Section 6 of the Terrorism Act in July 1976. He was suspected of transporting youngsters across the border to Botswana. We later came to understand that one of these young people was a security police plant. Mapetla died in detention, allegedly by hanging himself with his jeans from the grille of the door of his cell in Kei Road Police Station.

We were devastated. We refused to believe the story of suicide which was supported by a note on tissue paper written to Captain Schoeman (of all people). Why would he write a suicide note to his torturers and not to his loved ones? Mapetla had been resourceful and had only a day or so before his alleged suicide smuggled a note on a strip of toilet paper to his wife Nohle, reassuring her of his ability to cope. We suspect that in spite of a later Supreme Court finding, which accepted the suicide story, he was throttled by his captors and then hung up when they realised they had gone too far. I was asked to attend his postmortem examination on behalf of the family. Fortunately, Dr Dubs Msauli also came along and gave me much-needed moral support. It was one of the most painful duties I had to carry out as an activist medical practitioner. It is bad enough losing your friend and colleague, but to stand by as his body was being cut up was very traumatic.

To add insult to injury, I was detained on the late afternoon of 6 August 1976 as we were preparing to bury Mapetla in Sterkspruit, in the Aliwal North district. And so I was prevented from taking proper leave of Mapetla – a double blow. I was one of the first activists to be detained under the newly promulgated preventive detention clause of Section 10 of the Terrorism Act. Also detained were Malusi Mpulwana and Mxolisi Mvovo. I remember parting from them in the reception area of the brand-new King Williamstown prison, convinced that we would be kept in detention until the day of liberation, which we naively imagined was around the corner. We had a long way to go to 'around the corner'.

I had fortunately been advised by a visitor to Zanempilo, as I was being led away by an impatient Captain Schoeman, to take a small cuddly blanket I had bought to wrap myself with on the trip to Sterkspruit. That blanket became a constant companion during my detention, especially on the first night when I was still unsure about the cleanliness of the prison blankets. I had heard horror stories of lice-infested bedding, but I need not have worried. It was hard sleeping on the thin felt mat on a cold cement floor, but at least the blankets were clean. I remember my fury as I heard the convoy of buses drive past on their way to Sterkspruit. Mapetla was no more.

It was a day or two before I identified a supportive black female warder who lived in Ginsberg township to help me communicate with the outside world. She brought me newspapers, cigarettes and messages from Steve. Steve reassured me that he had briefed a lawyer, Mr Griffiths Mxenge, to look after us in detention. The warder remained a lifeline keeping detainees informed on what was happening outside, until she was trapped by her white colleagues, and later charged and dismissed from her job.

Subsequent police swoops netted Steve and Thenjiwe Mtintso, Seolo Solombela, Thoko Mbanjwa, Pumla Sangotsha, Nobandile Mvovo and many other activists across the country. Replacements had to be found to keep vital services and projects going, and in some cases the very replacements would promptly be detained in a determined effort to bring all our efforts to a standstill. Thenjiwe and Steve were held under the dreaded Section 6 of the Terrorism Act, a clause that licensed torture to extract information. The majority were held in preventive detention. Some were beaten on their way to prison by vindictive policemen bent on getting their own back by assaulting the 'cheeky Bantus' who had outsmarted them at every turn in their surveillance.

Though I had started off alone in the female section for about ten days, more detainees came in during the following nights. I remember hearing the heavy metal gates open and then becoming aware of voices, which I strained to recognise. After the warders had gone I would shout in an effort to establish contact with the new arrival. After two weeks of this trickle, we requested and were granted permission to share a common cell. We were thrilled.

Our communal cell did not have a toilet but we had access to one during working hours, by attracting the attention of the warders to let us in and out of the cell. We later learned to use this system to discipline the warders if they were uncooperative. We would take turns – seven of us at one stage – in calling them. As soon as the warder had locked the cumbersome door, we would call her back to let the next person out. In the end they kept the door open throughout the day, locking us in only when they went off duty in the evenings.

The three warders who looked after us were different in both physical stature and personality. The eldest was an old unhappy woman with such a deep voice you would swear it was a male talking. She neglected herself and was smelly and unpleasant. She used foul language and always invoked prison rules to turn down reasonable requests from prisoners. The regular prisoners called her 'Hodoshe', a Xhosa word for a large green fly.

The most senior of the three women was a cold-hearted, mousy woman. She played the game by the rules and did not allow any friendliness to develop between herself and the prisoners. In contrast we named her other colleague 'NoNice' because she was such a nice person. She talked to us whenever she had a chance to do so, and was generally helpful.

We had access to an exercise courtyard where we walked around and enjoyed the sunshine for an hour or so each day. We took up yoga, learning from a book which was brought to us from the male section. It belonged to Gibson Kente, a well-known playwright, who was unfortunate enough to be arrested in the vindictive swoop on anything black that moved in the Eastern Cape. Having brought his show *How Long* on tour to the Eastern Cape, he got caught in the crossfire. We loved yoga and some of us got quite good at it: head and shoulder stands, relaxation postures, and long stretches.

We were also allowed to order our own food on set days; it was bought with the rest of the prison supplies, and delivered to us individually – not a bad service, and a remarkable improvement from the first two weeks of prison food. Prison food has a bad reputation throughout the world, but in South Africa it was worse, because of the racial discrimination involved. Africans got the worst diet. Breakfast at about 7.30 a.m. was a large tin mug of sweet black coffee and soft porridge with no milk. Lunch at 11 a.m., samp with no beans, and tomato-sauce colouring added to it. Sometimes there would be shredded stewed meat or vegetables. Supper, between 4 and 5 p.m., was soft porridge with beetroot, cabbage or a slice of bread swimming in it. It would on some occasions be served with vegetable soup which looked appetising, until you got to the bottom of the mug and found carrot ends complete with soil.

Nobandile suggested that we should drink the otherwise tasty soup without looking at the contents of the mug, and be prepared to stop when our tongues felt gravel! As at Bethesda Normal College, I could not bring myself to eat food which was an affront to my dignity. I spent the first ten days of detention living on diluted coffee in the mornings, and whatever I could rescue of the slice of bread before it drowned in the soft maizemeal porridge at supper-time. I lost weight rapidly. When I was released I weighed no more than fifty kilograms. But I was healthy because of the yoga exercises and the later dispensation which allowed us to buy our own food.

We soon established a thriving prison community with an efficient system of communication with the men on the other side of the divide. We were allowed many privileges, including weekly visits from friends and family. We were grateful for small mercies and got used to the presence of policemen during visits. Occasionally, we would be fortunate enough to bump into a visitor as we were being shown to the glass cubicle. The treat of hugging someone from outside would be the talk of the week.

Fr Aelred Stubbs of the Community of the Resurrection visited us regularly at Zanempilo. He brought me news of the detention of my youngest brother, Molepo, who I had brought with me to King in December 1975. I was incensed! He was only fourteen years old, and had gone to live at Steve's home under Mamcete's care after my detention. How could any adult stoop so low as to detain such a young person? I raised hell with the prison authorities. They initially denied that any minors were being held in prison. I remember that NoNice, whose husband was deputy chief of the prison, assured me that she had been given his word of honour that they did not have fourteen-year-olds in the prison. She added confidently: 'And I can assure you, Dr Ramphele, my husband never lies to me.' I told her I had news for her, and that she might just as well brace herself for her husband's first lie. Armed with hard facts from our good 'prison telegraph system', I insisted that they produce him.

Molepo appeared at the visitor's window uncombed and unwashed. He had been brutally assaulted by the security police, who initially held him and his friends, about five of them, in the local police cells. He told me that his legs were so swollen that he could not wear his pants for days. He also complained that they were all infested with lice. I demanded that he be seen by a medical doctor immediately, together with the others, and that they be deloused and given toiletries, for which I provided money from my deposit account at the prison. They were kept for a few more days, to let their injuries heal, before being released. They had been detained by Captain Schoeman in desperation after he had failed to find evidence to nail Steve during his detention.

My sister Mashadi, then a senior nurse at Baragwanath Hospital, came by train from Johannesburg to visit me at about the time that Molepo was also imprisoned. It must have been a trying time for my family, particularly my mother. So many people were dying in detention that relatives had every reason to fear the worst when they got news of an arrest. Mashadi was relieved to find that our circumstances were relatively comfortable and could take comforting news back to my worried mother.

As detainees we spent hours playing card games and Monopoly to amuse ourselves. We became quite addicted to these games, and in some cases people would have serious conflicts over cheating or losing. It is remarkable how much institutionalised people regress in their behaviour. You easily lost perspective on the importance of things in your life, and over-reacted to ridicule or teasing – a sign of increased vulnerability and insecurity. The excitement about food and other treats from outside, visitors and letters also reflected the increasing emotional deprivation.

But there were benefits as well from being forced to spend time away from the type of lifestyle we had established. Although those of us who were smokers continued the habit, there was no alcohol for the entire four and a half months that we were out of circulation. Our bodies could be detoxified and regenerated. I had also benefited from the first ten days on my own. I needed time with myself after the hectic months in the constant company of others. I had the opportunity to take a long hard look at myself in the solitude of my cell. There were some things I liked, but others I didn't.

I had been registered as a part-time student with the University of South Africa, a correspondence university, for a Bachelor of Commerce degree since the beginning of 1975, but had made little headway because of my work and social circumstances. For the first time since my earlier university days, I enjoyed the time alone with my books, and consequently did extremely well in the end-of-year exam, which I wrote at a venue arranged by my gaolers. I gained a first-class pass and won a scholarship to continue my studies in 1977. That came in handy in the next few years as I pursued my goal of learning to understand the world of business management and administration.

Two or three weeks before our release in December 1976 a number of significant things happened. Firstly, we received a visit from the International Red Cross. They questioned us about our prison conditions, and must have been appalled to find us sleeping on thin felt mats on the cold concrete floors. A few days after their visit we were pleasantly surprised to get beds and linen, including pillows. There were also improvements in the quality of the food.

In the second place, we got to know through our 'prison telegraph system' that Steve had been released from detention. Thenjiwe, who had received the worst treatment from the bully boys in the security forces, had joined us a week or so earlier. She was traumatised physically and emotionally. She had ended up in the Libode Police Station cells in the

Transkei, after the security police were done with her, and was later brought to join us.

I remember my excitement at the thought of seeing Steve again after four months! I could not contain myself before his visit to me in prison. He had lost a considerable amount of weight – almost regaining his slender, youthful body which I associated with the beginning of our relationship. He looked devastatingly handsome and sent my heart into a mad spin. I was also fortunate to bump into him before he was shown into the glass cage, and could get a long-missed embrace.

Our release was swift once the process was initiated. It came as a welcome birthday present on 28 December 1976. We were all reunited at the gate of the prison and Steve organised transport to Zanempilo for a big celebration. Thenjiwe was the only unfortunate exception. She was taken straight to her mother's home in Orlando East, Johannesburg, where she was restricted under a banning order. Her absence put a damper on our celebration, but there was still a lot to celebrate: couples were reunited, lovers renewed intimacies suspended over the months, and the joy of just being able to walk about in the open or ride in a car was intoxicating. Two marriages were contracted within a day or so of our release: Malusi married Thoko, while Seolo Solombela and Pinkie tied the knot. The township community soon came to join in the festivities.

Steve and I had a long, frank discussion at the earliest opportunity. He had also had time for reflection after he had deflected the heat of his interrogation, and had physically stopped Warrant Officer Hattingh from an attempt to assault him. He realised how much he had hurt me in a vain attempt to force me to sever our relationship, which was complicating his life both as a married man and as a national political leader. He was amazed at my lack of awareness of the many affairs he had had, which he claimed had been in part aimed at disgusting me and forcing a showdown. He acknowledged that he found me very challenging as a partner because of my strong personality and my insistence on certain basics where others would turn a blind eye. He recognised how important this was as a braking mechanism in his life, and knew that uncritical admirers were a danger to him in the long term. He also knew that he could rely on my loyalty whatever happened. We renewed our commitment to each other, and agreed to work gracefully but speedily to resolve the triangular relationship.

He also realised that no one could sustain a marriage if you felt guilty about choosing the wrong partner. Attempts to protect his wife from the pain occasioned by his continued love for me had not been successful anyway: all three of us were constantly hurt by the tensions inherent in the triangular relationship. He had been criticised by his political colleagues for his unfaithfulness to his marriage vows, but he had made it clear to them that however much he had tried he could not conceive of a life without me. We shared not only a passionate love but also a commitment to the liberation of the oppressed in South Africa. Ours was a complete relationship in which we mutually nurtured our shared values. His dilemma was how to deal with Ntsiki, the mother of his two children, without doing violence to her dignity. Solitary confinement gave him ample opportunity to reflect and realise that he could not continue to live a lie. He had to harmonise his life and publicly and formally commit himself to his heartfelt desire to share his life with me as my marriage partner. On his release he told me that he planned to institute divorce proceedings as soon as possible so that our relationship could be formalised before the end of 1977.

This was music to my ears. It vindicated my conviction that he and I were destined to share our lives more fully. But the continued hesitation on his part had begun to erode my trust in him. I came out of detention determined to force him to choose between his loyalty to his wife and his love for me. I was not going to perpetuate the untidy mess that our lives had become.

Our relationship reached new heights. The sense of comfort in belonging to each other was all-embracing. The song which had been silenced over the trying past months came alive. My heart danced for joy. This time we were not going to let anything stand in the way of our happiness together. We grew back into each other at all levels. Every day became a treat.

'Well, Dr Ramphele, goodbye, you bitch!'

O N THE POLITICAL FRONT, THUNDER CLOUDS WERE GATH-ering. Captain Schoeman intensified his disruptive actions in the Eastern Cape. Surveillance on Steve increased. Schoeman brought many unsuccessful cases against Steve for breaking his banning order. In desperation he also began to add traffic offences to his list of charges, but they were thrown out one by one by the courts.

Schoeman charged youngsters in Ginsberg for arson committed at their school, Forbes Grant, and forced my brother Molepo and his friends to become state witnesses. The only strategy that would protect Molepo from perjuring himself by contradicting his confession obtained during detention was to invoke language as a delaying tactic. Molepo was too young to defy the courts and refuse to testify without risking imprisonment, a fate which befell one of his friends. I advised him to insist on a Northern Sotho interpreter before he would agree to testify in the Grahamstown Supreme Court. It was a tall order in a Xhosa-speaking area to find a suitable person. I was, in fact, the only one within the jurisdiction of the Grahamstown Supreme Court with the competence to assist the court, but I was not going to volunteer. I did attend the hearing to support him. In the end the frustrated security police had to ask for Molepo to be released, but not before threatening him. He was resolute. The police were furious but powerless.

The security surveillance continued. The final blow came for me in April. I had received an uncharacteristic call from the security police offices in King asking me to present myself that afternoon. I smelled a rat. I phoned Steve and asked that we meet at 15 Leopold Street. No sooner had we arrived than Captain Schoeman came in with my banning order, which he suggested was as good as a warrant of arrest. He commanded me to follow him to his office. I refused. He then tried physically to force me, but Steve intervened and warned him to keep his hands off me.

Undaunted, Captain Schoeman radioed the regular South African police, who were often in awe of the security police. South African policemen above a certain rank had the legal authority to arrest citizens without a warrant: they only needed to assert that they had reason to believe they were acting in the public interest. They wasted no time in dragging me out of my office and throwing me into the back of the police van, which they drove around at a hellish speed, intending to create maximum discomfort for me. I was thrown from one end of the van to the other until the sudden stop at the police station. My angry but feeble attempts to lay a charge of wrongful arrest and assault were laughed at by the policemen in the charge office.

A satisfied Captain Schoeman came in a few minutes later and curtly ordered me to his office upstairs. He triumphantly read out the banning order. I was stunned! I was being restricted to the Naphuno district of Tzaneen in the northern Transvaal, an area I had never heard of before. I thought that there was an error somewhere. Indeed there was. My name had not been spelt correctly – a common occurrence. But I pinned my hopes on the identity number, which was clearly not mine. I was convinced that they must have confused me with someone else, whose home was in Naphuno. I pointed this out to Captain Schoeman. He simply asked me to indicate the corrections to him, and proceeded to alter the document accordingly, making a mockery of the legal requirement that the banning orders be given 'under the hand of the Minister', as the document piously proclaimed. He was to pay for this indiscretion.

As a desperate last-ditch measure I asked what was to happen to my responsibilities at the health centre and to my possessions. After all, I had a younger brother to make arrangements for, personal effects to pack, and patients and colleagues to take leave of. Schoeman would not hear of any such things. He said the police would take care of the packing and removal of my possessions. All I needed to do was to give them a list of the clothing I would require on the trip to Tzaneen, which was to start in an hour or so. I was outraged. How dare he imagine that I would let them get their paws on my personal effects! Schoeman replied that in that case I would have to leave as I was. His parting shot was: 'Well, Dr Ramphele, goodbye, you bitch!'

I sat in his office numbed by the events of the past few minutes. How could they send me to Naphuno? Where was I to stay there? How was I to manage without clothing on this long trip into the unknown? It is remarkable how much residual reasonableness one expects even from the worst of torturers and repressive regimes. I had not imagined that their desire to control and isolate would extend so far.

I was dressed in a full-length sleeveless cotton dress and a jersey which I had bought from our home industry in Umtata earlier that year. It was torn, having been caught on a nail at the door of our offices in Leopold Street as I was dragged out that afternoon. I was also at the tail end of a menstrual period, and dreaded the prospect. I had a handbag in which I had less than five rand. Warrant Officer Hattingh, who was put in charge of my removal from King, also relished what he saw as the final triumph over me. He implored me to accept their offer of packing some things for me from Zanempilo, but I held to my earlier view, hoping that they would relent and take me there. Indeed, Steve had driven to Zanempilo expecting that they would at least let me collect a few belongings, but it was not to be. Hattingh, who we nicknamed Maxolo, a Xhosa reference to the scaly appearance of his neck, assured me that they would buy me cigarettes and food on the way. We finally left King at 4 p.m. Another policeman and his wife had been asked to accompany Hattingh and assist him in driving and policing.

The trip turned out to be one of the longest in my life, both physically and emotionally. The policemen engaged in small talk and tried to be as friendly as possible, but I was too preoccupied with my own thoughts to respond. We stopped overnight at Zastron, in the north-eastern Cape. It was bitterly cold. They locked me in a police cell in the town, and went to a local hotel for the night. The policeman who was put in charge of me was appalled to learn that I had committed no crime, and was a medical doctor, and yet had been made to sleep on a concrete floor in a police cell. He promised to give me a liberal supply of new blankets, which he did, and to make me as comfortable as I could be under the circumstances.

The rest of the trip the following morning was exhausting. Hattingh got lost and ended up on an even longer route than intended. Schoeman, who originally came from the northern Transvaal, had directed him to take the back route along the eastern part of the country, perhaps to avoid the main cities, where I could possibly be spotted by someone who knew me. If that had been the intention, then it was an impeccable route – completely unfamiliar to me. We arrived at Tzaneen Police Station around 10 p.m. I was smelly and exhausted from lack of washing and proper sleep.

Hattingh was about to repeat the previous night's performance of signing me into a police cell overnight. I flew into a rage, which was not difficult at that point, as I was at the end of my tether. I demanded to be taken where they planned to take me. There was no way I was to sleep without a bath for one more night. Hattingh contacted the local security police, who came and formally took charge of me as a restricted person in their area of jurisdiction. I only then learnt that I was to be taken to Meetse-a-Bophelo (literally, Water of life) Hospital – an ironical name for a person in my circumstances. As I was to learn later, the irony extended to the locals, who had been forcibly removed from the fertile Makgoba's Kloof area and brought to this arid land.

I was relieved to be finally delivered by the two black security policemen, after an hour-long bumpy ride on a gravel road, to Sister Thubakgale, who had been a schoolmate at Bethesda Normal College. She was shocked to see me there under escort by security police but quickly showed me to my new home – a small flat in the nurses' quarters. She also got a former neighbour from Kranspoort Mission Station to visit me. Matsela Seko helpfully lent me toiletries, nightwear and, the following day, a dress to wear. After a long-awaited bath, I fell asleep.

Chapter 16

A brief interlude

PEOPLE OFTEN ASK ME HOW I SURVIVED THESE DEGRADING situations. The short answer is that if you are faced with adversity, you have no choice but to strive for survival. It is amazing what internal reserves come to the fore under stressful conditions – mostly reserves you did not even know you possessed.

In his moving book *Man's Search for Meaning,* in which he shares his experiences of a Nazi concentration camp, Viktor Frankl eloquently discusses those attributes that make for survival on one hand, and those that condemn victims of abuse to an 'existential vacuum', a feeling of emptiness and meaninglessness, on the other. He points out that the most important survival strategy is to turn personal tragedy into triumph: 'Even a helpless victim of a hopeless situation, facing a fate he cannot change, may rise above himself, may grow beyond himself, and by so doing, change himself. He may turn a personal tragedy into a triumph.'[21] I was to learn this the hard way.

My first thought when I awoke the morning after my arrival at Meetse-a-Bophelo Hospital was to make contact with Steve. I was sure that none of my colleagues knew where I had been taken. Captain Schoeman would have made sure about that. I also needed clothing, toiletries and money while I decided on my next move. Above all I longed for the comfort of friends in my predicament.

---

21 V. Frankl, *Man's Search for Meaning* (London, 1984), p. 147.

It seemed that my best bet would be to get to a church establishment, Anglican or Catholic, the two most likely to be sympathetic to my plight. On asking, I was told that there was a community of the Sacred Heart Mission in Ofcolaco, near Trichardtsdal, some five kilometres away. I had no money, but armed with my only possessions, a banning order and my empty handbag, I set off in a taxi to Ofcolaco, promising the driver that I would ask the priests there to pay him the fare.

The first people I met at the mission were two African nuns, Sisters Mary-Theresa and Emily. Sister Mary-Theresa was the more forthcoming of the two. She knew what it meant to be banned and understood my plight. She was a vivacious woman with a gentle matronly manner. Sister Emily was less self-confident and tended to let Sister Mary-Theresa take the lead. Both wore traditional habits which revealed little of their physical attributes, but one could see that they were on the large side and had strong legs which carried them around the difficult terrain they worked in. The nuns quickly responded when I asked to have the taxi man paid, even before they had heard my full story. I was then shown into the sitting-room where I proceeded to tell them how I had landed there. I showed them the banning order as evidence of my plight. For the first time since this ordeal had started, I allowed myself to cry. For a while I could not stop. They were tears of anger and self-pity.

Sister Mary-Theresa then went to call Fr Mooney, the priest-in-charge at the time. He listened sympathetically and agreed to put me up and allowed me to use the phone. When Steve's voice came on the line, I burst into tears, but calmed down after a while to give him the details of where I was. I also told him about the errors in the information on my banning order and how Schoeman had treated them. He promised to arrange for the things I needed to be brought to me as soon as possible, and to get a lawyer to assist me. He also gave me news of others who had been banned in the last few days, among them Mxolisi, his brother-in-law. Steve reassured me and asked me to remain calm.

A sense of relief descended on me after this call. I could now face the reality of my circumstances. At least people who mattered to me knew where I was. There is something frightening about being in 'non-space' – unknown and among people who do not know you. I experienced the frightening emptiness of it all during the two days while being transported to my place of banishment. Many narratives of ex-detainees and ex-prisoners attest to the same overwhelming sense of not feeling like a complete human being until you have some contact with those you know, those who define your humanity. It is not surprising that solitary confinement is used as a mainstay of torture.

The ease with which Fr Mooney accepted me caused some of his colleagues anxiety. How did he know that I was not a security police plant? They found my story an improbable one. How could I have been dumped in an unknown place? Even allowing for the cruelty of the security police, banishment to unknown lands was not their usual weapon. They also were concerned that I looked too sophisticated to fit the bill of a desperate person. The borrowed dress I wore was a pretty, full-length floral outfit which more suited someone attending a dinner party than one stranded in the outback. It was also too much of a coincidence that I should make my appearance on the very day they were discussing how to respond as a community of priests to the growing political tension in the country.

Of the priests Fr Thomas Duane was the most vociferous in cautioning against my acceptance. Ironically, Fr Duane later became my greatest friend and supporter. Fr Mooney's final position was that he would accept me at face value and would not turn a deaf ear to my plea for help. Should I turn out to be a fraud, that would be on my own conscience. Fr Mooney informed me that he would arrange for me to live with the two African nuns at Tickeyline village, closer to Meetse-a-Bophelo Hospital. He drove me in his open van to Meetse-a-Bophelo to fetch my only dress, which I had washed and left to dry at the hospital, and return Matsela Seko's borrowed dress. Matsela kindly gave me the set of toiletries she had lent me earlier, and we headed for Tickeyline.

Tickeyline was a poor village, hence the name derived from the 'tickey' coin (worth three pence in the old South African coinage, later 2½ cents), which reflected the residents' sense that their lives were regarded as cheap. The houses were mainly thatch-roofed rondavels built by the locals according to their means. There was no electricity or piped water, and no proper road system. A primary school and the chapel, which formed part of the nuns' mission base, were the only public facilities for this village. There were about a hundred households in the village at the time.

The nuns' residence was a humble one. It merged into the surrounding homesteads in its simplicity. It was a two-bedroom house with a kitchen-cum-dining and living area. They used a primus stove for cooking or else made a fire outside on an open hearth. Simple as it was, I was relieved to have such a supportive place to stay. For Sisters Mary-Theresa and Emily were very kind. They made me feel welcome, and understood my predicament because of their own backgrounds and their contact with activist priests such as Fr Smangaliso Mkhatshwa. They generously let me have the use of one of the bedrooms for myself. They also promised to pray for me and with me.

Naturally the local security police were disappointed by my decision to leave Meetse-a-Bophelo Hospital, but I told them that they could not expect me to cooperate in my own imprisonment. After all, if they had been so keen to have me treat patients at the hospital, they should have had more compassion for the patients I had been treating. They were a tame lot and no match for an activist steeled by the thugs in King Williamstown.

I spent the next few days hitching lifts to and from Ofcolaco, a distance of a few kilometres, to make phone calls and to send messages to my family. On some occasions I had to walk the last kilometre or so. This was most unpleasant. The weather was very hot in typical Low-veld fashion, and the temperature reached 40°C on some days. The grass on both sides of the path was high, and on more than one occasion a snake slithered across the path, leaving me utterly beside myself with fear. Once I was so scared that I ran all the way to the mission house. Not that I could be described as a sprinter, but fear gave me wings.

Three days after my arrival I was thrilled to see Mziwoxolo Ndzengu, the ambulance driver at Zanempilo, drive up with my suitcase full of clothing and some money. He had flown to Johannesburg, and then hired a car to Tzaneen. It was good to be with someone who was part of my broken community. Mziwoxolo was never very social or talka-tive. He gave me a sketch of the events since my departure from King, in headline fashion. In this way I got to know who had been detained or banned, what the latest developments were at Zanempilo, the response of the security police to the anger generated by my banishment, and other essential news. I was grateful for his loyalty. He left the same day.

A day or so later none other than Thenjiwe Mtintso, herself restricted to Johannesburg, arrived at Tickeyline late in the evening. I was over-joyed. With Baba Jordan she brought me a VW Beetle to help me become mobile again. That was Thenji at her best, in one of the many daring missions in her life as an activist. We had a wonderful time catching up on the state of the nation. They brought news of the intensifying repression which had claimed many more people. Yet despite the ban-nings and detentions there was no sign of the political struggle letting up. The activism of the urban youth was increasing, many were leaving the country for military training, and boycotts of schools showed no sign of abating. We all felt that 'the system' was on its last legs – we just had to hang in there for the final push. It was after midnight when Thenjiwe and Baba finally tore themselves away.

The following day Mr Raymond Tucker, an attorney from Johannesburg, then popular in activist circles, called on me at Steve's request. After carefully reading my banning order, he told me that it was in fact a banishment order, restricting me to a foreign part of the country – a treatment which had up to that point been reserved for troublesome chiefs who refused to cooperate with the white authorities in imposing controls over their people. Banishment in this new sense was a distinction I was to share with Winnie Mandela. Later in 1977 she was banished to Brandfort, a small Free State town.

Raymond Tucker became visibly excited when he heard about the way in which Captain Schoeman had handled the errors in my banning order. His conclusion was that I was not banned legally, and could go wherever I chose. He also felt that there was a case to be made for wrongful arrest, and he was accordingly instructed to institute legal proceedings against the Minister of Justice and Police, Mr Jimmy Kruger. I was thrilled. My first thought was naturally to go back to King Williamstown. I decided to make contact with Fr Stubbs at the Community of the Resurrection Priory in Rosettenville in Johannesburg, for he was the best person to help me return home. But I first had to get directions to the Priory from him, without giving away too much on the telephone, for it was known to be tapped by the police.

When I called Fr Stubbs I pretended to need the directions for Raymond Tucker. My story was that Tucker wanted to visit him that evening to report on his discussions with me. Fr Stubbs was vague. He could not understand why Raymond Tucker needed directions to the Priory, where he had been a visitor many times. In the end I had to make do with what he finally gave me. I confided to Fr Mooney my intention to leave that night. He was concerned about my safety, but blessed me and let me go.

Back at Tickeyline I found my younger brother, Thomas. He had been asked by my concerned mother to see me. He was then a twenty-year-old student, and was visibly shaken not only by my new place of abode, but by my plans to leave that night for Johannesburg. In fact I told him that he would have to drive me out of Tzaneen: it was unusual then for a black woman to be seen driving a car, and I did not want to arouse suspicions or draw attention to myself. This was a case of naked bullying by an older sister, but it was not the time for gentle negotiations.

We left Tickeyline after dusk. Unfortunately, a typical Lowveld thunderstorm descended on us as we entered Tzaneen, and Thomas's considerable driving skills were severely tested on the sharp curves of the Makgoba's Kloof area. As soon as we emerged on the straight towards Pietersburg, he stopped on the side of the road, visibly shaken by the stress of events. We had passed through the danger zone, both physical and political, so I drove for the rest of the way. The trip was uneventful except that we got lost near Rosettenville and had to ask directions from a national serviceman. He was blissfully unaware that I was the embodiment of the very threat to national security which he was supposed to counter.

When we arrived at the Priory, Fr Stubbs was caught completely off guard. He could not believe his keen political antennae had missed my hinting. In his typically methodical way he made us comfortable for the night, especially my poor brother Thomas, who was still overwhelmed by the day's events. Thomas had no idea of what it meant to be banned and banished when he was pressed into breaking the orders of those restrictions. For a young man with no political education it was too much, but necessity is the best teacher, and he rose to the occasion. Fr Stubbs arranged with Fr Leo Rakgale, one of his brethren, to drive Thomas to the Johannesburg railway station to catch the train back to Pietersburg the following day. He also arranged for our trip to King, which was to start early the next morning.

The journey offered us time together. We had a long, frank discussion about our individual backgrounds, our fears and personality traits, which drew us closer together than would have been possible otherwise. Fr

Stubbs stopped being just another priest to me; he became a human being, friend and counsellor. When we arrived at Zanempilo, the staff couldn't believe their eyes. There was joy and celebration as people came to embrace me and welcome me back to the fold. The joy of reunion was everywhere in evidence. Steve was called urgently by phone without much explanation. He was absolutely astounded. 'Fr Stubbs, I thought I told you to keep her where she was!' he said. We flew into each other's arms and forgot the nightmare we had lived through during the past few days. The comfort of familiar surroundings and faces had the desired effect and the tension which had settled into my frail body began to ease.

After a discussion on the best way to extract maximum political benefit from this blunder by the security police, Steve and I sat back and enjoyed our reunion. Many of our colleagues and friends in the region heard about my return. Yet the vigilant security police remained blissfully unaware for the entire four days I spent in the King Williamstown area. They were embarrassed to read about my presence for the first time in the Monday morning edition of the *Daily Dispatch*. Donald Woods, the editor, had been one of the first people we alerted. He came to Zanempilo for a breakfast meeting on the Sunday. Thrilled to get the scoop, he announced it with a vengeance. The red-faced security police came to Zanempilo that Monday morning to find me revelling in my new-found freedom and acting in my usual capacity.

It was a short respite, but a crucial one on two counts. Firstly, I settled the score with Captain Schoeman: 6-0, game, set, but not yet match! Secondly, I received a gift I was not to know about until a month later – the conception of my beautiful son, Hlumelo, who became the embodiment of all the happy memories of 'A Love Supreme', the poem Steve had written for me during our student days. The rude interruption of our lives had upset our plans not to have another love child until our triangular relationship had been resolved, but my contraceptive pills had been left behind in King together with my other essential items. Abstinence was not a proposition. Passion took its course.

With Captain Schoeman nowhere in sight, the police apologised for the manner in which I had been treated earlier, but made it clear that I would be taken back to Naphuno in the end. They made elaborate efforts to get everything right the second time: spelling names correctly and giving the right identity number. They also made adequate preparation through mutual consent for transporting my personal effects. I was also allowed to wind down my responsibilities in King Williamstown, which included securing my brother Molepo's release from another spell of detention. Captain Schoeman had been trying to press him to turn state witness in yet another of his crazy cases against Steve and other activists.

I even had time to take proper leave of the people of the village, who I had got to love so much. The staff organised a party for me, and Mamoswazi led the women in singing and dancing. Lein van den Bergh, an official of the Dutch development agency ICCO, was one of the guests who shared this bitter-sweet farewell with me. He was to become a lifelong friend. There was a sense in which the sadness of my departure was tempered by the hope of my return sooner rather than later. It was farewell, but not goodbye. I was convinced that I would be back in King before the year was ended. At least that was how it looked from Steve's point of view and mine after a discussion of our future plans. However, history had other things in store for us.

I finally drove back to Tzaneen in my own Peugeot sedan with Mziwoxolo at my side to help with the driving. We followed the security police car to Pretoria, where we spent the night sleeping in my car parked in the basement of the Compol Police Station. Here we were given access to staff bathrooms in the morning and prepared ourselves for the remaining drive to Tzaneen.

There was a sad reunion with Fr Mooney and Sisters Mary-Theresa and Emily at Ofcolaco. They were happy to have me stay in Tickeyline while I sorted myself out, but my return signalled the permanence of my restrictions. The Tzaneen security police were thoroughly ashamed of their ineptitude at not having kept me in check. They had only learnt from their King colleagues on the Monday morning with the publication of the news that I was out of their jurisdiction. What a disgrace! But it suited me fine: I was one up on them.

That fateful day – 12 September 1977

I FOUND SETTING UP HOUSE IN LENYENYE TOWNSHIP, WHICH I had made an absolute condition of my return to the area, an interesting exercise. It gave me insights into the people I was to deal with for the next few years of my life. The security policemen, having made such fools of themselves, now kept me under constant surveillance. But they were so inexperienced that I would vanish in front of their eyes, and they would later catch up with me with desperation written on their faces. They were also confused by my friendliness. I treated them with courtesy and made a point of greeting them, even when they did not notice me, at the supermarket or other public places.

Nor did the local township superintendent, Mr Letsoalo, know how to deal with me. He had never seen an African woman medical doctor, let alone one who was said to be a danger to the security of the state. His dealings with me were also bedevilled by the open involvement of the security police in the administration of the township. He did not know the boundaries of his limited authority, but was as helpful as he could be under the circumstances. I was given a house on the edge of the township, with two bedrooms, a living room, a kitchen, and an inside toilet and shower.

The local magistrate, from whom I had to obtain permission to go outside my area to shop or attend church services, also found it difficult dealing with me. Later he became quite friendly and would share his ambivalences with me. He was very helpful in seeing that my requests were met. He was also instrumental in my move to a better house in a newly developed area. This was to be my home for almost eight years. He had come on an inspection visit to my first house and was visibly shocked at its inadequacy. I was sad when he was transferred out of the area during 1978; perhaps he was seen as too friendly. I shall never know.

The people in the area were amazing. Sister Mary-Theresa arranged with a local parishioner in Tickeyline, Mrs Mangena, to let one of her daughters, Makgatla, then about sixteen years old, stay with me in Lenyenye. The trust accorded me as a stranger has never stopped to amaze me. Makgetla Mangena has stayed with me and my family up to today, except for a brief interlude when she lived in Pholokwane. When her marriage failed, she returned to us as full-time housekeeper.

My neighbours in Lenyenye, all policemen in the regular service, were very curious about me. I have no doubt that they had been warned about me, and that some of them informed on me to the security police, who they saw as their superiors. I nonetheless decided to behave as normally to them as you do to any neighbour, which added to their confusion. Why was I not spitting flames of rage, as they may have been made to expect? I had decided on a deliberate strategy of vigilant self-preservation with the least expense of energy unless matters of principle were at stake.

Gradually individual members of the Lenyenye township community started warming to me. They would stop and greet me less nervously than in the first few weeks. I became particularly friendly with some families. Most important among them was a young couple, the Mokgashis – Mapula was a teacher, while her husband, Matthews, was a local catechist in the Roman Catholic church. I had been introduced to them by Fr Mooney. Our ties were later cemented by the friendship which developed between my mother when she later came to stay, and Mapula's mother, Nkabati Mamorobela, who also lived in Lenyenye. We visited each other's homes, and shared many meals together. Mapula introduced me to the delicacies of the area, particularly pumpkin leaves prepared with tomatoes and a liberal amount of freshly ground peanut meal. Delicious!

In addition to friends, there was the support of my family. My mother came to see me soon after I got back to Tickeyline. She was saddened by the reality of her daughter as a virtual prisoner in a foreign district. She hated the idea of the constant surveillance by security police, and feared for my safety. Later the ambivalences she experienced would surface: she was grateful that at least I was now more accessible to her than I had been for the previous ten years. Soon she acquired a reputation among the local security policemen of a tough, uncompromising woman. She could not hide her loathing of them and their work. She reacted negatively to their greetings and would fly into a rage if she detected any rudeness on the part of a policeman towards me.

Repeatedly she reminded them that they were uneducated in comparison with her daughter: 'You are as good as Sub A's[22]. Are you not ashamed of your behaviour towards this doctor?' I was at times embarrassed by my mother's outbursts, but she left the security policemen in no doubt about where they stood with her. One rude security policeman, Warrant Officer Ehlers, got a fair share of this treatment. On one occasion he ended a verbal confrontation with my mother by remarking that it was not surprising I was so stubborn; I came from tough stock. My mother retorted, 'What did you expect? She comes from here' (pointing to her abdominal area). That sealed it.

During the first few weeks of my stay in Lenyenye, I relied heavily on an old-fashioned public telephone located in a bus depot to communicate with the world beyond the Naphuno district – 'the back of beyond', as Donald Woods so aptly commented in the *Daily Dispatch*. I talked to Steve every three days or so, in violation of our banning orders,

---

22 My mother spent most of her professional life teaching Sub A (Grade 1). Thus for her this was a convenient metaphor for the lowest educational level.

which prohibited communication between banned people. I can't imagine that the police were unaware, but what could they have done about it? They could have taped our conversations and used these tapes as evidence but this alone could not secure a conviction even in repressive South Africa. I also spoke to other activists whenever possible after making prior arrangements. But I had to rely increasingly on my personal resources for spiritual sustenance and sanity.

One of the most important ways of maintaining sanity is real work. Without it, as many unemployed people so painfully know, life can be extremely difficult. The network of support that developed around me in the first few months, despite its value, could not provide the intellectual stimulation and meaning in my life which were essential to survival. I had spent too many years leading a very full life to tolerate endless days of doing nothing. I could not continue to sit and wait for my return to life with Steve.

I was to have another opportunity to see Steve in June 1977, when I gave evidence in his defence. A case had been brought against him for defeating the ends of justice. Such opportunities for meeting were used to the full by political activists across the country, to the great annoyance of the security police, who were powerless to stop us. After all, you were entitled to a proper defence, even under the draconian legal system of apartheid South Africa. I flew to East London.

It was good to be back in Mamcete's house. We were soon joined by Thenjiwe, who also arrived ostensibly to give evidence. The expected police swoop came earlier than we anticipated, but they failed to nail us in one another's company – a trophy they coveted. They nonetheless spoilt our fun. We were temporarily detained and released only on the promise that we would stay in different places. I was by then expecting Hlumelo, and could share this happy event with Steve without the awful distance between us. We also discussed my intention to start a small local health project to keep myself busy while awaiting new developments.

We had a huge party in Ginsberg in a house near Steve's home, in celebration of old times. It was attended by all the old party faithfuls, banned or unbanned, who were within twenty-five kilometres of Ginsberg. It was a nostalgic occasion which invoked a past we could not recreate. It was also an important symbolic statement about the bonds which tied us in spite of the distances imposed upon us. At the end of the hearing it was sad to leave King and all the friends. I had to tear myself from Steve, who was, as usual, reassuring and urged patience.

Upon my return to Lenyenye, I decided to occupy my time with something creative. I started a clinic at the back of the local Roman Catholic church, in one of the general offices, in July 1977. Ironically, Fr Thomas Duane, initially a sceptic, had become most supportive of me and negotiated with the priest-in-charge of the parish for the space. The Black Community Programmes, through its banned director Bennie Khoapa, generously made money available to me to purchase modest medical supplies in keeping with the temporary nature of the enterprise. The supportive network of political activists continued against the odds. I was able to start with the help of a local nurse aid, Morongwa Puka, who had been unemployed for some time.

Due to my lack of understanding of the local dialect – Selobedu – I relied on Morongwa to interpret patients' symptoms. Many people stayed away from the clinic in spite of their needs. This only became clear later when I got to know the area better. They could not risk the displeasure of the security police, who were clearly trying to discourage this initiative. It sounded too familiar, and smelled to them like trouble. They were right. But they need not have worried – not yet, in any case.

———— ◈◈◈ ————

It is difficult to explain the series of coincidences which happened after my return to Lenyenye, other than in terms of what I believe must be telepathy. I started experiencing discomfort around my lower abdomen towards the end of August. I went to see a Swiss missionary doctor who was the superintendent of Shiluvane Hospital, a local hospital. He reassured me about my pregnancy, and advised bed-rest. My attempts to contact Steve over the next week drew a blank. I became concerned when he did not return my calls. (I had by then installed a telephone in my house.) A few days later I learned that he had been detained en route to King from Cape Town. I was not overly concerned. He had, after all, survived many brushes with the security police and could take care of himself. It would just be a matter of time before they charged or released him.

My admission to Shiluvane Hospital with a threatened abortion coincided with the beginning of Steve's brutal interrogation, which was to lead to his death on 12 September 1977. I was then sixteen weeks pregnant. His death coincided with the intensification of the threat to the life of my expected baby. With much reluctance, and after threats of defiance from me, the security police agreed to my transfer to Pietersburg Hospital, a relatively better-equipped institution with specialist services. I remember weeping on the way to the hospital in the ambulance, which left Shiluvane at 4 a.m. on 12 September 1977. I ascribed my weepiness to anxiety about the safety of my pregnancy.

Dr Van den Ende, the obstetrician, was assigned to look after me. He was a well-built, kindly man with soft eyes and a strong Afrikaans accent. He explained to me after a thorough history and examination that I had an irritable uterus which was reacting to both the growing baby and the multiple fibroids (benign tumours) in its wall. He cautioned me about the chances of success in maintaining the pregnancy to term, but promised to do his best. I was put on treatment to suppress the contractions, and confined to bed. The nurses were wonderful. I relaxed towards the end of the day, permitting myself to regard this as a time to be nurtured.

The following morning I was taken aback when the nursing sister in charge of my care insisted that I breach the order of strict bed-rest and speak to my sister on the phone. She had a major family problem to share with me. I told the nurse that this was precisely the reason why I should not go to the phone: my family had to learn to solve their problems without me. I had problems of my own, I said. But she persisted.

Eventually I was wheeled to the phone. Thenjiwe was on the line. I thought that she had succeeded again in fooling 'the system' and settled down for an update on the state of affairs. After impatient niceties, she asked me if I was sitting down, and then she said the impossible: 'Steve is dead.' It was as if someone had put a high voltage current through me. A searing fire burned inside me. 'No, it can't be true' was all I remember saying.

I went into a state of profound emotional shock. 'It can't be true' was my refrain. Dr Van den Ende had to sedate me. I fell in and out of a state of nightmarish sleep and wished that I could die. But death does not come to those who need it most. There was no escape from the reality of loss.

I owe the survival of my son to many people, above all to the undying loyalty and love of Thenjiwe. She had correctly anticipated that I might learn about Steve's death when I opened the newspapers on the morning of the 13th. The paper, with bold headlines, was indeed lying on my bed when I returned from the fateful phone call. Thenjiwe visited a day or so later to grieve with me. The risks she took were enormous, but characteristic of this very fine South African.

I also owe a debt to the skill and patience of Dr Van den Ende. He constantly reminded me over the next few days to pray to God for 'Serenity to accept the things I cannot change, Courage to change those I can, and Wisdom to know the difference'. This prayer remains my constant companion. I owe much as well to the support and good care of the nurses at the hospital, who went beyond the call of duty, and to Fr Duane, who came to sit at my bedside day in and day out for two weeks after this tragedy. He just sat there, ready for a smile or tears on my part. I felt utterly lost. My world had collapsed. Gone were the anchor and the security I had become so accustomed to.

The seismic event which shattered me on that fateful morning had many aftershocks. It was not just the end of the vibrant life of a gifted person with a sense of destiny; it was the death of a dream. The dream which was killed had both personal and national dimensions. But it was the personal anguish which preoccupied me in my lonely hospital bed. I had none of the traditional support which you get from family and friends. My sister's visit, though brief, helped. But the worst aspect of the loss was not burying Steve. I remember being even more distraught the day after his funeral on seeing newspaper reports and photographs of the ceremony. There was a finality about the pictures. But my exclusion from the rituals made acceptance of this finality difficult. I kept hoping for a miracle to restore him to life.

There were other aspects to the exclusion. Not only was I banned and unable to travel to King Williamstown, but I was too ill to travel. I had to refrain from burying him to protect the life of his unborn son. What is more, I was not his widow. How would I have fitted into the rituals? It was a bewildering time for me.

The Biko family were also bewildered, not only by Steve's death but by the fact that he and his wife had already separated as part of the divorce proceedings which Steve had instituted a few weeks earlier. In fact they reversed his decision to end his marriage, by fetching his wife to participate in the mourning ritual as his widow. This reversal of Steve's wishes has run like a thread through the continuing confusion about his life. His widow was put in the uncomfortable position of mourning as a wife someone who had taken steps to end their marriage. It is not surprising that tensions often surface within the Biko family around the ambiguous position they made her occupy.

The film *Cry Freedom* was in one respect an inaccurate portrayal of

Steve's political life, which Donald Woods had not understood in the relatively short time during which he knew Steve. It also misrepresented his personal relationships. The peripheral role in which I was cast belied the centrality of my relationship, both personal and political, with Steve. What the film did was to perpetuate the lie of Steve as a Gandhi-type person respectably married to a dedicated wife who shared his life and his political commitment. It distorted his life story. When I tried to stop the filming of this movie in Zimbabwe, my attempts were sabotaged by the eagerness of a number of people in the liberation movement, including senior ANC leaders, who were primarily concerned with the anti-apartheid statement it made. It all added to the pain of loss by inventing memories which were not true to the reality of his life.

But life had to go on, and would go on, with or without my co-operation. I spent the rest of my pregnancy on strict bed-rest, nursed by my caring family and Makgatla Mangena. My sister Mashadi took leave for the whole of October to come and take care of me in Lenyenye after my discharge from hospital. My mother also came to see me over weekends, when freed from her teaching duties. Brothers stayed at various points, and Molepo finally came back from King to stay permanently with me in Lenyenye from the end of 1977.

The Nationalist government was not satisfied with having killed Steve; they also sought to kill his ideas. All the Black Consciousness organisations were banned on 19 October 1977, together with many other organs of civil society such as the *World* newspaper. Organisations like the Christian Institute were declared 'affected' and could no longer receive foreign funding. Major political actors were detained and banned. The season of repression intensified.

I endured the worst summer of my life in 1977/8. The emotional distress was matched by the harsh physical conditions of my new home. Temperatures hovered around 40°C on most days, relieved only by occasional violent thunderstorms. I had to remain indoors in a house with no ceiling to protect me from the low asbestos roof. I relied on an electric fan, which I kept on for almost twenty-four hours, for some comfort. There was no garden to take refuge in, or trees to shade me from the relentless heat. I also had to contend with the constant screeching of crickets at night. I thought that I would lose my sanity. Captain Schoeman had clearly chosen the worst place for me as part of his extended torture.

Hlumelo, 'the shoot that grew from a dead tree trunk', was born on 19 January 1978. It was a long and difficult labour. In the end Dr Van den Ende had to use a pair of forceps to aid the delivery of the head, which was in a posterior position. I was overjoyed when I saw him – a true shoot from that indomitable tree trunk, an exact physical replica of his father, right down to the fingernails. Malusi prophetically gave Hlumelo his name soon after Steve's death. He said that it was suitable for the baby, be it boy or girl. I forgot the immediate pain of delivery and savoured the bundle of life next to me.

I was fortunate to have my mother with me to help with the care of my son. Hlumelo was a difficult child and cried incessantly. The old women of the village ascribed it to my having cried too much during pregnancy. They were convinced that foetuses pick up the mother's unhappiness and become tense and irritable. It was exhausting coping with my son, but I was so grateful to have him that I could put up with anything. Nobandile Mvovo, who came to see him soon after birth, tried to talk to him: Xhamela intoni uzo sihlaza hide kangaga? Ba za kuthi singabantu abanjanina xa be kujongile? Ilali yonke intantele isikhalo sakho. Thula mtana ka Dadebawo. Thula Mgcina. (Xhamela [the Biko clan name], why are you disgracing us so much amongst these strange people? What will they think of us? The whole village is listening to your cry. Please quieten down, my child.) Hlumelo remained unimpressed.

The period of forced inaction gave me the opportunity to mourn and to see my plight in a broader perspective. Many people had lost sons, husbands and loved ones to the repressive system. I was at least in a better position to take care of myself than most other victims of this wanton destruction. The poverty of the people around me and their generosity filled me with humility. I had to stop feeling sorry for myself and get up and walk.

I planned my life anew soon after my son was born. I arranged for my furniture from King to be transported to Lenyenye.

It had been left there in anticipation of my return to join Steve after we had resolved the triangular relationship. That dream lay in ruins.

I had to scratch around for the relics of the past and piece my life together somehow.

Fortunately we moved house to a better area in Lenyenye at the beginning of 1978. This house had three bedrooms, a living room, a kitchen and a proper bathroom. We soon established a garden with flowers and lawn in front and fruit trees on the rest of the property. Fr Duane brought me a number of rose plants which flowered throughout the year, providing a delightful array of colours and beautiful aromas for the brutalised senses. My house became a place I could call home.

Before long I realised I had to set up a longer-term project in the area. I found a base in an old shopping centre and started work in April 1978 with the support of the Roman Catholic Church and Fr Stubbs, then a prohibited immigrant, who arranged for financial support from British Christian Aid and Oxfam. Many other previous supporters re-established contact, notably Mr Lein van den Bergh from ICCO.

Morongwa Puka, the energetic nurse aid who had worked with me before, was happy to join me again. But soon more hands were needed. Leah Mafuna, a slightly built woman from Kranspoort Mission, my childhood village, also joined us as a nurse aid. Mankuba Ramalepe, a large woman whose heart matched her size, and a qualified nursing sister, completed the complement for a while. Mankuba was later to become my brother Sethiba's sister-in-law. Mmaisaka, a woman whose malnourished child drew our attention to her, became a vital member of the team as a cleaner.

Lenyenye is situated in a basin surrounded by hills dotted with small village settlements. Outstation services were virtually demanded by the villagers in outlying areas of the district of Naphuno, which was about 150 square kilometres in size. People also came on foot from Tsonga-speaking areas of the Tzaneen district and in buses and hired open vans. They braved the dusty heat and occasional thunderstorms to reach the clinic and outstation points. We bought a van with a canopy for the clinic activities, and for fetching and carrying supplies from the local railway depot. We soon outgrew both our premises and our energy.

There was real hunger among the impoverished locals for a caring primary health service. They loved the personal, dignified care they received, and enjoyed my attempts at speaking the local lingo. When the old ladies came to tell me how much better their arthritis had become with my treatment, I would challenge them to demonstrate by participating in the local dances – and would join in myself.

I learned a great deal about local beliefs: explanations of the causes of disease, indigenous healing methods, and many other things which helped me understand the people I was to live and work among for many years. I also built on their own knowledge to introduce new concepts and healing strategies. For example, a child with diarrhoea would be brought to the clinic with incisions made around the fontanelle and a black substance smeared over it. This local healing method is based on a recognition of the effect that loss of fluids has on the fontanelle of the baby, which becomes sunken. Their remedy, although ineffectual, at least provided a basis for introducing the more effective oral rehydration treatment (ORT). I expressed my respect for their diagnostic skills before suggesting a change in the method of treatment. In this way, the old women healers responsible for the traditional treatment were not made to feel stupid, but affirmed in their astuteness at having made the correct observations – which was a sound basis for introducing innovations.

The local population was typical of the impoverished rural areas in apartheid South Africa: predominantly women and children, older or disabled men, a few professionals – nurses, teachers, policemen – and a growing breed of civil servants in the 'homeland' government services. Old women played an important role as heads of families in the absence of their sons, who were migrant workers. I had to learn to work with them, because they made all the important decisions, including those about health care. It was not difficult to establish a rapport. I had been popular with old women in King and became quite good at knowing how to relate to them, affirming them, yet slowly moving them from their tendency to rigidity.

I also learned how to forge better relations between older women and their daughters-in-law, which empowered the younger women without making the older ones feel that they had lost control. I helped the younger ones understand the game of power between the generations, and to appreciate the real fear older women had of being abandoned by their sons. There were far too many unhappy cases in the area for the older women not to feel vulnerable. I showed their daughters-in-law how little it cost to smooth ruffled feathers by providing inexpensive treats for the older women, such as preparing a warm bath or a favourite dish or even dancing around and making them laugh. But it was not always easy.

The popularity of my work did not please the security police. They intensified their surveillance and introduced further restrictions. In 1979 my area of restriction was reduced from the Naphuno district to Lenyenye township, which had no more than 850 houses on a dusty piece of land. The security police captain who served the order on me found me breakfasting before leaving for one of the outstations. He refused to sit down or to accept the cup of tea I offered him. He stood near the front door, literally shaking in his shoes, as he read out the offending additional clause to my banning order. I continued my breakfast, listening and watching him. He could not believe my cool reaction, and thought that I had not understood that the order was to have immediate effect. I assured him that I understood, and he left. The security police were used to dealing with anger, but found civility confusing.

Their attempts to limit my influence met with little success. People made simple calculations about what was in their best interest, and decided to continue visiting our clinic in even larger numbers. The initial hesitancy was soon replaced by greater boldness. Even local chiefs in the area – paid functionaries of the state – defied the authorities in the matter of development projects in the villages under their jurisdiction and listened to us when we talked to them. Chief Maake, who was also my patient, went as far as writing a blanket permit for the Ithuseng Community Health Programme to undertake any project it thought fit to promote the health of her subjects. This was a blow for the system from the least-expected quarter.

In desperation, the security police tried to encourage me to go into exile. They sent Lisa Williamson, sister of Craig Williamson, the notorious security police captain who infiltrated the international student movement in the 1970s, and later worked for the International University Exchange Fund (IUEF), which he was to destroy. Lisa, unbeknown to me at the time, was also a police officer. She came to the clinic unannounced one morning, wearing a woollen hat to cover her white hair, and accompanied by a young black man, who she referred to as 'a comrade' from a neighbouring township. She brought me much-needed support from the IUEF: a thousand Swiss francs. Over lunch at my house later that day, she suggested that should I want to 'skip' the country illegally, she would be more than happy to assist. My first re-action was anger at the impertinence of a young liberal white woman to assume that I wanted to go into exile or that I would need her assistance. But I also needed to make one point very clear. I was going to be a pain in the neck of the security police and their masters, and was not going anywhere. This was my country and I would help liberate it. Little did I realise that the intended audience was indeed receiving the message.

The pressure of popular demand on our premises led to the building of the Ithuseng Community Health Centre, a scaled-down but much better planned version of Zanempilo. It was not an easy task, given the scarcity of financial resources for large development projects. A com-bination of dogged determination, supportive friends inside and out-side the country, and sheer luck made it possible. Desmond Tutu, then general secretary of the SACC, rescued me from serious contractual problems when the World University Service (WUS) reneged on a prom-ise to fund the building costs. If it had not been for his help I would have landed in legal hot water.

I had happily signed a contract for R78 000 on the basis of the WUS's 1979 promise of support. I was later to learn that the WUS was under pressure from some ANC exiles not to support any activity in South Africa unless requests for such support came through the ANC. I was then, and am still now, opposed to development being held hostage to party politics, and would not have agreed anyway, even if I had been given the opportunity. But the pressure may well have been part of Craig Williamson's plan of sabotage to prevent the emergence of another major community development project. History will have to judge this one.

It was fitting that Desmond Tutu, then still Bishop Tutu, came to open the Ithuseng Community Health Centre in September 1981. I was grant-ed permission to attend the festivities. It was a marvellous occasion. Friends came from far and wide to celebrate the resilience of the human spirit. Members of the old King community were represented by Nohle

Mohapi and Nobandile Mvovo. Francis and Tim Wilson, as well as the president of the Carnegie Corporation, were also present. It was a bitter-sweet occasion for me. Bishop Tutu had to remind me several times to relax and celebrate, but I remained tense. There were too many mixed emotions about this sphinx that was rising from the ashes.

That weekend the conservative Anglican parishioners of Tzaneen created a scene which left a bitter taste in the mouth. One of the guests at the opening festivities was Mr Venables, a fellow Anglican parishioner. He suggested that Bishop Tutu should come and worship at the local parish on the Sunday morning. He offered to arrange it with the parish. We were appalled when we heard that the parish council refused to have Bishop Tutu worship with them. Some even said that Bishop Tutu would enter their church over their dead bodies. I was furious and vowed never to set my foot in that church again. The arrogance of the parishioners in debarring a bishop of their church from worshipping with them was unprecedented in my view. I had up to then received little support from the priest-in-charge, who bore me as a cross. He had turned down the invitation to the opening festivities – he had prior arrangements, he said. Bishop Tutu was hurt but took it in his stride.

Top: My maternal grandparents, Sethiba Michael Mahleaela, an evangelist of the Dutch Reformed Church, and Matlala (Mamphela) née Masekela.

Bottom: My mother, in front of our family home at Uitkyk in Limpopo.

Top: Making a point at the first meeting of the Black People's Convention held in Hammanskraal in 1972.

Left: The doctor at work. At Zanempilo Community Health Centre in Zinyoka village outside King Williamstown.

With Steve Biko in 1977 outside the magistrate's court in East London after another of Steve's numerous court appearances, a result of the legal restrictions placed on him which he often ignored.

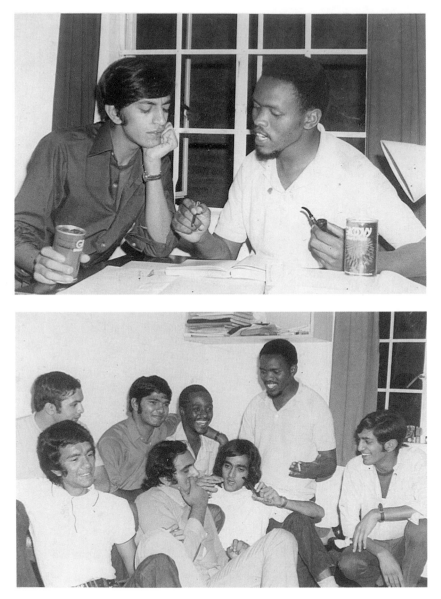

Top: Steve and Rashid Goolam in discussion as students.

Bottom: Steve with fellow students, including Barney Pityana to his right, next to Salaam Sulaiman and Bupendra Madhavjee. In front are Fazel Parker, Goolam Abram, Suliman Bhaila and Rashid Goolam.

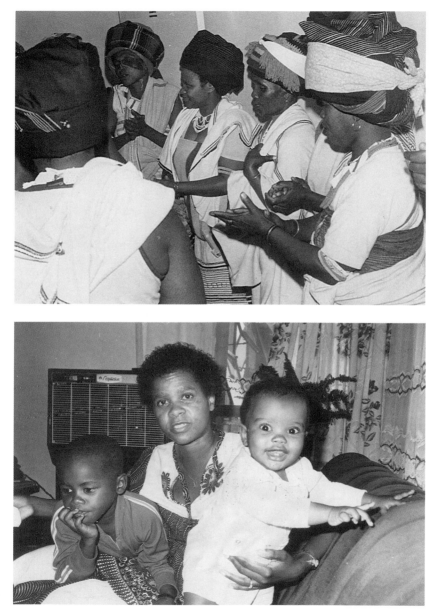

Top: Local women saying goodbye at my farewell from Zanempilo when I was banished from King Williamstown in 1977.

Bottom: With Hlumelo (6) and Malusi (1) in 1984 in Lenyenye, our new home.

Top: With some of the Tickeyline villagers among whom I worked at Ithuseng, the health project we started in Lenyenye.

Bottom: Father Aelred Stubbs, who was a great support to me after Steve's death, with Hlumelo.

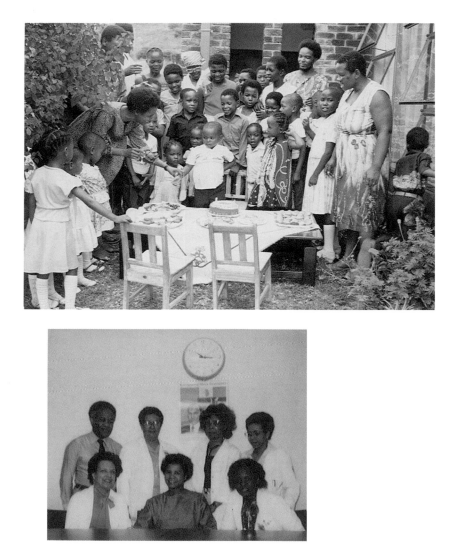

Top: Hlumelo's birthday party. Makgatla Mangena, right at the back, had become part of the family in 1977.

Bottom: With some colleagues as a young intern at King Edward VIII Hospital in Durban.

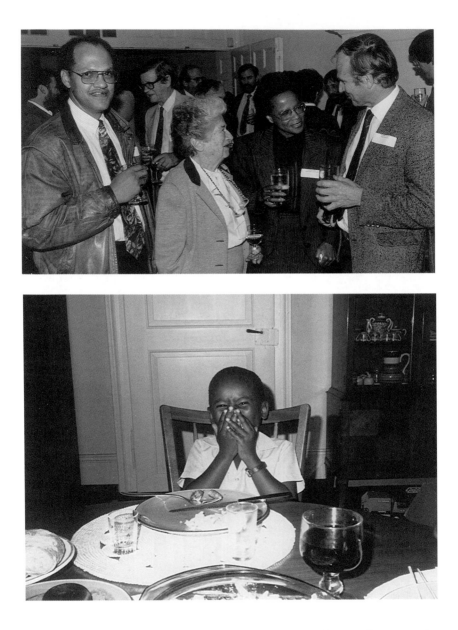

Top: With Wilmot James, Sheila van der Horst and Francis Wilson at a function at the University of Cape Town in 1992.

Bottom: Hlumelo in Cape Town.

Top: With Mamcete, Steve's mother, visiting me in Cape Town in 1995.

Bottom: With my siblings at Uitkyk: Thomas (Malesela) and Mathabatha are standing behind Nick (Phoshiwa), me, my mother, Mashadi and Molepo.

Left: At my inauguration as vice-chancellor at the University of Cape Town in 1996 with the chair of the council, Ian Sims, on my right, and Professor Wieland Gevers on my left.

Bottom: On our way to the inauguration banquet with my mother, Hlumelo and Malusi (middle). My niece Mamphela Chilwane and nephew Letladi Ramphele are on the left.

Top: At the entrance to the World Bank in Washington in 2000, in discussion with a colleague.

Middle: With Jim Wolfensohn, who appointed me at the World Bank.

Bottom: With Kofi Annan of the United Nations.

Top: With Richard Attenborough, Chancellor of the University of Sussex, when Sussex awarded me an honorary doctorate.

Bottom: In 2002, when Harvard University awarded me an honorary doctorate.

Top: Launching my book *Steering by the Stars* in 2002. I was fulfilling my dream of reading and writing after my return to Cape Town from Washington.

Bottom: Malusi's graduation from the University of Southern California in 2006.

Karina Turok

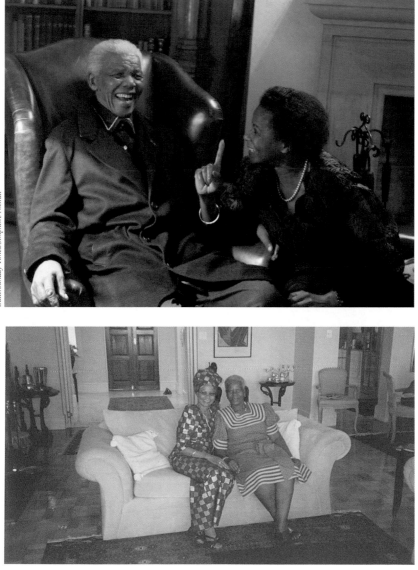

Top: With Nelson Mandela at a party for Graça Machel in 2010.

Bottom: At home in Camps Bay with my sister Mashadi.

Opposite top: With my grandson Luthando.

Opposite bottom: With my beloved mother in 2006.

Gallo/Buisness Day/ Paxley Makgatho

Gallo/Foto24/Lisa Hnatowicz

Top: In 2013 I was back in Lenyenye, where in 1977 I had been banished to. This time I was there by choice, to listen and talk to residents about the launch of Agang.

Bottom: Launching Agang in Pretoria in June 2013.

A matter of survival

Putting down roots in Lenyenye was a matter of survival. I had no other option. So Lenyenye became home in every respect. There were three taproots: work, social relationships and intimacy. As regards the first of these, I consolidated my primary healthcare project. Even though I was restricted from working among the people in the surrounding villages, I learnt to work through, and with, other people on the basis of trust and faith in their abilities. Mr Lazarus Lekgolo Ramalepe, husband of Mankuba, the nursing sister-in-charge, came to join us as Programme Officer and Administrator. He had enormous energy, initiative and courage. He focused more on the nascent income-generating projects we were struggling to strengthen and expand. The brickmaking cooperative was the biggest challenge. It was built on existing capacities and skills within the community. Women who were working in local commercial brickyards at slave wages were brought together to create their own wealth. It took some learning on our part to understand the complexity of communal ownership, particularly by people who had never wielded power or controlled much in their own lives.

Development activists like myself had to learn the hard way that the capacity of poor people to own both the successes and failures of projects they are engaged in is severely limited. You need self-confidence and self-esteem to acknowledge your failures and weaknesses. The humiliation of conquest, racism and poverty had undermined many people's self-esteem by labelling them mistakes of God's creation. How could we expect them to own mistakes? But development work entailed a trust in systems, and consequently a move away from personal politics, which was the hallmark of survival strategies for poor people. Poor people's experiences of systems, both official ones and those run by people fighting for freedom, have not inspired them with trust. They have been let down too often, and have too often seen corruption operate in the name of regulations and procedures, to believe that there is reason to trust systems.

Yet there were many successes. Vegetable gardens blossomed everywhere. Child care as a social responsibility was explored and finally accepted by a community used to viewing child care as women's responsibility and 'granny' as the only support for overextended mothers. Many child-care centres have since been built with community participation and support, and are being run by representative village committees.

Projects aimed at the empowerment of women also took root. Many women suffered from the burden of the endless search for firewood in areas that were becoming more and more denuded of vegetation. The building of mud-stoves, the making of wonder-boxes,[23] and the improvement of housing all helped to conserve fuel and developed a better self-image among poor rural women.

Preventive health-care strategies took many forms: literacy classes and oral rehydration treatment (ORT) for diarrhoea became popularised;

---

23 Mud-stoves are cleverly designed mud hearths which provide for the making of fire in enclosed space, complete with chimney, just as in a metal stove. A wonder-box is constructed out of a cardboard box with a tight-fitting lid, which is lined inside with cushions made from insulating material. One need only get food to a brisk boil for a few minutes, then leave it to cook in the box. Wonder-boxes are particularly good for slow-cooking foods such as samp and beans, which are popular amongst the poor.

immunisation and 'Road to Health' cards became a status symbol of good parenthood. Women learnt to work together and to shed their powerlessness at many levels. There were also many opportunities for fun: Christmas parties for the elderly, and outings for younger women, some of whom had never been outside their immediate surroundings.

In Lenyenye I also put down roots in social relationships. I had up to then survived by losing myself in work. In fact I worked myself to a standstill on many occasions. This worried my mother, who was then staying permanently with me. I would be so tired by the end of the day – having seen on some occasions eighty patients and also attended to other project needs – that I would barely have the energy to eat and bath after getting home. As soon as my head touched the pillow I would be asleep. Such a lifestyle protected me from facing the pain of loss, but I could clearly not sustain it.

Fr Thomas Duane was a lifesaver. He was the only person in the area with whom I could have serious intellectual discussions. His regular visits were crucial. In 1979 I started visiting the Ofcolaco Mission, where he was then based, under cover of darkness. I got to know and like the other priests, and enjoyed their Irish sense of humour. With increasing confidence, Fr Duane started taking me out on day-long trips to see the beauty of the Lowveld. We drove through the Strijdom Tunnel and ventured farther east towards God's Window – a true window into a valley of beauty surrounded by rolling hills covered with lush vegetation. The Three Rondavels, three near-identical round hills set apart in the landscape of what is now Mpumalanga, were also spectacular. We would sit facing them and surveying the horizon beyond for hours on end. The Echo Caves, with their tall, flowing rock formations and many recesses, were also a favourite visiting place. We mixed with the predominantly white tourists without a hint of the illegality of our action. On these trips I would ride with Fr Duane in his pick-up truck. His view was that he had nothing to lose if we were caught. He would never give evidence against me or any politically persecuted person. We took the necessary precautions to avoid detection without becoming neurotic about security.

Later I took the staff at the Ithuseng Community Centre, my family and other friends to these scenic areas, and I would then ride on the back of Mr Ramalepe's powerful Ford truck wearing jeans and a cap. We were amused that the security police, who we would encounter on rare occasions, did not recognise me because they did not expect me to defy my orders so openly in broad daylight. They also would not have expected a medical doctor to ride on the back of a truck like a labourer, as was the practice in this farming area. It is interesting how easy it is to fool people who think in rigid stereotypes.

A protective community developed and consolidated around me. They came from all walks of life: my family, their friends, fellow workers at Ithuseng, local residents and patients. The security police could not penetrate this protective wall, and, when they did, they had no chance of securing a charge for my breaking my banning order. On one occasion we had such a rowdy party that my neighbour, who was the sole known informer among my other police neighbours, called his masters. They burst into the house, but in the nick of time I was pushed into my bedroom by my younger brother, Molepo. I quickly got into bed, shoes and all, and was found by the security police only a few seconds later, reading a book. They were frustrated, but knew that they could not get any of my guests to give evidence against me.

There was also an increasing flow of outsiders who came to visit me in Lenyenye: journalists, national and foreign politicians, diplomats, fellow activists and friends. It was fairly easy for them to find me. Many came without any prior arrangement. In fact, sometimes prior arrangements by telephone simply alerted the sleepy security police.

Helen Suzman, then MP for Lower Houghton for the Progressive Party, was the only South African parliamentarian who took an active interest in the plight of political prisoners, detainees, banned people and their families. She visited me and we had a good laugh about her failed attempts in parliament in mid-1977 to have the Minister of Justice, Jimmy Kruger, explain why he had served a banning order on me. What security threat did I pose to the state? Kruger simply said, as was the practice, that it was not in the interest of state security to disclose the information. She even asked him to inform me of the reasons privately by letter. Well, it was impossible to beat that. Such was the importance of state security that citizens had no right to know why their rights were being violated by the state.

The legal suit instituted by my lawyer, Raymond Tucker, against the Minister of Justice for wrongful arrest failed on a technicality. My lawyer had lodged the papers with the Johannesburg Supreme Court instead of the Pretoria Supreme Court. The former had no jurisdiction in the matter because the route of the first journey into exile with the security police from King Williamstown had gone through the back roads of the then eastern Transvaal, and had not traversed the Johannesburg Supreme Court's area of jurisdiction. Such is the luck of evil ones.

Helen Suzman remained a tower of strength for me through all the years. She was particularly helpful after my banning order was lifted, and I needed to secure a South African passport to travel abroad. A passport was regarded by the National Party government as a privilege, not a right, for black South Africans. Your access to a passport was treated as a reward for good behaviour, and of this the security police were the sole judges. I would phone Helen frantically a week or two before departure on an overseas trip after having waited in vain for an answer to my application. A phone call from Helen to the minister's office never failed to secure an assurance that my passport was waiting for collection at the local office of the ministry. What power 'the system' had. But also how fortunate I was to have the leverage provided by Helen Suzman. Many people were frustrated in their efforts without this assistance. She will certainly go down in history as someone who did not shy away from helping ordinary South Africans in times of great need.

Fr Timothy Stanton's regular visits were also an important source of strength. The coldness of the local Anglican parish priest in Tzaneen between 1977 and 1982 stood in sharp contrast to the caring ministry of Fr Stanton. He drove all the way from the Community of the Resurrection Priory in Rosettenville to visit me. My family grew to appreciate his quiet presence and the Eucharist he celebrated with us. My mother would remark that we were lucky to be visited by one so close to the Lord – she referred to him as 'the Visiting Christ'.

Bruce Haigh, the Second Secretary at the Australian Embassy, was also a great supporter and regular visitor. He was a handsome man in his early thirties, always dressed in jeans and Australian boots, with compassion and a commitment to supporting those fighting against the system of apartheid. He would come for a weekend and participate in parties and picnics. We got to be very close over the years.

Bruce once took me on a daring mission in October 1978 to visit Steve Biko's grave in Ginsberg. It was a vain attempt on my part to complete ritually the unfinished business between Steve and me. The mission was not successful on two scores. Firstly, there were people digging a grave near Steve's, most of whom I recognised even at a distance. I could not take the risk of my presence becoming known. I had to be content with a distant view of the grave that had swallowed Steve. Then again, the return to the Eastern Cape exacerbated the pain. King Williamstown looked so desolate and defeated. Any romantic notion I had of returning, even without Steve, died at that point. I knew it was no longer my place. I had to add it to my list of losses.

The trip did, however, offer me an opportunity to see Malusi and Thoko, with whom we stayed. Malusi was then restricted to Zwelitsha township and was going through a difficult transition from political activist to religious convert. His last detention in the middle of 1977, during which he was tortured, had precipitated his conversion. He rejoined the Order of Ethiopia, a church where his late father had been a leading priest. Malusi continued to grow in his religious commitment, and eventually ran a successful grassroots Pastoral Institute in Grahamstown, which trained lay people in leadership for the development of themselves and their communities.

I tried to fill the intellectual wilderness in Lenyenye with structured studies. In 1983 I completed my Bachelor of Commerce degree, which I had first registered for in 1975 with Unisa. I also studied part time with the University of the Witwatersrand for a postgraduate Diploma in Tropical Hygiene in 1981, and a Diploma in Public Health in 1982. These studies were made possible by a special dispensation for which I had applied, and which was granted. Conditions of my banning order were varied to allow me to travel to Johannesburg for a week four times a year for classes, and a week at the end of the year for examinations. I had to report to the Tzaneen Police Station on departure, and at John Vorster Square Police Station on arrival in Johannesburg, reversing the order on the trip back to Lenyenye.

◇◆◇

Re-establishing intimate relationships while nursing my wounds was the most difficult process of my time at Lenyenye. I spent the years between 1977 and 1981 without daring to explore close relationships. Everything had died inside me, including dreams. There was not a single dream I can recall from this period except for the first few weeks after Steve's death when I had dreams of denial of his death. I would have vivid conversations with him, telling him that people were claiming he had died. He would laughingly say in his usual manner, 'You know, Toto, that I cannot die', and I would peacefully continue my sleep, only to wake to the harsh reality. My system shut out all dreams after that.

It took Sister Liz Elberts, a caring Dominican nun based at Villa

Maria in Johannesburg, to help me come to terms with Steve's death during 1987, ten years after the event. I was introduced to her by Fr Duane. We immediately clicked spiritually and were able to communicate in ways which words were inadequate to express. That she was close to her father and yet had given up close family ties as part of her religious journey enabled her to recognise the depth of my pain.

The frenetic pace of work which had helped me channel my anger into creative endeavours had only been successful in dulling the pain. But the ease with which the wound bled was an indicator of how raw it still was. I would become physically ill from the tension and pain of reliving Steve's death every September. I would go over the circumstances of his death in my mind. I would imagine the pain he must have suffered while being tortured. I would see his attractive physique reduced to an inert confused pile by the brain damage he suffered. I wept for him. But I wept more for myself, and the sense of loss of what could have been.

Moreover, I got upset each time some distortion of Steve's role or political philosophy appeared in the media. It was as if I had to protect him personally from defilement. I was not yet ready to let go of the unfinished business between us. But I had to learn to say goodbye to him finally. Sister Liz helped me lower the protective armour I had donned, and forced open the door I had closed to keep Steve's place in my heart sacrosanct. I remained in love with him and was determined to remain faithful to him. She assured me that Steve would not like me to remain trapped in a love affair with a corpse. He was big enough to share me with others.

The process of saying goodbye involves an acceptance of the pain of loss, its incorporation into your psyche, and an ability to integrate the pain with the memories of shared joys with the departed person. It involves making peace with the unfinished business instead of dwelling on what could have been. It is a difficult process, which I accomplished only with the skilful assistance of Sister Liz over a number of months. I can never thank her enough for this.

I had to accept my loss and stop clinging to what was no more and would never be again. But there were no easy answers to this greatest human problem – the reality of death, which was a companion of all life. Ultimately, you are left with no option but to wait in the hope that everything you have lost will come flooding back again out of the darkness of your grief, and that your relationships with the departed loved ones will be transformed into new, non-clinging relationships. I knew that mine was to be a long process of healing.

To tell or not to tell my son, Hlumelo, about the fate that had befallen his father? This question was an additional source of pain and anxiety for me for four years after he was born. His physical and personality likeness to his father added to the burden. How was I to tell him that the person from whom he drew his very being was no more and would never become known to him? Of course, if he had understood the meaning of his own Xhosa name he would have known that the passing away of his father was incorporated in his name – shoot from a fallen branch – and thus marked him as a son who was never to meet his father.

His own instincts must have told him that something was wrong. He took advantage of the preparations for his annual visit to his grandmother in King Williamstown in 1982 to announce to his uncles (my brothers) that he was at last going to meet his father. My brothers reported this to me and insisted that I talk to Hlumelo about his father.

I set the scene in my bedroom with an album on my bed and behind a closed door we sat on the bed in a tender embrace. I showed him a series of photographs of his father, and commented how much they looked alike and told him what kind of person his father was. I then said that his father had been banned just as I was, and that he had been killed by the police after being arrested outside his area of restriction.

Hlumelo just turned, looked at me directly and said: 'Ag shame, Mama.' Then after hugging me tightly he said: 'Just be careful not to leave your area without permission.' Having secured my promise to be careful, he jumped off the bed and announced that he was going out to play. It was as if he was relieved that the big question had been answered for him.

I lay down and cried softly – both out of relief and in awe at the ability of one so young to absorb so deep a pain.

◇◇◇

During the course of 1981, a group of old friends from the University of the North started visiting Lenyenye on weekends. They were a rowdy lot who added to the raucous parties we had. Sipo Magele, a tall, well-built, handsome man in his early thirties, who lectured in pharmacy, was one of the regular visitors. We developed a relationship, which resulted in marriage in 1982, and a son, Malusi Magele, born on 16 March 1983. I had no illusions about my relationship with Sipo. On the contrary, I probably had too low an expectation of what was possible. I was unashamedly seeking a companion with whom I could possibly grow old. The door to the special place in my heart was still shut. I was not yet ready to share Steve's place with anyone else at that stage.

Malusi's conception also served to reduce my hyper-anxiety about losing Hlumelo, my only connection with my past. I was neurotic about Hlumelo's safety. I would jump out of the bathroom semi-clad at the sound of a car in the driveway. I could not trust that others would take sufficient care to ensure that he was not standing behind a moving vehicle. My family would laugh, but understood my neurosis. I had, after all, lost my first child, Lerato, and was not going to let this one slip away. I had in a sense made too much of an emotional investment in one child: this could not be good for either of us.

My third pregnancy was even more difficult than the first two. Malusi was born prematurely after eight months, when Dr Van den Ende decided to save me from internal bleeding. Malusi was a mere 1,7 kg at birth; he hardly moved after delivery, and was disposed of by my doctor as non-viable. Unbeknown to me, he was rescued by the nursing sister in attendance at the time.

I mourned Malusi for twelve hours before I knew that he was alive. Surprised nursing staff found me crying the following morning. I had to be wheeled to the nursery with my blood transfusion drip to see with my own eyes that he was alive. There he was – a tiny soul with an obvious bruise on one of the ankles. I cried more now because I thought that his legs were damaged. My medical knowledge escaped me at that point – babies born legs-first (in the breech position) have blood stasis signs afterwards, which clear after some days. Dr Van den Ende had used Malusi's head as a device to apply pressure to my bleeding placental site, to stop me from bleeding to death.

Hlumelo's comment on first seeing Malusi in an incubator two days after his birth was that he was no larger than a Niknak. But Malusi was a survivor. He survived neonatal diarrhoea in the overcrowded Pietersburg Hospital nursery which was crawling with cockroaches, and a period of underweight as a toddler because of chronic tonsillitis and enlarged adenoids which made eating almost impossible for him, and grew into a thriving boy and successful adult.

After this brush with maternal death Dr Van den Ende would not countenance anything but a hysterectomy post delivery. He told me what I already knew: I was a bad incubator. I had to lie virtually over my foetuses to ensure their survival, like a brooding hen, and even then I had been barely successful. The physical pain of a large abdominal operation wound was compounded by the need to keep Malusi alive by feeding him myself.

The paediatrician in charge of Malusi was brutally frank with me: 'You can lie there and nurse your pain, but then your son will surely die – I cannot control his diarrhoea.' There were no second thoughts.

Dragging a drip two days after the operation, I had to stand in a hot nursery every three hours expressing my breasts, and feed Malusi through a slow nasal drip. I would go back to my private ward, drenched in sweat from heat and pain. I demanded pethidine, an injectable pain-killer, which had been ordered for my post-operative needs. When I used up the usual number of permitted dosages, I demanded more, and offered to sign for them myself. The alternative was too ghastly to contemplate.

I fortunately had Dr Lelau Mohuba to take care of the clinic during my pregnancy, and could afford the luxury of a few months off work. Meanwhile Sipo had an unsuccessful time as a pharmacy master's student in the United States. He was too embarrassed to go back to his previous job, and ended up as a pharmacist at Livingstone Hospital in Port Elizabeth, his home town. Cracks began to appear everywhere in our relationship, but I put them down to physical distance.

I decided to leave Lenyenye in 1984, and join my husband in Port Elizabeth in a vain attempt to strengthen the relationship. My banning order had been lifted in 1983 in the first wave of attempts to reform apartheid. I had stayed on because of the need to strengthen the Ithu-seng project and ensure its long-term survival financially. Yet I had no anxiety about the abilities of my colleagues to continue the work without me. After all, my entire leadership style at Ithuseng was to work myself out of a job. I worked each day as if it would be the last, and made sure that my colleagues could pick up where I had left off if anything happened to me.

The community of Lenyenye organised a big farewell. A reception was held in the local Lutheran church where many speeches were made and presents heaped upon me. The most notable were two wooden carvings from my colleagues at Ithuseng Community Centre, the products of a self-taught local artist, Mr Makwela. One was a traditional healer with his divining bones: he was in a squatting position focusing on the messages given by the tools of his trade. The other was an old woman walking with a straw dish on her head, deep in thought and leaning on a walking stick. These two figures were to stand guard over me – the diviner to let the community know if things went wrong, the old woman to walk me back to Lenyenye if need be. It was a measure of the ambivalence of the community about letting me go. I was sad too.

My own family was bitterly disappointed. My mother had tried desperately to burn the bridges behind me in a vain attempt to stop me from ever going back to the Cape. I discovered the lengths to which she had gone during the last few days of my stay in Lenyenye. I had entrusted a box with valuable historical documents spanning my activist years in Natal and the Eastern Cape to an illiterate woman in the village, knowing that she was unlikely to be a target of security police searches. She had, unbeknown to me, disclosed this to my mother. I do not know when and how they destroyed the documents. I was shocked to discover that they were nowhere to be found when I went to fetch them prior to my departure. After an uncomfortable silence and exchanges of shifty gazes, she confessed that they had been destroyed at my mother's suggestion. I was furious. But what could I do? A mother's love is both life-giving and destructive. In her eagerness to protect me from danger as her child, she had destroyed valuable links with the past.

I finally left Lenyenye for Port Elizabeth in May 1984. It was a sad occasion. My family was distraught. They mourned the end of my easy accessibility to them. The community in the area could not understand why I had to leave. How could I walk away from my beautiful house, thriving project (which they referred to as Mamphela's Clinic) and such love and popularity? But it was time to move on.

Forging an independent lifestyle

B EING BLACK, WOMAN, MOTHER AND PROFESSIONAL PLACES you in a challenging position anywhere in the world, but more particularly so in South Africa. The boundaries between the various spaces which you have to traverse, and within which you have to negotiate complex relationships, impose constraints on your approach to life. To stretch across the boundaries of race, class and gender, while remaining creatively engaged in relationships across the generations, was and remains a monumental task. 'Stretching' had the potential for creative expansion, but also of rupture, and yet it was the ultimate, inescapable challenge facing every citizen in changing South Africa.

When I became freer to make decisions about my future role, I had to take stock of the skills and capabilities which I had developed over the years of student activism, professional activism and life in the wilderness as a banished person. Some of the survival strategies developed in the furnace of activism had steeled and strengthened me as a person, affording me skills to deal with new and difficult environments with greater confidence. Others were appropriate to the demands of the hostile contexts I had found myself in, but of no use in the changing world I encountered after my departure from Lenyenye. They could become liabilities if not judiciously harnessed.

I had not bargained on what it meant to be a wife after living independently for so long. Negotiating this role was complicated for a number of reasons: firstly, Sipo Magele had not arranged proper accommodation for us in Port Elizabeth. I realised at the last moment before leaving Lenyenye in June 1984 that he had not, as promised, got a house. So I had to make arrangements with Livingstone Hospital, where I had been offered a job as a medical officer, to obtain a staff house. The authorities could only provide a flat in the doctors' quarters with two bedrooms, a kitchenette and living area. It was hard to adjust to this small space with two children who were used to a bigger house and a supportive neighbourhood. I was back living in almost the same space I had occupied as an intern ten years earlier at the same hospital. We even ate in the same dining room where I had eaten as an intern. Something was not right, but I hoped that it would be a temporary inconvenience until my husband got his act together.

Then again, I had up to that point always been surrounded by supportive helpers. Makgatla Mangena, my housekeeper and childminder for both my children, who had become a true companion, had stayed on in Lenyenye to complete her schooling for the year. My mother, too, with her indomitable spirit and maternal love, had moved in with my brother Sethiba in Pietersburg. I suddenly found myself coping with all the demands of housekeeping, child care, professional work, and being a wife and partner. It was strenuous.

What is more, like so many women, I did not negotiate our respective roles with my husband before our marriage. My feminist consciousness was still fairly underdeveloped. I had not yet acquired the sophistication which would have enabled me to negotiate an equitable partnership. I had been content to play the traditional woman's role in the domestic arena, provided it did not clash with my public role, and did not involve abuse and disrespect. Even during my King days, my approach to gender roles in the domestic arena had largely been traditional.

Two events stand out. Firstly, I remember being uncomfortable with Fr Stubbs's offer to wash up after sharing a meal with me. I did not mind younger people – my colleagues – pitching in to help with domestic

207

chores, but a priest was another matter, particularly one who was clearly my senior in age and a guest. Secondly, Desmond Tutu, on a visit to Zanempilo in 1976, tried unsuccessfully to get the chauvinists among my male colleagues to regard domestic chores as part of the responsibilities of being adult. He told them about the joy of washing his own children's nappies while his family was living in England in the 1960s. That shocked me too, but I hoped in vain that my colleagues would at least consider dishwashing acceptable.

Sipo's expectations of the role of a wife were traditional. We would both come back from work at 4.30 p.m. Sometimes we fetched the children together, or else he would do that while I was busy with some household chores. Although I employed a part-time cleaner and washerwoman, I still had housework and did the cooking because we disliked the food in the communal dining room. It never occurred to Sipo that I was as tired as he was after work. I remember one particularly frustrating evening while I was cooking, Malusi, then a tiny one-and-a-half-year-old, cried next to Sipo, who was blissfully asleep in an easy chair. He could not understand why I was making such a fuss about his lack of attention to his own son.

The pleasurable moments we spent together – and they were not insignificant – were not enough to stop the nagging feeling that I had made yet another monumental error in choosing a partner. The differences between us became ever more pronounced. There was no sign of a house materialising in the foreseeable future, and Sipo didn't regard this as an urgent problem. For as long as we did not have better accommodation, I could not arrange the household properly, and that was intolerable for me. Sipo had a casual approach to many other things. I organised my life in a manner that anticipated problems as much as was humanly possible. To live with someone who could see nothing wrong with running out of petrol in a car that had a working gauge was too much for me. We had incompatible approaches to life.

My stay in Port Elizabeth was not all bad news. My job as a medical officer was very enjoyable and rewarding both intellectually and financially. For the first time in my working life I was paid an adequate salary, which was augmented by overtime pay for call duty once a week. I also did not have to worry about where the money would come from to run the hospital – a welcome relief after almost ten years of struggling to balance the budgets of institutions in which I had worked. I benefited, too, from being in a more intellectually challenging environment after a life of isolation in the wilderness. I learnt a lot from my colleagues, some of whom had been my juniors at Natal Medical School. They had specialised during the years when I pursued my professional activism, and it was a pleasure to be guided by them. There was mutual respect between us.

During August 1984, after about only two months in the role of working wife, I decided that such a life was not for me. I made plans to leave. I contacted Francis Wilson, a Professor of Economics at the University of Cape Town (UCT), who was then directing the Second Carnegie Inquiry into Poverty and Development in Southern Africa, and he promised to help me obtain an appointment at UCT to work with him on the study. Francis had been one of the friends who kept in touch with me during my years in Lenyenye. He came several times to discuss the poverty study with me, and had kept me abreast of developments in the wider society. He was an attractive, energetic, creative thinker, who always seemed to find a way out of tricky corners. He assured me that he would do his best to help me.

My departure from Port Elizabeth and the end of my marriage were sad affairs. Sipo was distraught. He could not believe that I would take such drastic action without giving him a second chance. Although I did not like hurting him, I had to tell him that there was no hope of either of us changing our very different personalities or of us ever developing an acceptable *modus vivendi*. We had to accept the painful fact of our incompatibility. I had lived for too long as an independent person to play the traditional role of a wife.

I had difficulties living with unresolved problems. As far as I was concerned, our relationship did not have a chance. Neither of us, I felt, was ready for the major commitment that would be necessary to renegotiate the marriage contract, and face up to the personal compromises that would inevitably follow if we were to give our relationship a chance to grow. Although my career was not negotiable, I could have been content with a slower pace of change. However, this would have required a willingness on my husband's side to face the risks of ridicule from his peers, most of whom were childhood friends and would have had difficulty supporting his break with the traditional macho habits of Port Elizabeth men.

Most young men in Port Elizabeth townships at the time, and probably in most other townships as well, spent their free hours in shebeens or each other's homes drinking and boasting about their achievements, their women and their cars. The fact that in the status-conscious and hierarchical society in which we lived my profession was ranked higher than pharmacy, also complicated the prospects for a changed lifestyle for us as a couple. My high national profile as a political activist was another 'liability' in this regard. The chances were too great that Sipo's friends would misinterpret *any* change in his behaviour as bowing to the demands of a dominant woman. It would have taken a much stronger and more secure person to resist such peer pressure.

Bruce Haigh, my Australian friend, once observed that the very characteristics which men find attractive in strong women are ironically the ones most threatening to men. Non-traditional marriage relationships with set gender roles are difficult to negotiate under these circumstances. Women all over the world are often compelled either to play down 'the threatening aspects' of their personalities to preserve their marriages, or to negotiate terms which suit both parties even if these may put the marriage at risk. Most women, given the limitations of their circumstances, opt for the former. But I chose differently.

My brother Sethiba, then a teacher in Pietersburg, flew to Port Elizabeth to help me with the physical move to Cape Town, and to provide support in the event of Sipo attempting to obstruct my plans. The drive to Cape Town on the last weekend in September 1984 was tiring, but I was relieved that I had made the decision to move, and followed through with it.

Cape Town

M Y ATTRACTION TO CAPE TOWN HAD BEEN KINDLED BY previous visits. The first was at the beginning of 1976, in my capacity as the Eastern Cape Regional Director of the Black Community Programmes. There are not many cities set against a magnificent mountain and caressed by two oceans, as one finds here. I was struck by the beauty of Cape Town.

The second visit was during 1982 while I was still banned and expecting Malusi. I had been encouraged by my lawyer, Kathy Satchwell, who was then working in Raymond Tucker's law firm, to apply for permission to go on holiday, a possibility I had not entertained before. She told me that other banned people such as Beyers Naudé had already taken advantage of this privilege – another example of how you could use biases within the system to your advantage. I had never heard of a black banned person ever applying for a holiday, let alone being granted permission. But I did not wait for a second prompting. I grabbed the opportunity to get out of Lenyenye. Sipo and I drove to Cape Town on what I hoped would be an opportunity to be alone together as man and wife for the first time in our married life. It was an interesting trip which partly fulfilled my expectations. I was again deeply impressed by the wonderful setting of Cape Town with its striking combination of sea and mountain.

On this trip the limitations of my husband became more obvious to me, as too did our expectations of what being together meant. I had hoped that we would use the time to explore the beautiful environment and get to know each other better without the distractions of family and friends. His idea of fun was sitting with friends over drinks. There was nothing I could do to create a better balance. I spent the time with friends or resting and reading.

◇◆◇

The conference of the Second Carnegie Inquiry into Poverty, held in April 1984, provided the third occasion for me to visit Cape Town. I was then also able to experience a little of the physical beauty of the University of Cape Town (UCT), where the conference was held. The campus setting on the side of Devil's Peak lends a majestic aura to the university. I liked what I saw and enjoyed the intellectual energy which I sensed flowed through the institution. After years in an intellectual wilderness, I became attracted to the possibility of being part of an academic community.

During the first three months in Cape Town, from October to December 1984, my sons and I stayed with the Moletsanes, Thami and Nontobeko, at the Anglican rectory in Langa where they lived with their four children. They were a generous couple, always ready to open their home to many people. It was also a joyous reunion. Nontobeko had been the first sister-in-charge of Zanempilo until their departure in 1976 with Thami's transfer to this parish.

We had an easy relationship as a compound family. Hlumelo found playmates in two of the Moletsane sons who were the same age. He also joined them at the local school. Malusi enjoyed the pampering of the many people who came through the household. I could not have asked for more from friends in time of need.

Langa township is the oldest of Cape Town's African 'locations'. It was a mixed bag. Family houses of all types stood alongside derelict migrant-labour hostels. The educated and uneducated shared community life together. There was stability and order in the midst of apparent chaos. The filthy streets contrasted with the meticulous cleanliness of the interiors of individual homes. Appearances were deceptive in this setting. Services at the local St Cyprian's Church run by Thami Moletsane were joyous occasions of fellowship with other Christians. The music was glorious. There was a sense of security in Langa.

I spent two months bargaining hard with Lester Peteni, an acquaintance from my Eastern Cape days, who had become the local manager of the Urban Foundation's Housing Division in Guguletu, to secure a house that we could lease there. At the beginning of December 1984 we moved into a comfortable three-bedroomed house which Lester had been using as a staff house. It was a relief to be in our own home again.

We lived on the main road in Guguletu, NY 108 (Native Yard 108, the nomenclature deriving from colonial days). The township had a mixture of housing types. Firstly, there were old-style houses like long train carriages, subdivided into two- or one-bedroom family units with living-room and kitchen space. These were by far the most numerous of the family housing units. Secondly, after the 1976 Soweto riots, freestanding houses were constructed by the Urban Foundation to ease the pressing housing problems in the townships. These were few, given the limited land available and affordability problems faced by prospective owners. Thirdly, there were the single-sex migrant-labour hostels where men supposedly lived on their own, though more and more women and children began at great risk to join them in the squalid, dormitory-like accommodation.

Guguletu, like many similar townships, had poor social services. The few, overcrowded schools were hardly functional during the 1980s, an era of school boycotts and work stayaways. Hlumelo attended a primary school not far from our house. He would often be dismissed early when trouble was expected, and so he had little effective education in 1985. On one occasion he was nearly run over by a taxi speeding down NY 108, as they did. I was horrified by the lack of safety for children in the area. I lived in fear.

Guguletu became caught up in the vicious cycle of political violence – a common experience of most townships in the mid-1980s which persisted until the 1994 non-racial elections. It also had the dubious distinction of having the highest per capita murder rate in the world, higher than that of Chicago's ghettos. Political violence simply fuelled the existing fires of criminal violence. Some criminals assumed the political metaphors of the time, and became known as com-tsotsis. They adopted the term 'comrade', popular among political activists, while pursuing their tsotsi (criminal) behaviour. Living in Guguletu in the mid-1980s was not easy.

Our problems were compounded because the house fronted on NY 108, which was the funeral route. During the many mass funeral processions of that decade, which often turned into running battles between the police and mourners, we would be caught in the crossfire. On one occasion, a hole with a diameter of about three centimetres was made in our roof by a burst of buckshot from police firing at fleeing youths. The wafting of teargas fumes through our house was also a regular occurrence. A military vehicle used to park in front of the house. We welcomed it privately when buses with ordinary commuters would come under attack from township youth without any provocation. But we hated the security forces' bullying of ordinary people and the ease with which they resorted to live ammunition.

Encounters with the 'comrades' were not pleasant either. One Sunday we were sitting in the dining room having a family lunch when a young man burst into the house. He did not respond when I asked how I could help him. He simply vanished into one of the children's bedrooms. Hot on his heels were vicious-looking policemen who demanded to know where he had gone. We could genuinely say that we did not know.

For the next hour or so – it felt like a whole day – the police searched through the property, in and around the house, and eventually settled on the only bedroom which was locked. They demanded the key from me and I told them truthfully that I did not have it. They then threatened to use teargas to flush out the fugitive. I pleaded with them and pointed out that it would be unfair for my family to be subjected to such unpleasantness simply because someone had run into our house.

The police sought authority from the local police commissioner to break into the bedroom. They kicked the door in and found a frightened young man in one of the cupboards. He was arrested for allegedly having thrown stones at the police. The police promised to come back and have the door repaired but they never did. The young comrade was later to claim that I had betrayed him – a dangerous statement in the days when 'necklacing' occurred in the townships. Fortunately there had been enough witnesses for the claim to be seen for what it was.

Malusi, then only two years old and very tiny for his age, became so insecure in this war zone that he lost faith in my capacity as his mother to protect him. Whenever he heard the sound of gunfire he would slide under a bed and refuse to come out. He also bit his nails. Such was the terror of living on the frontline.

My work environment was, in contrast, calm and peaceful. It was amazing how successful the apartheid cities had been in separating the lives and problems of black township residents from those of whites in the suburbs. It was hard to believe that we all lived in the same city. This effective separation in part explained the ease with which most white South Africans could pretend to themselves that there was nothing wrong with the society in which they lived.

SALDRU, the Southern Africa Labour and Development Research Unit, started and run by Francis Wilson, provided a warm, supportive base for my re-entry into the academic world in October 1984. I was given a cubicle, for which I was grateful, in view of the pressure on space in SALDRU. I also had access to Francis Wilson's office whenever he was out of town, a not uncommon occurrence. I spent the first three months of my life at UCT reading all 310 papers presented at the Carnegie conference earlier that year, in preparation for my co-authorship of the report. It was wonderful having all the time to myself in a stimulating intellectual environment.

The year 1985 was one of real growth for me and crucial for the development of my academic skills. My initial intention was simply to sit back and take in what I could from the richness around me while regenerating my energy. Years of activism had left me drained in ways which are difficult to describe to anyone who has not had the experience. It was not simple burnout; rather it was being programmed for action to such a degree that total relaxation became a rare and strange phenomenon for the body and mind – almost painful. I had to learn anew how to relax – just to stop and smell the flowers.

Moreover, I felt a deep need to reflect on what I had been involved in over the previous decade or so. Developing critical thinking, reading and writing skills became urgent. Writing the report on poverty with Francis provided an excellent training. We spent most of the first half of 1986 working on the structure of the book: tracing the central themes, deciding on the level of detail we wanted to include, the audience we were targeting and the layout, particularly the boxes in the text, which became effective in highlighting case histories and quotations. The title was the most difficult: it was decided upon just before publication at the end of 1988. You get to know when a title sounds right, and *Uprooting Poverty*[24] did just that.

The collaboration with Francis during the writing of the book strengthened our friendship. He helped me discipline my stream of conscious-

---

24 Francis Wilson and Mamphela Ramphele, *Uprooting Poverty: The South African Challenge* (Cape Town and New York, 1988).

ness and transform it into meaningful phrases, sentences, paragraphs, and eventually themes which hung together logically. I learnt a lot about the English language, the difference between the written and the spoken word, and the added care you have to exercise with the former. Split infinitives, a common problem for non-mother-tongue speakers of English, especially those from an African language background like myself, were a constant theme which Francis harped on. My admiration for the convenience of computers was kindled over the months while I sat next to Francis as he punched in our thoughts, to have them emerge at the end of four years in book form.

I brought to the project my insights into the reality of poverty and the survival mechanisms which people develop to cope with their difficulties. I was able to inject a less romantic notion of poor people than one which would have flowed from the pen of a male, liberal English-speaking South African. We were also able to present an integrated analysis of race, class, gender, age and geographic location which went beyond what was politically correct in the mid-1980s. In this way we could present a sympathetic case study of a poor, unemployed, rural African man and his misery without denying his own role in the oppression of his wife and children as part of the patriarchal system. Francis's economics background was crucial to the quantitative analytical enterprise. We complemented each other's strengths and weaknesses well.

In 1987 we produced *Children on the Frontline: A Report for Unicef on the Status of Children in South Africa*.[25] In so doing we stepped on many sensitive political toes. The report gave both statistical and case-study data on the plight of South African children caught in the double jeopardy of structural violence, created by a racist political and socio-

---

25 Francis Wilson and Mamphela Ramphele, *Children on the Frontline: A Report for Unicef on the Status of Children in South Africa* (New York, 1987).

economic order, and physical violence, which scarred not only their bodies but their psyches as well.

In the 1980s many children as young as seven were caught up in the frenzy of political activism. Stompie Seipei was a case in point. His kidnapping and murder had a sequel in the widely publicised case involving Winnie Mandela. He was one of the many children in the 1980s who were involved in violence as political activists, innocent passers-by, detainees or victims of indescribable police brutality. But we also dared to suggest that children, particularly black children, were also victims of political movements which took advantage of their enthusiasm and dare-devil mentality to fight battles that adults were too scared to pursue. White children too were fighting in the apartheid war as conscripts, pitted against black children in the townships.

We cautioned against the brutalising impact of violence on the children of South Africa, both as its victims and as its perpetrators. We cited Archbishop Tutu's prophetic stance and his outright condemnation of both police brutality and the 'necklace' murders of suspected police informers as equally dehumanising

There was outrage among political activists. How could we criticise the self-defence of powerless oppressed people? Were we not aware of the danger of blaming the victim and thus strengthening the hand of the victimiser? Some critics even suggested that we were allowing ourselves to be used as agents of American imperialism. How else could we explain our acceptance of the Carnegie Corporation's funding without prior consultation with 'the people'? The fact that Francis Wilson had indeed consulted widely before accepting the sponsorship was a factual inconvenience that was dispensed with lightly. We were both satisfied that we had presented an intellectually honest case of the impact of oppression on children, and the dangers of liberation strategies which further dehumanised those caught up in a repressive system.

Our collaborative work brought our different personalities into sharp relief. I had difficulty living with an unfinished product for four years, whereas Francis was relaxed, and would quote his mother, Monica Wilson, as an authority who believed that writing up research should take as long as its collection had done. I was frustrated by this, but could do little to change the pace of work. It was fortuitous that I could channel my energy into other things between our writing appointments.

I did some session work at the Guguletu Day Hospital, which gave me an opportunity to practise my medical skills and become acquainted with the local primary health-care system. It was depressing. On any one day 600 patients would be crowded into the inadequate waiting room. Some had arrived at the gate as early as 6 a.m., only to be seen for about five minutes by caring but overwhelmed medical doctors after five hours or so of waiting. It was a typical apartheid health facility. I struggled to cope with being part of such an inadequate system, but stayed on because it was important for me to keep in touch with the realities of poor South Africans. Not only did my conscience as a political activist dictate this, but it also made academic sense to maintain a research base.

◇◇◇

At about this time I entered the world of anthropology, through a back door. After working for some time I found my cubicle in SALDRU had become too small. It is interesting how you outgrow physical spaces. What once looked perfectly adequate became intolerable later. Francis used a combination of his old boy network and ancestral ties with the Department of Social Anthropology at UCT to secure me an office in the department at the beginning of the 1986 academic year.

My new colleagues in anthropology were supportive. It was a well-run department under Professor Martin West, with well-established rituals. There were regular morning and afternoon teas, a bequest of good English upbringing which Professor Monica Wilson, Francis's mother, passed on during her term as head of department from 1955 to 1973. The department also had a well-run weekly seminar programme at which staff and graduate students had the opportunity of presenting their work. These seminars provided a collegial, yet critical, environment for personal academic development. But like many academic settings, critical comment can, and does, run the risk of destroying an argument without due regard for a vulnerable person's self-confidence. There were rare occasions when stinging attacks on students' work only succeeded in demoralising them. On one occasion I felt strongly enough about the attack to intervene – to the embarrassment of my colleagues, who felt that I had broken ranks.

During the course of 1986, I took an interest in the plight of people living in migrant-labour hostels in the townships of Cape Town. David Russell, then the Anglican priest assigned by the Cape Town diocese to minister to the needs of migrant workers, introduced me to hostel dwellers. They were at the bottom rung of the socioeconomic ladder of South African society, and viewed as temporary sojourners in Cape Town. This was in keeping with the dictates of apartheid which tolerated Africans in the white urban areas only while they were usefully employed.

Africans in the Western Cape also faced additional problems from the constraints placed on job prospects and social services by the Coloured Labour Preference Policy, which sought to make the Western Cape the preserve of white and 'coloured' people. African townships such as Langa, Guguletu and Nyanga were deliberately neglected and underdeveloped so as to discourage family settlement. Large hostel compounds were built to house single African men, and vicious policing of the pass laws was used to criminalise attempts by African men and women to lead normal family lives.

I decided to start a project with the newly established Western Cape Men's Hostel Dwellers' Association (HDA) with a view to strengthening their own efforts to secure their rights to family life and better living conditions. The men in the leadership of the HDA were courageous people with interesting names reflecting their unsophisticated backgrounds: Johnson Mpukumpa, Welcome Zenzile, Super Nkathazo, and so on. I did not anticipate the challenges that lay ahead. With Francis Wilson's help I obtained financial support from the Ford Foundation to fund my own research post until I was given tenure by UCT later in 1986.

The Anglo American Corporation and De Beers Chairman's Fund funded the research costs of my project. It was symbolically appropriate that this mining giant, which organised and benefited from migrant labour, should make some contribution to the study, and hopefully to the elimination of the vicious system they helped create in South Africa. It is a battle which I am still fighting.

Learning to do research in a methodical way was taxing for one more accustomed to the world of activism. It took time for me to come to terms with the demands of scholarly rigour. There was a big psychological hurdle to cross regarding the importance of academic work in the wider scheme of things. I had joined the ranks of arm-chair intellectuals who occupied the ivory tower of academic life, the very people we as activists used to view with scorn. How could I justify my presence at UCT and claim it would make a difference?

There was a sense in which intellectual work was not regarded within activist circles as *real* work. Activist intellectuals often had to engage in other activities to justify their credibility within these circles. It was a difficult problem to tackle in a country where the majority of people had been denied educational opportunities to develop the skills to engage in intellectual work. A deep sense of guilt by the survivors of a discriminatory system drove them to overextend themselves in an attempt to respond to the expectations of their fellow oppressed people, while also trying to meet academic demands. Political activists often exploited this guilt to extract the maximum out of them, sometimes with devastating consequences for all.

My choice of a research area and the use of a participatory research methodology were in part aimed at reducing the level of discomfort I felt in my new position – my guilt as a survivor. In this way I could convince myself more easily that my academic work was a continuation of my previous work and did not subtract from my political commitment. It was more difficult to convince former co-activists and others who feared that my energies would be sapped by the demands of academic life, and that I would be neutralised as an agent of change. Many regarded my entry into the academic world as a loss to the struggle.

In addition, the association of anthropology with colonialism, a charge political activists often made, did not sit comfortably with me. I could, however, take comfort from not being a professional anthropologist, but merely using the Department of Anthropology as a convenient base from which to work. But it became clear as I learned more of the discipline of anthropology that it was much more than the 'handmaiden of colonialism'. I learned to distinguish between the prostitution of anthropology by racists and colonialists to serve their own ends, and anthropology as a social science. Although a particularly vicious form of anthropology operated in some Afrikaans-speaking universities, which provided ethnological justification for segregation, there was also another tradition which had earned South African anthropology a place of honour internationally. A.R. Radcliffe-Brown, Monica Wilson, the Mayers and many others had done valuable work that led to a greater and more sophisticated understanding of South African society.

I also noticed that the method of anthropology – participant observation – was not very different from what I had used as an activist in community development work. I had to live among the people I worked with, observe what they did, why certain things made sense to them, and what motivated them. Participant observation was a prerequisite of any action which would try to change people's life circumstances. I could build on the skills I had developed earlier to sharpen my research work: communication in the people's own language, empathy and the ability to win the trust of others.

But I was still not ready to become an anthropologist. In one of my first presentations to the departmental seminar in 1987, I drew on my reading of feminist literature from the United States to understand the dynamics of gender which I had observed in the migrant-labour hostels of Cape Town. One of my colleagues objected to my use of the term 'patriarchy' to refer to the system of male-dominated power relations I saw in operation. Patriarchy was not a widely used term in South Africa at the time. He told me that anthropologists did not like using such terms. I reminded him that I was not there to become an anthropologist, and that I would continue to use the term anyway.

Anthropology in South Africa had until the mid-1980s not embraced gender as an important construct in social analysis. Many ethnographic texts had indeed documented the inequalities of power between men and women in the communities they studied, but little theoretical discussion had developed around gender politics, nor was there any serious discussion of feminist literature. The exchange between my colleague and me was indicative of the tensions which existed between traditional and non-traditional approaches to social science in our discipline. As a newcomer to academic life, I could go where angels feared to tread.

Among many other political activists, Thabo Mbeki, then foreign relations spokesman for the African National Congress (ANC), also questioned my choice of academic base, when we met at a conference at Duke University in 1989 to launch *Uprooting Poverty*. He asked, 'Et tu Mamphela?' To which I replied confidently that he needed to distinguish between good and bad anthropology. I was becoming more comfortable with the nature of my new academic base.

As my academic work progressed, the migrant-worker research project proved much larger and more demanding than I had anticipated. Not only did I have to cope with the demands of fieldwork for data collection, but I also ran into serious conflict with the authoritarian tendencies in the Western Cape Men's Hostel Dwellers' Association (HDA). The demands of fieldwork were exacerbated by the horrible conditions in which people lived. I became physically ill at the end of 1987 from sheer exhaustion and anger at the dehumanising conditions of the hostels where I spent about three months observing the daily lives of hostel dwellers. As in the case of Unni Wikan, who worked in a Cairo slum, your psyche takes punishment under such conditions.[26]

But the conflict with the leaders of the HDA was more exhausting. It challenged all the romantic notions I had about the capacity of poor, oppressed people to organise themselves out of their position of power-lessness and become part of the process of shaping a more egalitarian society. In the first place, the assumption that all poor, oppressed people would keenly embrace any well-thought-out participatory programme to change their lives underestimated the power of years of oppression in conditioning subordinates to accept their fate as unalterable.

Also, the leaders of the HDA displayed a style which reflected, rein-forced and replicated existing power relations in our society. Older men who were more articulate saw it as their destiny to lead, and their right to be listened to with little or no questioning. And there was little evidence of questioning from the ranks of hostel dwellers. Yet the com-mitment of the leaders to changing the conditions of life for their fellow hostel dwellers could not be faulted. They took enormous risks at a time when state repression of any movement for change was vicious. Some of them, such as Super Nkathazo, paid with their lives in the vio-lence of the 1990s. Their followers granted them the reverence they felt they deserved.

---

26 Unni Wikan, *Life among the Poor in Cairo* (London, 1980).

It seemed to me that the high risks involved in political leadership in an authoritarian system had the potential to breed authoritarianism. Such authoritarianism was not only tolerated by the oppressed, but expected. The feeling of insecurity and the danger of infiltrators led to demands for strong leadership, even if it came at a cost. The need for leaders who would not look back when danger loomed was a major concern of powerless people.

But I could not come to terms with these realities. Having worked myself into the position of adviser to, and fundraiser and advocate for, the HDA, I experienced a deep crisis when I realised I had to withdraw from this role. I could not continue to be associated with something which was likely to perpetuate inequalities between men and women, and between old and young, and had demonstrated its potential for ruthless suppression of dissent. But withdrawal would put at risk the possibility of the physical upgrading of the hostels into family units which was being negotiated at the time. Who was I to put my moral stance between poor people and the social services they were waiting for?

It was only after reflecting on the distinction between my role as a facilitator for change in social relations, and that of local authorities as providers of social services, that I was able to free myself from guilt. My conscience was clear. I withdrew from the HDA at the beginning of 1988. That withdrawal had some positive effect on the leadership style of the HDA. I had called their bluff. I felt that their victim status was no excuse for undemocratic behaviour. We resumed our relationship on a much healthier basis; but I was left drained.

At this time I also had to make important decisions about finally leaving township life behind me. We were now living in a university staff house in Lovers Walk, Rondebosch, having fled Guguletu in June 1986, when the violent repression of the local population by the security forces became open warfare. This included the burning of shacks in squatter areas in a vain attempt by the police to flush out political activists.

One day in June 1986 I got a call from Nomvume Sotomela, my housekeeper at the time, that there was a rumour of a threat to burn the Uluntu Community Centre, which was situated on the property adjacent to our house. In my view there was just one appropriate response. I drove straight to Guguletu, terrified by the thought of impending danger, but determined to get my son Malusi and Nomvume out of harm's way. We thrust a few personal belongings in the back of the car and dashed to Francis and Lindy Wilson's house in Rondebosch, where we remained as refugees until UCT allocated us the staff house in Lovers Walk.

At the beginning of 1987, after many battles with the racist housing system in Cape Town and the UCT bureaucracy, I finally purchased my own house in Mowbray. It had to be registered in the name of the university to circumvent the legal barriers to black ownership of property in white suburbs. Many other black South Africans had to have 'fronts' to acquire property in the land of their birth. My white neighbours, after initially protesting against our presence to the local police, relaxed when they realised that the heavens were not going to fall in One of them said to the local police that they had not realised I was a medical doctor! How my profession made me less black only white racists can explain.

Chapter 21

As mother and professional

ARLY IN 1988 MARGARET TOUBORG, THEN PERSONAL AIDE to Dr Martina Horner, President of Radcliffe College at Harvard, came to South Africa to identify potential applicants for the newly established Carnegie Distinguished International Fellowship for the 1988/89 academic year. The thought that I could be chosen did not even occur to me. I did not see myself as an academic, but as someone who had come to seek refuge in the academic world to reflect on a new path for the life ahead of me, and therefore I did not imagine myself qualifying.

However, Margaret not only convinced me that I was the person Radcliffe College was looking for, but made arrangements for my eventual arrival at the Bunting Institute in September 1988, where we were to remain until April 1989. We lived in a two-bedroom flat in one of the Harvard University housing complexes. It was three minutes' walk to the Bunting Institute in Concord Avenue, and five minutes' walk to Buckingham Browne and Nichols Lower School where my sons went. They were 'latch-key children' but would often stop at my office on their way home.

I was able to call upon a stipend and research money to employ a student assistant and regular baby-sitting services. Tracy Walton became our baby-sitter and a valuable support for all of us. She generously used her own car, a station wagon, to drive my sons to movies or to places of interest. Such luxury I had never known before. I sat back and immersed myself in the community of women scholars and the wealth of Harvard

University's library resources. I had the opportunity to engage in discussions with powerful women of all ages who were making a name for themselves in their careers: poets, painters, sculptors, astrophysicists, mathematicians, political scientists, anthropologists, and many more. It was an intellectual feast.

The idea of creating a safe, supportive space for women in academic life had long been recognised by feminists, but it was fair to say that the generosity of the Bunting Fellowship was in a class of its own globally. Men had always created such spaces for themselves, even though they do not generally have to deal with the competing demands of a career and raising a family. Think of all the major fellowships and scholarships that were exclusively reserved for men until a few decades ago. It was a measure of the low value placed on women's contribution to high-level jobs in society that these spaces were such a rarity for women throughout the world.

One of the books which I had the good fortune to read on the recommendation of Jane Cooper, a poet and Bunting Fellow, was by Gaston Bachelard, a philosopher and poet, entitled *The Poetics of Space*.[27] Jane later gave me an autographed copy when she realised how much it meant to me. Bachelard combined his philosophical and poetic skills to produce an eloquent exploration of space and its symbolic impact on people's lives. It suddenly dawned on me that space had many dimensions: psychological, intellectual, political, social and economic. What the Bunting Institute provided was this multi-dimensional space for women to develop their skills.

Not only did that realisation infuse a new meaning into my own life, but it provided a thematic tool for the collation and analysis of my migrant-labour hostel data. It helped me understand that hostel dwellers' capacity to act as active agents of history was constrained by their

---

27 G. Bachelard, *The Poetics of Space* (New York, 1964).

limited political, social, economic, intellectual and psychological space. But I also recognised the way in which those same constraints, as they had done in my own life, enabled people to develop important survival strategies that ensure their ability to live within the constraints and to transcend them. I realised that the various constraints worked together to set off a vicious cycle, but once such a cycle was broken, the transformative capacity of human beings came to the fore.

Risk-taking is an important element and a necessary condition for people to break the cycle of powerlessness and submission. Making choices in our lives is one of the characteristics which make us human beings, and choice remains with us even as we face death at the hands of torturers – the choice to submit or to die in dignity. I have had to learn that the courage to take risks was not given to all of us. This realisation enabled me to develop a better approach to the process of empowerment, and also encouraged me to have more compassion for those who were unable to become transformative agents.

One outcome of my time at the Bunting Institute was a decision to write up my research data as a PhD thesis entitled 'Empowerment and the Politics of Space'. This was accepted at UCT in 1991. A book of the thesis, *A Bed Called Home*, was published in 1993.[28] I had become an anthropologist after all.

For women in my position the 'superwoman syndrome' was an ever-present danger. Terri Apter, among others, has explored this syndrome at length. Women trying to juggle the multiple roles they have to play in life – as partner, mother, career woman – face enormous challenges to remain human. 'The trap that the superwoman falls into is the belief that she can have everything because she can do as much as two or three people.'[29]

---

28 Mamphela Ramphele, *A Bed Called Home: Life in the Migrant Labour Hostels of Cape Town* (Cape Town, Edinburgh and Athens, Ohio, 1993).
29 T. Apter, *Why Women Don't Have Wives* (Basingstoke, 1985), p.118.

There was an assumption in this statement of Apter's which resonated with what many of my sympathetic critics sometimes say to me, that women in this position elect not to exercise the choice they have between the various contending demands, and thus avoid the trap. How did I as a single woman with two sons choose between a career and motherhood? Moreover, as a South African in a country where black people had limited skills, how did you exercise this choice when faced with the relentless pressure to engage in many national and community activities? And, as a black woman in a changing South Africa where even fewer black women could participate meaningfully in shaping future social policies to ensure greater equity, how did you make the choice between engagement and non-engagement?

From my own experience, 'superwomen' did not necessarily believe that they could have everything because they could do as much as two or three people. It was a condition of being black and female in South Africa that you had to be a 'superwoman'. My mother did not choose to remain a primary school teacher while bringing up seven children with little help from her traditional husband. She had to do *both*. She had to learn to do as much as three people. This was a survival strategy. Many ordinary poor women in South Africa were presented with the 'superwoman' title by the historical accident of their birth, not because they sought it.

As a mother, however, I had a very different set of attitudes from those of my own mother. It had struck me that my biological incompetence to carry my pregnancies to term without assistance might have been an important factor in my attitude to motherhood. I did not have the illusion of being programmed for the nurturing role. The discomforts and frustrations I experienced in having to lie on my bed with its foot elevated at an angle for months on end did not leave me with romantic ideas about pregnancy. Then again, even allowing for my particular problems, there was something truly invasive about pregnancy. Its invasiveness was particularly pronounced as the baby grows, shaping and dictating the mother's every movement.

The birth process was a major challenge to your body. Whatever form the delivery took, there was the ever-present danger of death lurking behind the exhilarating prospect of a new life beginning. There is a saying in Sesotho that tswala e bolaile tšie (birth has killed a locust). In other words, once a female locust is fertilised it is destined to die as soon as it completes the process of laying its eggs. In spite of that knowledge, many other female locusts will still engage in the process of giving their lives so that new life can be brought forth.

This locust metaphor had more than a physical aspect to it. There was also the invisible (sometimes not-so-invisible) death of aspects of women's lives as they engaged in the necessary sacrificial action to give birth to children and to raise them. The indignity of the birth pains, for those of us who gave birth to our children before epidurals were considered safe and generally accessible, I found humiliating. As Francis Wilson told me, his mother Monica once commented that the whole engineering and plumbing job around the birth canal left much to be desired. I passionately believed that the designer would have been failed if this had been an engineering graduate project.

The compensation of seeing a bundle of life next to you immediately after birth makes up for the mess you experience after delivery. But I had bitter-sweet experiences around the birth of all three of my children. In none of the cases could their fathers be there with me.

Nor does nursing young babies fill me with a glowing feeling. I enjoyed watching them tucking into my breast and relishing the flow of milk. But breast-feeding beyond six months was not for me. I also resented the interruption to my sleep, which had to be endured for the first six to twelve months. Both my first two babies were screamers, and gave me little time for rest. I was glad to have family support.

I never feared the empty nest syndrome. On the contrary, I developed a relationship with my sons which was nurturing but encouraged independence. From very early on, I made my children know that much as I loved them dearly, I was but a normal human being who got tired and irritable and made mistakes. I encouraged them to appreciate how important my own personal space was to me, and how vital it was for my best functioning. It was hard for children to understand this, but it was the only way I could retain my sanity as a parent. Once my bedroom door was closed, my room became out of bounds to them, unless there was an urgent problem.

My own parenting style attempted to take the best from my childhood experiences while shunning the self-sacrificial aspects which made my mother's life a misery. I learned from her how to be a good cook, keep the house tidy, including kitchen corners, and still have quality time. The importance of discipline and getting children to take responsibility she perfected to an art form. I never had to go as far as she did, because I was not as desperate for quick action as she was with the seven of us. She also could not afford the luxury of negotiation, which I used to great benefit with my sons. My mother's use of physical punishment was a reflection of both its acceptance in her own environment and time, and the pressure under which she was operating that made tolerance of mistakes difficult. She had to run a tight ship. I have watched myself slipping into impatience under pressure, and know how easy it is for parents to be intolerant.

I made sure that occasionally I prepared the apple-pies, pancakes and waffles which my sons loved. But I discovered, and could afford something which my mother could have done with – having wives! I accepted that I couldn't fulfil all the expectations of motherhood and parenting, nor did I wish to. I did not enjoy some of the chores essential for a normal well-functioning family, but made sure they were done to perfection by those capable of doing so.

Unlike a lot of other women in my position, I had no guilt feelings about my domestic arrangements. I believe that I compensated adequately those who made my life comfortable, within my limited means. I am indebted to all those women who played this effective wife role in my life. It was not an accident that men have over the years protected their privileged access to the services of their wives. Wives have throughout history freed men to succeed outside the domestic arena. Until society is better organised, I see no end for the essential role of the 'wife', male or female.

Widowed well-to-do African matriarchs in the former Pietersburg region, where my parents came from, used to marry wives late in their lives to secure essential support in their old age. This applied in particular to childless women. The marriage involved customary bride wealth and all the other traditional rights and obligations. The young married woman was free to have male friends and bear children, but the children belonged to her 'husband', the older woman. It may not be an egalitarian model to follow, but it illustrates the complexities inherent in dealing with the problem of adequate domestic support.

❖❖❖

Balancing my role as mother and professional became more of a challenge over the years. While I was still a professional activist in a supportive domestic scene with extended family members around, it was not a major problem. It became a problem in Port Elizabeth. My move to Cape Town did not initially present major problems. But as my work became more demanding, the balancing act grew more taxing. It was, however, perhaps fair to say that the biggest problem for me was not being a working woman, but the competing demands of national agendas, which impinged on the delicate balance between mothering and work-time achieved through trial and error over the years.

The complexities of negotiating the role of a woman executive are, however, dwarfed by those facing black women executives. These women share the frustrations of their black male colleagues, having to survive in a cultural environment which is alienating in its arrogance. But unlike their male counterparts, black women executives have to fight cultural stereotypes held by many people in society, including their own colleagues, about the place and role of black women. Black women executives fit the role of the witch perfectly: they are the ultimate transgressors. One way in which people attempt to deal with the transgression is to find a male connection with whom to identify the woman executive. The male connection resolves the enigma of a successful woman – she is seen as acting because of, or on behalf of, him. Her own discomforting agency is thus denied. In my case I am often amazed at how Steve Biko was dragged into whatever was being reported about me – almost forty years after his death. Would the same have happened if our genders were switched?

A most effective way of establishing this male connection is through the status of widowhood. A widow's status cannot be seen independently from that of the man to whom she is connected. In my particular case, the fact that I was not Steve Biko's widow was treated as a minor inconvenience, easily brushed aside. Over the years I acquired the dubious status of 'a political widow who could never be'.

Political widows who do not qualify to be widows in the ordinary sense find themselves in a curious social space, and are faced with a particular set of problems. In fact the eagerness to label a woman who was linked to, but not married to, a deceased political personality signals society's anxiety to re-establish its own equilibrium by symbolically removing her from the liminal unknown to the liminal known where social tools exist to 'deal with' her.

References to me in the media illustrate some of these issues. One of many such instances, a *Boston Globe* article (20 April 1994), ran under the heading 'Biko's Lover: Banished and Pregnant'.

Ramphele was prohibited from leaving the remote village of Lenyenye, a thousand miles from her lover. Lenyenye was sweltering, desolate, and pointedly impoverished, a dumping ground for 'surplus' unemployed black South Africans who were no longer viable members of the country's labour pool. And she was pregnant with Steve Biko's child.

Her tenuous emotional and physical state almost resulted in a miscarriage. It was during that ordeal that Ramphele, struggling to keep her child alive in a neighbouring hospital, heard the news of Steve Biko's death.

This material was extracted by the *Boston Globe* from the South African journalist Allister Sparks's book *The Mind of South Africa*, published in 1990. On my arrival at the Kennedy School of Government in January 1994, where I was a visiting scholar, I had to force the publications section of the school to retract a similarly worded introduction. My professional interests and achievements had received no mention in the article proposed by this academic institution.

Similarly, in 1991, when I was appointed as deputy vice-chancellor at the University of Cape Town, one of the country's leading glossy magazines, *The Executive*, introduced me as 'The mother of Steve Biko's son becomes UCT executive'. I asked them if they would have introduced any male executive with a comparable reference, and forced them to publish an apology. I also objected to the extreme insensitivity to my son. Little thought seemed to go into how a teenager would feel about being described in the public media as a 'near miscarriage'.

I could only infer that my public persona was an uncomfortable one for patriarchal society to deal with, and had to be given 'respectability' by summoning Steve from the grave to accompany me and clothe my nakedness. In summoning him to my side, society chose to forget the multi-dimensionality of the relationship I had with him as colleague and fellow activist, and only dwelt on the aspect which presented me as an instrument of his nurture and a bearer of his son. My comments were not intended to deny the important role Steve played in my personal life, but to pose the question about the extent to which that relationship had become a marker on my body to enable society to relate to me.

There were, however, other inferences which I could draw from this eagerness to bestow the label of widow on me. The public role of the political widow derives from her relationship with her husband, and thus she is there not as a woman, but as someone standing in for a fallen man. She becomes the ultimate honorary man. Her relationships are supposed to be shaped by, and flow along the contours of, her late husband's relationships. His friends and comrades become her friends. So too his enemies become hers. Her agency is not completely eliminated, but constrained. It is an effective form of social control of women who may be too independent for the comfort of existing social structures.

The agency of the political widow is by definition constrained by those sponsoring her role. To the extent that their goals, strategies and tactics and her own converge, a political widow continues to enjoy the patronage which comes with the role. Any major divergence, particularly if it takes on a public nature, poses major threats not only to the continuing relationships, but to her very public status. In so far as she can re-negotiate the terms of her engagement with public affairs, she is able to enlarge her socio-political space as a public figure in her own right. It is a tough balancing act fraught with risks and danger. The support society offers to you comes at a price. I have taken risks in losing social support which tended to come at a cost to my independence as an individual.

There is a final difficulty which many black executives, male and female, often face when they find themselves in the public limelight. It is not difficult to be a celebrity when a vicious discriminatory system has prevented many from succeeding. Being the first this, that or the other should also be seen as an indictment of a society which has denied black people the opportunity to excel. The double jeopardy of being black and female compounds the problem for me. It is not false modesty, but I cannot help recognising the historical realities which have made it possible for me to be a pathbreaker in many areas of our society.

The choice of my first career was a product of historical necessity. My passion for independence was the major driving force, and a medical career was the ideal choice at that time. It is noteworthy that my father did not question the suitability of my choice of career on grounds of gender, but on rational, domestic, economic ones. He had full confidence in my intellectual abilities, and often lamented my lack of application to do better. The only sexist remark I ever heard my father make with reference to my ability was that he lamented the waste of brains on a female child, which could have been better bestowed on a son. But I was never made to feel that I could do other than achieve the best possible.

The self-confidence I developed as a child served me well. Fear of success has never been an issue. For some women, femininity and individual achievements are mutually exclusive.

The double jeopardy of being black and female in a racist and sexist society may well make you less afraid of the sanctions against success. A non-subservient black woman is by definition a transgressive – she is the ultimate outsider. But political activism, with its higher purpose, and the steeling effect of breaking most of the rules in a society desperately in need of transformation, have added an important depth to my adult life.

My professional life has been marked by real enjoyment. I have never had the misfortune, after my internship period, of not enjoying my work. I have almost always been fortunate to design my own jobs. But I also have enjoyed the relations with my colleagues. I have had little difficulty finding a satisfactory basis for a good working relationship with people: male or female, educated or uneducated, white or black.

These working relationships have not come without cost and tough bargaining. But I believe in bargaining at the beginning to avoid misconceptions and misunderstandings. I also realise that such open negotiations are not necessarily acceptable to people brought up in a different institutional culture from mine. My greatest difficulties have arisen with people coming from backgrounds where uncomfortable issues are not supposed to be raised, and differences remain unacknowledged. But in most cases I have found a resolution or a way of living with an open admission to agree to differ.

———— ◇◈◇ ————

I have been able to negotiate good working conditions and thrive in circumstances in which I would not have expected to do so. For example, after I joined the UCT executive as a deputy vice-chancellor in July 1991, some women colleagues at UCT were genuinely concerned about the impact my working environment would have on me. The all-white, male executive did not look like a supportive working milieu. They offered to form a support group for me in which I could unwind. But they were surprised and disappointed when I replied that I actually loved working with my colleagues, and needed no more support than they did as academics. I have no doubt that support groups are valuable for women finding themselves in hostile territory, and that the failure of the women's movement to make gains similar to those of organised labour stems in part from lack of solidarity action. But I have had to survive without them all my life. I was not going to have one simply to show that I was not being swallowed by the male culture around me.

This point raises an important issue. To what extent is the expectation that those who are outsiders to institutions will fail to 'fit in', the product of a self-fulfilling prophecy? What role does personal agency play in these situations? I hasten to add that I am not referring here to racist or sexist institutions which have no intention of changing; that would simply be like walking into a lions' den. I am referring to institutions that have made some declaration to change, however tentative.

My concerned women colleagues at UCT made certain assumptions. Firstly, that I was going to try to 'fit in' and would be frustrated – a reasonable assumption, given the many women who have been co-opted into honorary male roles. But I was employed in my executive job to take charge of the Equal Opportunity Policy Portfolio, aimed at changing the culture of the institution. Fitting into it the existing UCT culture would negate my mission. A second assumption was that as a woman I would find little support amongst my male colleagues. It is dangerous and limiting to exclude the possibility of real supportive relations with caring male colleagues wherever one goes, for they do arise. I have over the years developed a support network consisting of both men and women who are invaluable for my sanity.

Then again, my blackness in a white stronghold must have been an added concern to my women colleagues. One of the enormous benefits of having been steeled in the furnaces of Black Consciousness activism is that I have been liberated psychologically. I feel I belong in any part of my country, and I treat any major public institution in my society as part of my heritage. I do not have to apologise for being there for a legitimate purpose. This sense of belonging was particularly strong in my job at UCT, where I was invited to come and make a contribution. The knowledge that UCT, despite its history, represented an important national asset was sustaining and made the effort worthwhile.

It is interesting how many South Africans have failed to appreciate the importance of Black Consciousness in the historical struggle for justice in South Africa. The largest group of people in this category are those liberal white English-speaking South Africans who felt rejected by Black Consciousness activists in the 1970s. For them this was a slap in the face which they found hard to take. People like Dr Beyers Naudé, having experienced the humiliation of Afrikaners under English rule, had little difficulty in understanding and supporting the need for blacks to redefine themselves and their aspirations.

In contrast, Alan Paton died without overcoming his anger at being 'excluded' from the struggle by the Black Consciousness Movement. One also detects the same confusion in Nadine Gordimer's musings about her relief at 'the re-emergence of non-racial politics' in the 1980s.[30] What Nadine and others do not appreciate is the importance of the positive identity and self-confidence which Black Consciousness instilled in blacks, and its role in shaping the politics of the 1970s, as well as laying the foundations of the defiance politics of the 1980s.

Mongane Serote has aptly noted that the Black Consciousness Movement breathed oxygen into the moribund ANC operations in exile, particularly its armed struggle, which benefited from the young militants who had been nurtured by the BCM. One need only look at those who have played a significant role in both the BCM and the ANC to see the connection – Cheryl Carolus, Jay Naidoo, Frank Chikane, Cyril Ramaphosa, Murphy Morobe, Mosiuoa 'Terror' Lekota and Thenjiwe Mtintso, to name but a few.

The second group of South Africans who reject the importance of Black Consciousness comprises some of the older generation of ANC leaders, particularly those connected to the South African Communist Party. The late Mr Govan Mbeki, for example, was quoted in the *New York Times* of 12 February 1994 as saying that whilst performing his duties on Robben Island as a political educator during his imprison-

---

30 See Charles Villa-Vicencio's *The Spirit of Hope* (Johannesburg, 1993), p. 106.

ment there, he had had to confront young political prisoners from the BCM tradition with the meaninglessness of their talk about 'blackness' and move them to a higher level of appreciating the importance of class analysis. The fact is that those young activists needed to go through an understanding of racism in South Africa to be able to integrate it with class analysis.

Mr Mbeki and others of his generation, who grew up as members of a proud peasant class in the Eastern Cape, have never had to doubt their own worth as human beings in spite of the racism around them. But for those young blacks growing up in the squalid townships of the 1960s, it was much more difficult not to have self-doubt. A Black Consciousness perspective was essential for these young blacks growing up in a racist country.

The same imperative applies to women, who have to integrate an understanding of their 'womanhood' in a sexist society in order that they may be able to develop an appreciation of the dynamics of race, class and gender as these impinge on their lives. Belonging to exclusive women's organisations is a necessary step in the process of liberation and personal growth for most women. By the same token, worker consciousness, an important part of the protective armour against exploitation, is part of the same social reality.

———— ◇◈◇ ————

The added depth which political activism gives to one's professional work has embedded within it the seeds of self-destruction. The merging of one's personal professional life with the destiny of one's own country is a powerful but deadly combination. One's entire life becomes dedicated to national service and eventually one starts to feel as if one is being treated as, or has indeed become, national property. I had to face up to this sooner or later.

When the engine stopped

W HILE AT THE BUNTING INSTITUTE IN 1988 I WENT INTO overdrive trying to complete a major piece of work before going back to South Africa. This resulted in a breakdown.

My body has an excellent early warning system which tells me to slow down when the going gets tough. But I often ignore it. I went through adolescence without a single pimple on my face, but have to contend with acne in my mature years as a sign of stress. I have had two major breakdowns as a result of not heeding the warning signals. It is as though the engine of my body just stops after running on overdrive for too long.

When my engine stopped in 1988 I was admitted to the Stillman Infirmary at Harvard with viral meningitis. I had woken up one morning late in November with a high temperature and splitting headache. I kept hoping that it would pass. No amount of painkillers seemed to help. By midday, I realised that something was seriously wrong and called a colleague to help me. It took days for the doctors to diagnose my illness. The only treatment was rest, rest and more rest. I owe my recovery to the many colleagues at the Bunting Institute and to friends who rallied around me.

Unfortunately, I had to go on yet another punishing schedule to promote the book *Uprooting Poverty* in February 1989, only eight weeks after this episode. At the launching conference at Duke University I became impatient with what I perceived as the American arrogance of some of the panellists. I stood up during the last session of the conference and reminded American academics and foundation executives that South Africans had fought for their liberation, and would continue to do so, with or without American assistance. We do not need your help if it comes at the cost of our dignity, I declared. That dramatically spelt the end of the session and the conference. Some of my South African colleagues made apologetic comments afterwards, but I was unrepentant.

Francis Wilson captured the state of my mind when he bought me a coffee mug after the conference. The inscription on the mug read: Grant me patience, O Lord, but hurry! Clearly I had to do something to slow myself down and stop carrying the burdens of the world on my insubstantial shoulders. But from my UCT years onwards it was a difficult adjustment from a passionate all-consuming activism to a lifestyle more suited to a woman in her forties with growing children.

It was the opening of political space after Mr Mandela's release from prison in 1990 that added momentum to the urgent need I felt to create a better balance in my life. At the same time, I began to feel that my worst fears regarding the short-sightedness of the anti-apartheid politics of the 1980s were about to become part of the reality of the 'new South Africa' which was announced with such fanfare.

My misgivings about the direction taken by the liberation struggle started in 1983 at the time of the launching of the United Democratic Front (UDF). I remember meeting enthusiastic activists who had been to the Mitchells Plain launch of the UDF, saying how wonderful the occasion had been. Their response to my enquiry about what had been most striking about the conference was that 'It was just like the 1950s!' For romantics this was a wonderful sign that the politics of the 1950s were back with us. I was dismayed. I feared that the lessons of the 1960s and 1970s would be lost in the romantic quest to recapture the past.

Observers of the South African political scene would know that much of the liberation struggle in the 1980s was to reassert the political authority of the liberation movements which had been driven under-ground by repression. It was inevitable that the politics of the 1950s had to be re-enacted in large measure, including the reinstatement of the old leadership in community structures and the opening of the road to the ANC-in-exile in Lusaka to seek political direction, legitimation and authenticity for internal programmes.

Much good came out of this cross-pollination between internal and exile politics. But there were major costs as well. The quality of long-term strategic planning for a post-apartheid South Africa suffered. For the exiled political leaders, the major thrust of their strategies was to make the country ungovernable so as to force the Nationalist govern-ment to relinquish power in deference to the liberation movement. A large number of internal political activists shared this goal, but there were differences in the choice of strategies. Tensions arose and intensi-fied within communities between contending political ideologies, young and old, those working within the system and those outside it. Develop-ment of individuals and communities was sacrificed in the quest for 'the political kingdom',[31] in the hope that all else would follow its attainment.

Some of my friends and political peers from the 1970s regarded me as a prophet of doom whenever I criticised the retrogressiveness of anti-apartheid politics in the 1980s. I lamented the failure to build on the positive gains of the 1970s when some foundations had been laid for liberation politics that put development of individuals and communi-ties at the centre of political concerns. The 'bounds of possibility'[32]

31 The call to seek first the political kingdom is Nkrumah's unfortunate legacy to Africa. It was made in good faith, but based on a superficial analysis of colonial power relations, ignoring the cushioning effect of colonised people on lower classes amongst colonial settlers. A simplistic linkage was thus assumed between political rights and material benefits.

32 A metaphor coined by Barney Pityana to characterise the impact of the Black Con-sciousness Movement of the 1970s on South African politics.

which had been extended in the 1970s with a positive definition of what the struggle was about, rather than what it was against, were largely ignored in the heady anti-apartheid activities of the 1980s. The chickens of political expediency came home to roost with a vengeance in the 1990s.

Most of my life had been dedicated to the struggle for justice and freedom in my country. It had been an exciting time for me: a period of phenomenal growth, nourished by both joy and pain. It had its victorious moments as well as its frustrations. I have invested enormous psychic energy in 'the struggle'. This investment derived from a complexity of motives – idealism, altruism, the need for realising my potential and, most important, the need for personal healing.

It was understandable that when the end of 'the struggle' seemed so seductively near, I would be compelled to stop and take stock. Would my country finally be free? What quality of life would accompany such freedom? Would my ideals of living in a truly non-racial, non-sexist, egalitarian society finally be realised?

The signs gave me little cause for comfort. On the one hand, the Nationalist government of F. W. de Klerk did not seem committed to abandoning the past and redressing the injustices of the apartheid era. On the other hand, the liberation movement seemed to have been thrown into disarray by the suddenness and extent of the concessions by De Klerk's government. It was too good to be true! Not only did Mr De Klerk open up political space for the African National Congress and the Pan Africanist Congress, and agree in principle to the release of all political prisoners, but he legalised the South African Communist Party as well! There had to be a catch somewhere, some activists ventured. There had been little strategic preparation within the ranks of the liberation movement for such an eventuality. Small wonder that valuable ground was lost in the first few months. The challenges of negotiation politics required a longer period of adjustment than most South Africans had anticipated. Concerned South Africans questioned the capacity of the liberation movement to transform itself into a viable alternative to the Nationalist government.

For me there was also increasing tension between the demands of political activism and parenting. As a single parent I had to reassess the extent to which I was being fair to my children and myself in this regard. Hlumelo was most affected by my relative unavailability. He was often teased by his teachers and friends about my many absences. He once said to me: 'It is not nice, Mum, when people ask you if your mother is away again.' Poor child. I reminded him often that it may well be envy, rather than ridicule, which triggered the teasing. He admitted that there were many compensations to the lifestyle of our family. But it was hard for him as a teenager faced with cruel comments.

I had to suffer another breakdown before I could find a satisfactory resolution to the tensions which flowed from my failure to draw a clearer line between the personal and the political.

The following nightmare which I had one night in March 1990 was a mirror of my state of mind: I dreamt that I had been walking through a farming district in some unknown rural area in South Africa. As I passed a homestead, a pack of vicious dogs charged me. I tried to run, but they closed in, pinning me against a thornbush fence. I resigned myself to being killed. Just before the dogs could maul me, an old woman came to my rescue. She was half person and half donkey. She asked me to get onto her back and then carried me to safety by leaping over the thorn fence. She vanished as mysteriously as she had appeared.

I told Carol Abramowitz, a psychologist friend, about this nightmare the next morning. Being a practising Jungian, she smiled knowingly, but in her wisdom did not delve into the meaning of this dream at that stage.

I had woken up that morning in bad shape. I had a splitting headache which was found to be due to high blood pressure – a new development signalling the level of tension within me. I was also very weepy and saw nothing bright in the world. Something was horribly wrong. I spent the next few days resting in bed with little sign of improvement.

Eventually I went to see Father Ted King, Dean Emeritus of St George's Cathedral, where he had served for more than three decades. I had been entrusted to Fr Ted for spiritual direction by Archbishop Tutu in 1989. Fr Ted was a gentle giant physically, intellectually and spiritually. As soon as I told him how I felt, he realised what the problem was. He had been working hard since 1989 to get me to see my role in the perspective of my history and the complexities of South Africa. There had been little evidence of success. I had too much excess baggage which I was not yet ready to relinquish. In a sense this crash had to come. I had to hit the real bottom of the existential valley before I could take stock.

He ministered to me and recommended that I go somewhere away from the pressures of my life and relax for a week or so. He armed me with C. S. Lewis's *The Lion, the Witch and the Wardrobe*, and reminded me with a touch of his dry sense of humour that St Paul had counselled that a bit of wine was good for the stomach. Thanks to the generosity of the Browne family I got free access to Watersedge, their holiday house on Seaforth Beach near Simon's Town, to which I retreated that afternoon.

I stood on the stoep of Watersedge and took in the views of False Bay and the gentle sound of the waves. The tide was low, but slowly coming in. The salty smell of the sea was comforting. The sounds of the seagulls frolicking around were the only interruptions to the quietness which pervaded the atmosphere. I marvelled at the sea with its endless energy and a rhythm of its own. It was very comforting.

My first evening alone at Watersedge was tearful but peaceful. I was in bed at eight and read a few pages from C. S. Lewis's wonderful story, which I found absorbing in a strange way. I fell asleep to the sound of the waves, by then splashing quite hard against the bottom of the stoep, creating a soothing, rhythmic lullaby.

The next day I went for long walks along the sea past the Boulders towards the southern edge of Simon's Town. It was so restful to just be, without having to speak to a soul apart from greeting the occasional passer-by. I felt completely at ease on my own.

I realised that I was in the grip of a serious metaphorical postnatal depression. Had all the energy I put into the struggle been worth it? What if post-apartheid South Africa turned into a big disaster with violent conflict between the various contenders for power? I could not see myself living in such a society. I had invested too much physical and emotional energy in this society to countenance the possibility of a negative outcome of the liberation struggle. But what would I do if the worst came to the worst?

I spent ten days at Watersedge on my own, walking, sleeping, reading and reflecting. I could not see a way out of the historical trap in which I found myself. C S. Lewis's story of the children playing in the wardrobe and landing up in a fantasy world was a helpful distraction from the feeling that South Africa was heading for impending doom. The story also had important symbolic messages for me. Like those children, I was also caught in a fantasy world with real and imagined problems. I had to find a way of making sense of my life in the unfolding historical drama.

A visit by Hlumelo and Malusi during my first weekend brought more sadness and tears. Anxiety was written all over their little faces. There was a great emptiness inside me, which made it difficult to nurture even my own children. It was too painful a situation to bear. It was as if I had given away their entitlement as dependent children, and now had to send them away empty. I had nothing to offer them emotionally. What pain they must suffer with a mother like me: a single parent, career woman, an idealist given to running out of energy and collapsing in a heap, sometimes in the most inconvenient of times and places.

I went to the Kalk Bay Anglican church that Sunday. I was moved by the simplicity and warmth of the parish Eucharist. I shed more tears – bitter-sweet ones this time. If only I could have the space to lead a simple life! History had unfortunately shaped a different pathway for me.

That Sunday evening I felt a little stronger. I stood on the stoep of Watersedge and watched the waves again. They had an inner energy and logic which no human being could alter. Their rhythm derived from a force beyond anyone's control. Who was I to think that I could change the course of history through sheer determination? Why should I think that my shoulders could hold up the sky above South Africa? The lesson of the waves was slowly sinking in, and having a therapeutic effect on my depression.

H. A. Williams, a theologian, once wrote some particularly apt words to capture this crisis: 'That is the agony, both as pain and the Greek agon, which people of the deepest vision have to endure in order to find life and to give it. If my devils are to leave me, I am afraid my angels will take flight as well.'[33] My angels had taken flight as I struggled to make sense of my role in the emerging 'new South Africa' and of my response to the euphoria which gripped South Africa after the release of Nelson Mandela. 1 went back home frail, but a little wiser.

---

33 H.A. Williams, *The Simplicity of Prayer* (London, 1976), p. 38.

Smelling the flowers

TRAVELLING HAS A BENEFICIAL EFFECT ON ME. WHENEVER I am under enormous pressure I seem to benefit from stepping aside to get a better view of my country and my own role in it. Shortly after my Simon's Town sojourn I fortunately had some overseas visits scheduled which enabled me to retreat further from the activism I was involved in.

I had a trip planned for April 1990 to Bermuda for an Aspen Institute seminar, which was part of Senator Dick Clarke's programme to educate American legislators on foreign policy questions. About twenty congressmen and one congresswoman, senators and their spouses, as well as a few foreign politicians, were brought together in a luxurious setting to be 'exposed to a variety of opinions from South Africa presented by participants from all the liberation movements, Inkatha, the South African government and parliamentary opposition parties'.

I took it as an extension of my time out from the intensity of my life, and really enjoyed the luxury and relaxed atmosphere. Bermuda was spectacular in its beauty. The houses were all painted white, each with a water tank to catch rainwater, which was a scarce resource and the only source of drinking water. The place was clean, and great care was taken to service the tourist industry, a major contributor to the country's economy.

The trip also provided an opportunity to meet fellow South Africans. Cyril Ramaphosa, then ANC Secretary-General and Chairman of the

Constitutional Assembly in the new South African parliament, had been a passing acquaintance until then. I got to glimpse the person behind the tough mineworkers' champion. He was a very private person. I was tempted to stereotype him, for this deep privacy is common among the people from his area of origin, Venda. I remember how some of the children I grew up with in that area would deny any knowledge of the whereabouts of their parents, fully aware that they were in one of the huts in their homestead. 'Thidebe' (I don't know) was their first response to any question: an appropriate survival tactic in an uncertain world. Such a culture with its reverence for privacy must have had an impact on a person like Cyril Ramaphosa.

Colin Eglin also became more than just a public figure to me. A witty man, who was the strategist of the Democratic Party, he was also a typical South African male and became agitated by my frequent reminders to all and sundry that political transformation had to address gender inequalities seriously. He remarked that I sounded like a scratched record. I reminded him that the references to racism by South African politicians sounded equally repetitive, but were tolerated because they were seen as mainstream concerns by most opinion-formers, who were threatened by a gender analysis.

I also had the privilege to get to know Dikgang Moseneke, spokesperson for the Pan Africanist Congress (PAC), who went on to become Deputy Chief Justice in 2005. He was a charming, sophisticated person who had a hard time coping with my teasing about the PAC's 'One settler, one bullet' slogan. In fairness to him, though, he must have been struggling with the hardliners within his organisation, who were not yet willing to let go of the slogan. His resignation in November 1992, in the wake of the PAC's intensified terror campaign targeting white people, came as no surprise to those who knew and respected him.

Koos van der Merwe was by far the most remarkable of all the participants. He did not seem to doubt the righteousness of his cause. He put up an impressive performance defending the Conservative Party (CP) line, and invited all South African participants who disagreed with him for a meal back home to talk matters over: Neville Alexander of the Workers' Organisation for a Socialist Azania (WOSA) and Franklin Sonn, then Rector of the Peninsula Technikon, and later South African Ambassador to the United States of America, were among the first to be invited. Koos also staged a well-orchestrated political show at a local cemetery where Boer prisoners from the Anglo-Boer War were buried. He was armed with a video camera to record the ritual of his standing to attention, hat on chest, in deference to the departed Afrikaner heroes. I was even more amused when I heard him comment on Mr Ferdie Hartzenberg, a CP leader with whom he had differences that were to lead to his resignation from the CP: 'Hy is so verkramp, jy weet, jy kan met hom ploeg!' (He is so conservative, you know, that you can literally plough with him).

Bermuda was the best possible setting for me to stop taking my country and myself too seriously. I arrived back home after ten days feeling much better. It was fortunate that my long-standing invitation to visit Australia as a guest of the government of that country was scheduled for about the same period. I requested that it be postponed from April to May to enable me to catch up with my children before setting off again.

The Australian trip advanced my healing process. My old friend Bruce Haigh was my tour director. Bruce met me in Perth after the long flight from South Africa and immediately took charge of all arrangements for my comfort. It was bliss. Bruce is a nurturer by nature and had been a great source of support for me during the most difficult time of my life during my banishment to Lenyenye. I relaxed and enjoyed myself.

The programme was organised to suit my needs and interests. I met a number of academics from universities in various cities: Perth, Adelaide, Melbourne, Canberra and Sydney. I also visited interesting community and health projects in various parts of the country, including

Alice Springs. I must confess that I was disappointed in the approach some Aboriginal leaders adopted to development for their people. Understandably, most of them had no faith in integrationist approaches, given the disastrous consequences of forced integration in the past. It was logical that they should have a consciousness-raising campaign to ensure that Aboriginal people developed self-respect and valued their own culture. However, it was difficult to see how they could successfully pursue a 'homeland' strategy, as some of them advocated. Indeed, some of the leaders had difficulty understanding why South African blacks were clamouring for the dismantling of homelands.

I was also dismayed to see the level of dehumanisation, alcohol abuse and violence which plagued Aboriginals in most areas, particularly in Alice Springs. The sight of groups of extended family members gathered under a tree with a five-litre box of wine was a common one. The level of interpersonal violence among Aboriginals was also a major concern to me. The approach of the Australian government to redress by providing free housing and welfare cheques to all needy Aboriginals seemed to have exacerbated the feeling of worthlessness and dependency among most of them.

I also met some charming Aboriginal people. In Melbourne, there was an Aboriginal health centre run by a dynamic woman who prohibited any smoking or littering on the premises. It stood in sharp relief to other Aboriginal health centres I had visited. Her approach was that you had to set high standards of good behaviour, because people either rise or fail to meet expectations society has of them. Those treated like boys, behave like boys, as the missionary doctor Anthony Barker once observed in the South African context. There were also wonderful young women in Alice Springs who were going about the business of development. They were thrilled by my observations about male dominance in their community leadership system. I remarked that it reminded me very much of my own country. The women do most of the grassroots organisational work and carry the administrative burden, yet have a limited part in decision-making and negotiating with the federal and regional governments.

(I cannot do justice here to the complexities of the problems facing indigenous minorities globally. But I can note the dangers posed by the combination of guilt and deep-seated lack of respect shown by the white colonial authorities, and the role of victim adopted by the colonised. Coupled with this role is a glorification of indigenous culture which poses the greatest threat to the ability of indigenous people to transform their social relations. Modernity is a reality they cannot wish away, but engaging it creatively requires a critical appraisal of indigenous culture, and the retention of the good as well as the jettisoning of the bad.)

The Australian landscape is extraordinarily varied and beautiful. It provided the nourishment of the spirit which I sorely needed. The coastal areas with their lush vegetation and rivers are given stiff competition by the vast and rugged central desert. It was in Alice Springs that I saw a double rainbow for the first time in my life. It was here that I also woke up to the sense of depth and distance represented by the different hues of mountains and hills, which I was convinced was a particular feature of Australia. Bruce Haigh was amazed that I could have been unaware of this, coming as I did from a country like South Africa, which had many similarities to Australia. What kind of life was I leading that could have made me so blind to my own environment? This was a further indication of a lifestyle in serious need of balancing.

Sydney, my last port of call, was the highlight of my trip. It was a beautiful coastal city which had taken full advantage of its setting. The old harbour had an imaginative waterfront development with wonderful restaurants situated in refurbished old warehouses. Boat rides to neighbouring coastal settlements provided spectacular views and relaxed entertainment. The famous Sydney Opera House graced the evening landscape.

We had a dinner party on the penultimate night of my visit in the old part of Sydney with its handsome Victorian and Georgian houses. What a pleasant environment to be in. I met some of the 1960s Australian activists who were all professional people, probably struggling with the same kind of tensions I had to deal with myself. We danced the night away – my first real dancing party since I left Lenyenye in 1984. It was wonderful to do the bump-jive and other energetic dances again.

I was sad to leave, but it was time. I spent most of the first part of the trip home gazing out through the window at the country below us. I felt ambivalent about going home. But I knew then that if I wanted, I could uproot myself from South Africa and live elsewhere. I was free at last to explore a lifestyle beyond the 'bounds of possibility' which I had imposed upon myself.

It is symbolically significant that like many women caught in a dilemma, I too have suffered depression. As Terri Apter so aptly noted, 'it is the very sensitivity of women to other people's needs that is likely to produce the appearance and the consequences of mental instability – women's instability stabilizes the world'.[34] But unlike most women, my depression was occasioned by too close a merger between the personal and the political. My 'instability' was a reflection of my oversensitivity to the dangers I felt lay in store for the future of the society I lived in and loved so passionately.

The relationships which developed among activists were both supportive and stifling. Finding a healthy balance in such relationships was a major challenge. It was a lifelong quest. I had taken heed of the injunction of St Bernard of Clairvaux to a new pope: 'You too are a man [I assume my exclusion is not deliberate]. So then in order that your humanity may be entire and complete, let your bosom, which receives

---

34 Terri Apter, *Why Women Don't Have Wives* (Basingstoke, 1993), p. 203.

all, find room for yourself also. So remember to restore yourself to yourself.' As an ordinary mortal I had an even greater need to 'restore myself to myself'. There was no other option for the sake of my sanity. I had to stop more frequently and smell the flowers.

The pain of loss

IN THE WHOLE PROCESS OF ESTABLISHING MY PERSONAL boundaries I also had to negotiate greater independence from my close-knit family. This was relatively easier than the struggle at a national level. My family had been supportive of me through all the pains and joys, as well as the triumphs and failures. But the process was marred by many personal sorrows. There were many times when I felt that I dealt with more losses than most people.

A big scratch to the scars left by previous bereavement was the sudden death of Morongwa, my elder sister's daughter, in April 1991, on the operating table at Baragwanath Hospital. This occurred during a routine operation to clean out her womb after a miscarriage. No one has yet explained the cause nor was an inquest held into her death.

The loss suffered by her young husband, their daughter Mamphela, then only four years old, and my sister, who relied so heavily on her, was indescribable. For me it was like losing a second daughter. She had been under my care for seven of the eight years I spent in Lenyenye while she and my mother were living with me.

Morongwa's smiling face, her energy and sheer love of life were her strong features. I was shocked by her death but also angry that she should die in circumstances which suggested negligence on the part of her caregivers. I flew to Johannesburg the next day and dealt with the pain of the loss by immersing myself in practical arrangements for the funeral.

I spent many fruitless months afterwards asking for a definitive statement of the cause of her death from the hospital. Nothing was forthcoming. All we had was an emptiness where her life had been. More
was to come.

The next one was Sethiba, my 43-year-old brother. At his funeral
Dominee Maphoto's opening prayer in the Westernberg Dutch Reformed
Church on a morning in June 1993 said it all: 'Lord, you have reaped
when the field was still green, before the corn was ripe.' This admon-
ishment of the Lord was an attempt to communicate the overwhelming
feeling of disappointment at the turn of events. It was difficult to come
to terms with the death of someone so young and energetic and with
as bright a future as Sethiba's. His wife, Mamakiri, and his four-year-
old son Letladi attached an even greater meaning to the words of this
prayer. Their lives' plans lay in ruins in the wake of this untimely death.

Sethiba's life had all the features of a middle child. His childhood was
uneventful except for his remarkable physical strength: he was capable
of both delivering devastating blows to bully boys, and wrecking my
father's tools, which earned him many a spanking. He was always interested in things mechanical and tried to understand how they worked.

He was unfortunate in being taken to my paternal grandparents at
the age of twelve to help the ageing couple look after their livestock. It
was a cruel decision by my father who, like many of his contemporaries,
viewed children as part of their possessions with no independent voice.
The decision did not enjoy my mother's support, but women at the
time were given little choice in such matters – the children belonged
to their fathers. My grandparents were not nurturers by any stretch of
the imagination. My father's younger brother added insult to injury
when he and his wife made Sethiba feel unwanted and unloved. His
pain must have been immense then, but as a child he was not given a
hearing, and my mother's pleadings for him to come back to the family
home fell on deaf ears.

It was only after my father's death that my mother brought him back and sent him to Setotolwane High School to finish his Standard 8 and to commence matriculation. Tragically, because of financial problems my mother was unable to pay the fees for both Sethiba and Phoshiwa, his younger brother. The burden of sacrifice fell again on Sethiba. He was forced to leave school, and subsequently registered at a technical college. After qualifying he began an unsuccessful struggle to find a job as an apprentice.

My mother's brother, Malesela, on whom she relied heavily for support, offered to help. Sethiba moved to Sibasa to live with my uncle, and he was set up as a self-employed all-purpose car mechanic. He became proficient, and attracted a lot of business. Sadly, my uncle let him down by not managing the finances properly. Even though Sethiba worked hard, he had little money to show for it.

I was not surprised when he started suffering from what sounded like migraine headaches. The traditional healers interpreted these as signs that he was experiencing a 'call' to become a healer himself. I was unhappy about this turn of events, convinced that Sethiba was showing the strains of the many burdens which fate had forced him to carry in his youth. His abandonment by his own parents to the uncaring custody of our paternal grandparents, the disappointment of having to leave an academic school career and later his exploitation by an uncle who was supposed to help him establish himself as a tradesman, were all too much for one young person to bear, however resilient he may have been.

I took advantage of our meeting at my grandmother's funeral in 1975 to discuss my concerns with him, and offered to send him back to school. He was well prepared to rebuff me. He said his ancestors had warned him that as a medical doctor I would attempt to dissuade him from his chosen path, but he should and would resist. We parted on an understanding that should he change his mind, my offer stood.

It was with great joy in January 1977, when I visited my mother in Maupje after my release from detention, that I found him at home. He admitted that he had come to the end of the road with both my uncle and his unsuccessful struggle to find a job elsewhere. We agreed that he would do an instructor's course at the technical college in Mafikeng in 1978. It was a privilege to finance his education: his was an uncomplaining, gentle and hard-working nature.

His teaching career started in 1981 at the technical college in Hammanskraal, where he met his wife, Mamakiri Moleba. It was with pride that I arranged his wedding from my house in Lenyenye. Sethiba was promoted to the headship of a division at Shikoane-Matlala Technikon in Pietersburg in February 1992. He commanded respect as a meticulous worker, an excellent teacher, an active Christian, and a loving husband and father. Among my brothers and sisters he was an anchor for all of us.

It was with shock that I learned that he had alveolar cell cancer of the lung, which was likely to be rapidly fatal. I had just returned home from a trip to Pietersburg to see him, when I received the news from my sister Mashadi. He had been unwell for a number of months but in his usual uncomplaining way he had brushed aside my concern at the length of the illness.

I suspected that the shock of the diagnosis had contributed to Sethiba's rapid deterioration and death. He was, however, true to form to the very last. He spent most of his last day, just hours before his death, with his wife helping her get to grips with life without him. He even planned his own funeral programme, emphasising the least amount of fuss. His greatest regret was leaving his four-year-old-son, Letladi, who was particularly attached to him.

Coping with such a loss was extremely difficult. It was harder for his wife and son. They were recovering from the loss of their daughter and sister, Matlala, who had died in August 1992 of brain damage occa-

sioned by pneumococcal meningitis. The meningitis she had contracted at the age of two months reduced the beautiful, lively child to a
floppy sad shadow. It was not inconceivable that the stress of Matlala's
illness and death may be linked to Sethiba's own illness and death.
After all, his was a rare cancer, seen mainly in elderly people. Stress is
suspected by many analysts to be a factor in the loss of the body's capacity to deal effectively with potential cancer cells.

Each loss had its own individual meaning, but also invoked the mean-
ings of past sorrows. Wounds inflicted by these sorrows started to bleed
again after each new one. The resilience which enabled me to accept
the loss and to give up clinging to what was irretrievably gone was
diminished by each additional loss. Nevertheless, the finality of death,
which made physical clinging impossible, forced me to accept that the
lost object of my love was irretrievable. It was not as if I had an opportunity to negotiate the terms of the loss. I was presented with a *fait
accompli*.

In all this my mother was a tower of strength for all of us. She remained active and maintained her sense of humour up to her death in
2008. She had borne much pain in her life but also known much joy.

Stretching across boundaries

AN IMPORTANT PART OF ANY PROCESS OF TRANSFORMATION has to be the transgression of social boundaries. Those boundaries might once have made sense but they stand in the way of creative responses to a changing environment. South Africa had many transgressives who had brought the country to its current historical position: all those who had died in the struggle for liberation, those who had been involved in negotiations at various levels, whether constitutional or socioeconomic, and the many unsung heroes and heroines who continued to lead lives which stabilised society. But it was fair to say that Nelson Mandela was by far the most important transgressive at the time of the South African transition. Without his willingness to talk to his gaolers at a time when doing so was tantamount to mixing the profane with the sacred, our history would have been very different.

I was fortunate to have spent time with this remarkable man. I first visited him at his invitation when he was still in prison. This was too crucial an appointment to miss, so I took no chances. I set the clock for 6 a.m, to make sure that I would be on time for my 7.30 appointment. As I drove along the highway towards Pollsmoor on Sunday morning, 31 July 1988, I could hardly contain my excitement. Many questions raced through my mind. How was I to respond to this living legend? What kind of person was he? Why was he interested in meeting me at this stage? I had to wait to find out.

I was at the gate by seven o'clock. I was shown into a living room by a friendly looking warder, who sat down at a makeshift desk at the entrance of the room. Soon Mr Mandela's tall, trim, well-built frame, oozing authority and grace, appeared. His face had a softness and gentleness enhanced by his beaming smile. He was wearing an immaculately clean prison outfit – a long-sleeved khaki shirt, gabardine pants and spotless boots.

His sensitivity to others shone through in every encounter he had with people. The mark of greatness in people often manifests itself in the respect with which they treat others irrespective of social status. Mr Mandela's respect for his captors as human beings was also obvious in the manner in which he acknowledged the warder at the door and requested him to warn him in case we overstepped our time limit. This respect was in turn rewarded in most cases by the deference which they showed him, and which became more obvious to me during my visits to him between 1988 and 1990.

On my first visit, Mr Mandela's major focus was on establishing a relationship of trust between us. He chose to greet me in Sesotho, my mother tongue, Dumela Kgaetsedi yaka (Hello, my sister), to signify his wish to engage the human being in me. His great social skills were in evidence at every turn. He put me at ease without patronising me. He could see that I was in awe of him.

Our conversation centred on trivia but was peppered with penetrating questions which indicated his curiosity about the real Mamphela. He enquired about my career aspirations, my hobbies, the books I was interested in, and the well-being of my children. I was amazed at how well informed he was about events in the country, people in different walks of life in our society, international politics, and the world of arts and music. There was hardly a book published over the last few years that he had not read or heard about. I was in the presence of a giant.

Just before we parted he urged me to ensure that the history of the Black Consciousness Movement was properly documented, and that the place of Steve Biko was properly delineated. He said earnestly: 'Steve Biko must take his rightful place in the history of the liberation movement in South Africa. He has made an enormous contribution. We must not allow that to be forgotten.' I made a promise to him which I kept. The publication in 1991 of *Bounds of Possibility: The Legacy of Steve Biko and Black Consciousness* was testimony to that.

Writing the book was itself part of the process of healing. I had to record that part of my history as objectively as I could. The participation of former fellow activists in the project, particularly Barney Pityana and Malusi Mpumlwana, made it more meaningful as a collective process of healing. But like all collaborative projects, it took time and energy to keep it on course. Barney's methodical approach helped a great deal in facilitating the completion of the book.

There was also pain involved in the project. The Azanian People's Organisation (AZAPO) regarded themselves as the custodians of Steve Biko's legacy and publicly opposed this project. They asserted that we, who were not members of AZAPO, had no right to record and reflect on that history. They put pressure on people such as Harry Nengwe-khulu, who had agreed to contribute a paper and attend a seminar in Harare where draft chapters were discussed, to withdraw. It was to me a sad reflection of a failure to grow beyond parochial boundaries. Steve was larger than any one organisation – his life was dedicated to the struggle for liberation of the whole person, which included the freedom from being constrained by ideological or organisational straitjackets. It could in fact be argued that AZAPO's parochialism had done a disservice to Steve's vision of society and his memory as an important player in the liberation struggle. By claiming sole ownership of this man, they had made it difficult for others to acknowledge his contribution to the struggle. Those of us who were determined to let Steve take his place in history refused to be deterred.

Subsequent visits to Mr Mandela between 1989 and 1990 were made under very different circumstances. His accommodation at Victor Verster Prison in Paarl was luxurious by any prison standard. Major Gregory, his personal warder, was gracious and made sure I felt at home during the visits. Gone was the prison garb. Mr Mandela wore smart casual clothes with soft slippers to ease his swollen ankles – the aftermath of many years of hard labour in the cold Robben Island climate. He sat in an easy chair with his feet elevated on a stool. I got to know a little bit more about the person behind Mandela the symbol.

On one visit in December 1989, Hlumelo and Malusi accompanied me at his insistence. He took time to engage them around their own interests – tennis in the case of Hlumelo, and starting school and favourite TV programmes in the case of Malusi. It was the closest my sons have ever been to relating to a grandfather. They liked him enormously and valued his interest in them as persons. Their respect for him grew over the years as he continued to take an interest in their development.

With each subsequent visit, our discussions moved from the initial polite trivia to important issues confronting our society. We found great areas of agreement, but also agreed to disagree about a few questions of strategy. One question related to the role of traditional leaders in a democratic society. The first time I broached the subject I could see that he was deeply troubled. I asked him how the ANC reconciled its espousal of democracy and its commitment to non-sexism with the resuscitation of the Congress of Traditional Leaders of South Africa (Contralesa). Traditional leadership by its very nature was hereditary and left little scope for the democratic election of leaders. Male dominance was an ethos deeply embedded within African traditional authority structures. Mr Mandela's face darkened. He sat up in a regal posture, and said: 'The issue you have raised is too complex to be dealt with cold in the short space of time we have available during this visit. We have to defer it for discussion during the next visit.' I could see that he was troubled.

Two weeks later when I arrived, he went straight to the heart of the matter. He acknowledged that he had been upset by my raising the difficult issue of traditional leadership, but also that he had not until then reflected on the contradictions I had pointed out. He took his time to explain the complexities of mass political mobilisation in a country where traditional leadership was part of the political and social land-scape. Mobilising people entailed taking them from where they were, and that might be an uncomfortable place for their sensibilities, to where you would like them to be. The ANC also had to face the challenge posed by the National Party government's continued use of traditional leaders for the perpetuation of apartheid. The resuscitation of Contralesa was part of the ANC's strategy to bring traditional leaders into the fold of liberation politics. I could fully understand the logic of his approach but pointed out the long-term costs of such a strategy.

I have over the years noticed the extent to which Mr Mandela has taken gender equity seriously. It was one of the issues he highlighted in his inaugural address in May 1994 as the first democratically elected President of South Africa. He acknowledged the difficulties of changing the male-dominated culture of South Africa, but insisted that everyone had to learn to live up to the commitment to gender equity – 'starting with the President'. Listening to that made me glow with pride and admiration. I felt privileged to have shared more than just a casual acquaintance with this remarkable man. Our friendship continued to grow.

Mr Mandela made the task of lowering boundaries in our divided society much easier. This involved both stretching across well-established boundaries and transgressing them. Transgression also brought with it the danger of incurring the disapproval or rejection of people – your own camp – who might be harmed by the breaking of taboos. It was a risky enterprise, but it was driven by such compelling historical im-peratives that I was privileged to be part of the process.

My transgressive activities were focused on one central goal: transforming the major institutions of our society. Unlike many post-colonial societies in Africa, South Africa had a viable and extensive infrastructure: transport and communications, finance and banking, tertiary education, science and technology, and so forth. The major problem area was the development of human resources, which had been sacrificed on the altar of racial bigotry. The major task ahead of us in South Africa was making human development the centre of a process of reconstruction which would create a better fit between the infrastructure and the people it was intended to serve. Such a better fit would enhance the infrastructural base and make it more effective and efficient.

My areas of engagement were those shaped by my competencies: higher education, social policy, and uprooting poverty. My training as a doctor and anthropologist enabled me to stretch across the boundaries between natural or medical science and social science in interesting ways.

The danger of medical doctors being treated as, and behaving like, demigods has been the subject of many analyses, particularly by medical anthropologists. But the mystique has lived on because it serves an important psycho-social function related to the ultimate vulnerability of human beings – the fear of our own mortality. However, in my own case it was also fair to acknowledge the enormous psychological advantages which a doctor derived from being a member of a powerful, respected profession. It gave you enormous self-confidence, overconfidence in many cases. It was the ultimate proof of the expectations others had of your influence and how it shaped your own expectations.

My membership of this powerful club has stood me in good stead throughout my life. I had no idea how right my young instincts were in choosing a medical career. Security police in both King Williamstown and Tzaneen, conservative farmers and traders in Tzaneen, strangers everywhere, all changed their response to me because of my profession. They could easily dismiss me as a black person, a woman, but not as a medical doctor. This was strategically important, and remained so in my subsequent engagements.

My anthropological training had given me insights into my own behaviour as a member of a complex society, and tools for ongoing exploration. I could stand back as a participant observer in the many complex settings I found myself, and try to learn from the social dynamics I saw around me. The capacity to switch roles, and become a visiting anthropologist, was essential for my survival in some of the conflict-ridden settings in which I often found myself. There were often people with such differences in outlook that it did not pay to argue with them. Listening with empathy became a valuable step before taking decisions about the need for, and the nature of, further interaction.

I stopped practising medicine in 1988 when I went to the Bunting Institute at Radcliffe College. I returned to my part-time work at Guguletu Hospital towards the end of 1989, but after a few sessions it became clear that it was time to move on from the clinical practice of medicine. I found the endless problems of diseases of poverty exhausting. But even more distressing was the regular appearance of sexually abused children. I could not cope with my impotence in the face of such symptoms of social disintegration. I felt that I could perhaps make a better contribution by involving myself more actively in shaping creative social policies which would provide a safer environment for children. It was the right decision to make at the time. I do not miss medical practice at all.

Chapter 26

In my wildest dreams

I COULDN'T IMAGINE BEING IN A BETTER INSTITUTE OF HIGHER education in South Africa than the University of Cape Town. Its physical setting made it tower above its surroundings – an interesting symbolic statement which even Cecil John Rhodes, who had bequeathed the land, could not fully have comprehended. It also had a solid infrastructure which put it in a good position to make a significant contribution to higher education not only in South Africa but in the entire continent. It fulfilled the criterion I have alluded to, being one of the major institutions in our society which I believed needed to be harnessed for the better service of humanity. Without a vibrant higher education system capable of producing the best in high-level human resources, the development of South Africa in the context of the competitive, technologically based global economy would be at risk.

Even in my wildest dreams I did not, however, ever imagine myself as an executive officer at UCT. Not because I did not think that I had the ability to play such a role, but because after settling into my new-found position as a social science researcher, I was content. I enjoyed the space to read, reflect, write and interact with colleagues across disciplines, both nationally and internationally. What more did I need? The little I had seen and heard about the lifestyle of UCT executives and the demands on them was enough to make me believe that you would have to be self-sacrificial to accept such a job.

In the second half of 1990 I had surfaced from the depression. I was

270

enjoying my research projects and I had started a programme with young people which I found deeply rewarding. As far as I was concerned my professional life was rewarding and fulfilling.

To add to this sense of purpose I would go on three- or four-day retreats every six months at a Roman Catholic convent in Rondebosch. Father Ted King who had pulled me through the depression was my retreat conductor during these quiet periods. I was very strict about these retreats and not even my sons were allowed to disturb me.

I was on one of these retreats when the vice-chancellor, Dr Stuart Saunders, phoned. He had been trying to persuade me to join the university executive, and equally I had tried to emphasise to him that my job was to write and reflect on how the country would come to terms with its realities. But Dr Saunders kept on pushing and pushing. Eventually he said he would take the matter to council and if they agreed he could then make me an offer. I let the matter rest there and pushed it to the back of my mind. This was a Tuesday, and for the next few days I would be on my half-yearly retreat. Two days later he telephoned my Mowbray home and Hlumelo answered. He told the vice-chancellor that when I was on retreat not even they were allowed to disturb me. But again Dr Saunders would not take no for an answer. He told Hlumelo it was urgent and important and under this pressure Hlumelo relented and gave him the telephone number.

Dr Saunders must have hung up and immediately phoned the convent. A sister summoned me to the phone, and I went to take the call with all sorts of troubling scenarios racing through my mind: had something happened to my children? I answered tentatively and heard Dr Saunders's distinctive voice. 'Mamfele' – that was what he called me – 'Mamfele, I'm sorry to disturb you and I apologise for twisting your son's arm to get your phone number but council has offered you a position on the university administration as a deputy vice-chancellor.' I was flattered and thanked him, and said I would need to reflect on the offer.

Being a deputy vice-chancellor was not a position I wanted. The reason was not because I felt I was incapable of doing the job but because I was enjoying my research work and did not want a high-profile position. Why would I give up my rewarding research to be a part of a university's administration at a time when it was a site of contention? Universities were facing all the unresolved issues of how to transform a higher education system which was deeply embedded in a divided society. I did not want to be part of shaping that particular transformation. I had other projects in mind.

But Dr Saunders had persuasive powers and so did many people I respected who had heard about the approach. Immediately after I had put the phone down on that Thursday afternoon in the convent I sought out Father Ted King. I laid out my problem while he listened thoughtfully. Father Ted King was a deeply spiritual man and maybe because of this he was also a practical man. To realise matters of the spirit you have to be able to act, you have to be able to formulate a plan. I remember he said to me that I would know inside what was the right thing to do. 'You can make a good contribution by taking this position,' he said, adding, 'Whatever you decide, you will make a contribution to this country anyhow.'

After the retreat I discussed the matter with Hlumelo, who was then a teenager and for many matters a useful confidant. His reaction was a version of Ted King's: if I thought it was the right thing then I should accept. Over the coming days I talked to other friends and mentors and they all said more or less the same thing: the university had been exceptionally well managed by Dr Saunders but there were blind spots, and only someone with my background could recognise and attend to those matters. Like so many decisions in my life, I let it percolate until the resolution was not a Damascus moment but a gradual acceptance of what was being asked of me. This new development also required a realigning of my personal projects. Up to this point I had set the Cape

Flats as my site of transformation; now I changed this to the University of Cape Town.

I duly called Dr Saunders and asked to see him. We met in his wood-panelled office on campus and over a cup of tea I told him I would accept the position, but that I had conditions. I told him that my biggest obstacle in arriving at this decision was my dislike of public office. If I was to be a deputy vice-chancellor then I would have to act in a way that did not violate my integrity. I would not be a razzmatazz cheerleader (although, ironically, I ended up in this position when it came to motivating students and staff). I told him, too, that transformation would be a disruptive process. Often we would have to take positions that went against the grain. We had already experienced some of this.

Some months previously I had been asked to chair a committee that examined instances of sexual harassment and race issues on campus. The sexual harassment cases – often these were instances of rape – had met with a tough response from the university authorities. I had argued that it did not matter how poor a young man was or how bright his future might be, if he raped or harassed a woman he had to leave the university. I saw the issue clearly. Rape and sexual harassment were unacceptable. Men who violated fundamental decencies had to leave. Dr Saunders supported me in this, and the tyranny that young women had been subjected to stopped. For me, the way these young men were acting was symptomatic of a deeper problem, and it was this deeper problem that the university needed to address. Hence my caution that transformation would be disruptive. 'Ja, Mamfele,' replied Dr Saunders, 'it will be good for the university to go through an orderly transformation.' He well knew that change was coming and he believed that if it could be framed rather than randomly dealt with, the university would be a better place. This was prescient of him. I believe he was truly visionary in this attitude. At the end of our meeting I said if this was his conviction, I would be willing to serve on the university's executive.

But there was a further condition to be negotiated. I was not ready to give up my research, so I negotiated a fifty percent engagement. Dr Saunders accepted. Anyone with experience of executive jobs would have known better. There was no way I could do an executive job part time. It called for more than a full-time commitment. You might try to prevent this subsuming of your lifestyle but resistance was impossible. I had to learn this lesson the hard way. The part-time arrangement lasted only a few months. They felt like years. Doing a full-time executive job while still attempting to pursue my research was a recipe for burnout. I reluctantly decided that my research work had to be put on hold.

The naïve side of my nature had led me to believe that I could pick and choose aspects of this job which suited me and leave out the rest. It was perhaps true that unlike many of my colleagues, past and present, I had greater flexibility to shape my own job. As I was the first woman ever to occupy an executive position at UCT, there was clearly scope for flexibility. Similarly, as the first black person in this position, I could take certain liberties.

There is no doubt in my mind that Black Consciousness prepared me for this position. The BC philosophy had shaped my consciousness to the extent that I never felt threatened by white people. So, I might be sitting on a council that was totally white and predominantly male but I did not feel threatened or intimidated. I had decided that I would serve for three years and then bow out to return to my previous life. Of course, fate, destiny, call it what you will, had other directions in store for me.

Right now, though, my task as the executive officer in charge of the Equal Opportunity Portfolio presented me with both space for creativity and major challenges. UCT had until 1990 responded to its environment and its heritage, as part of apartheid South Africa, by changing aspects of its operation to become more open and accessible to blacks and women in South Africa. But it had not systematically set out to alter course radically. The emphasis of the leadership policies was on blacks gaining access to the UCT they had come to love and respect. Black advancement was the primary focus – a problematic approach, which implied that blacks were to be advanced by whites to where the latter already were.

The shape my portfolio took reflected my philosophical orientation, forged over the years, as well as my social analysis of the interrelationships between the various markers of power in society and my understanding of what was possible within the institutional framework of UCT. I placed emphasis on equity as the goal which should shape the vision of a transformed UCT. But equity could not only be seen in terms of blacks and whites, it had to include gender and class as important determinants of inequity in our society. It was also vital to ensure that whatever process of change my portfolio promoted should take cognisance of the realities which made UCT what it was and motivated those within it. People function at their best when they feel that their own interests are not being compromised and, if they are, that such compromises should be seen to hold long-term benefits for them.

My approach to equity was informed by the research carried out with my research colleague, Carla Sutherland, through the Equal Opportunity Research Project, which I established as part of my portfolio. The creation of greater equity in higher education, and indeed in all areas of our inequitable society, had to involve three thrusts: greater access, opportunities for personal development, and a change in institutional culture.

The criticism directed at me for joining UCT had died down by 1990 as more black South Africans realised the importance of academic work as real work, and the contribution it made to social policy and the general development of society. Nevertheless some people thought that my joining the UCT executive in 1991 was going too far. Was I not allowing myself to be used by white liberals, who had no intention of changing, but needed to protect themselves by having a token, high-profile black woman? 'They are using you,' said someone I respected, and who really cared for me. I was troubled by this perception, but remained convinced that my decision was the correct one.

I had no way of knowing the real motive behind Dr Saunders's invitation to join his executive team, but felt comfortable taking his motives at face value. If he was intending to use me, as some people said, then he would have a major problem on his hands. UCT would have changed with or without me. But I believe that the strategies for which my staff and I sought acceptance at UCT, and which I had the pleasure of seeing put into operation, had far-reaching consequences beyond UCT, and indeed helped shape the way South Africans tackled equity issues generally. The Equal Opportunity Research Project, through its outreach programme, played an important role in helping other institutions of higher learning, the private sector as well as nongovernmental organisations develop policies and programmes around issues of race and gender equity.

A major concern during my time as a deputy vice-chancellor focussed on the transformation meetings. Student politics wanted to emulate the negotiations that had occurred during Codesa and their transformation demands had to be heard and discussed. Invariably these meetings occurred over weekends and would last for an entire Saturday, sometimes running to twelve or thirteen hours. Occasionally we would be back on the Sunday morning to conclude. I think Dr Saunders had foreseen something of this nature occurring and wanted me to be available. Certainly, these discussions were intense and you needed to keep your wits about you. Even after the meetings I would sit at home pondering angles and tactics they would use to get their way. For me personally they were important meetings as they exposed me to the way students were thinking, and they allowed me to set boundaries. These boundaries were necessary because we could not have a situation where students had equal decision-making standing with academics and the university's administrative staff. I would make the point to them that they were transient whereas we were making decisions that would affect future generations of students. This was an important principle.

This pressure of multitasking various jobs and the physical demands on my body – as I've mentioned, I need eight hours' sleep a night and I often needed to catch up on sleep over the weekends – took a toll: unexpectedly I began getting migraine headaches. Migraines are debilitating headaches. I have known cases where people are incapacitated for days. Fortunately mine were of relatively short duration. My doctor had prescribed tablets and if I took these the moment I felt the telltale symptoms and slept for an hour, I could recover within a morning. Often I did not have the luxury of being able to sleep off the madness, especially during the transformation meetings. At one of those meetings I sat incapacitated and ill for the entire day at Dr Saunders's insistence as he felt I was uniquely able to respond to the students. Later I was prescribed a medicine which I could inject and it would return me to normal within thirty minutes. I recall once – during my time as vice-chancellor – waking with a migraine at 4 am, yet, sweating and feeling awful, I had to rush to the airport for a 6 am flight. In those days I did not have permission to have migraines or be ill.

Apart from those transformation meetings I had to set other boundaries with the students. One Friday afternoon the students marched on the administration offices in the Bremner building, intent on shutting down the university. They took over Professor Martin West's office and refused to let him leave until their demands were met. Dr Saunders phoned and asked me to try and remedy the situation. Unbeknown to the students, Professor West had been emailing status reports during the confrontation. At the time email was new and the students had no way of knowing he was sending messages; they thought he was working at his computer. Eventually Professor West was given permission to relieve himself and I met him in Dr Saunders's office. He informed us of the students' demands and my suggestion, together with other executives, was that we all go home and leave the campus security control to deal with the students. Dr Saunders and his colleagues were horrified at this suggestion as they felt it rude – such were the constraints of white liberal guilt! The students were well aware of this dynamic and certainly not averse to applying pressure where they saw an area of vulnerability. Of course my action did not endear me to the students, but they knew that I was right and that such aggressive methods were intolerable. These sorts of confrontations and my attitude towards rape and sexual harassment meant that I occupied contentious ground, but I saw my position as morally defensible and rational at a time when some universities elsewhere in the country were being far too accommodating.

Despite these occasional problems most of the aspects of my job were enjoyable. Unfortunately it was impossible to change all the things I found irritating and uncomfortable. And there was no escape from interminable committee meetings, appointments, and dealings with bureaucrats. These were all part and parcel of working with people anywhere in the world. But the only time I really felt uncomfortable and ill at ease, if not downright embarrassed, was the first occasion I had to wear the robes of office at an inaugural lecture. I had naïvely thought that I could elect to be part of the audience. It dawned on me later that in the same way that I enjoyed the pomp and ceremony of High Mass at St George's Cathedral, I too had to make academic rituals come alive for those participating in the life of the university.

I soon learnt to relax and see the funny side of donning robes designed for the cold weather of the Northern Hemisphere, and wearing hats which could only have been designed with men in mind. You do become willy-nilly an honorary man in these situations. The awkwardness of a woman in my position showed up more starkly in public ceremonies. At the first graduation ceremony I presided over in December 1993, the dean who was to present candidates to me for graduation had to establish how to address me. When he said he did not want to use a sexist form of address, I asked him how he would have addressed my male colleagues. 'Mr Acting Vice-Chancellor,' he stated confidently. 'Well,' I said, 'I am Madam Acting Vice-Chancellor!' You have to learn to laugh at yourself in order to remain sane.

Chapter 27

If you had all the cards on your side

ANOTHER IMPORTANT INSTITUTION IN THE TRANSFORMA-
tion of South Africa was the Independent Development Trust. I
was invited to sit on the board of the IDT in 1990 as one of its founding trustees and was appointed its third chairperson at the end of 1994.
The IDT was launched with R2 billion from the National Party government. Many people correctly pointed out that this was blood money.
But what money in South Africa or anywhere else in the world was
clean? Are the large American philanthropic foundations not the ben-
eficiaries of the bequests of robber barons of old? Of greater symbolic
significance was the Nobel Peace Prize, which derived its legacy from
a successful armaments industry.

In setting up the IDT, the South African government was for the first
time trying to acknowledge its responsibility for the poverty which it
and its predecessors had deliberately created among the majority of
South African citizens. The grant of R2 billion was one of the initia-
tives of a party trying to reform itself. I was initially hesitant to be part of
this initiative, for different reasons. I did not want to be overextended,
and having just emerged from a debilitating depression, I was not ready
to take on new commitments. But with the encouragement of Eric
Molobi, then executive director of Kagiso Trust, I agreed. Here was an
opportunity to implement a major development programme drawing
on my previous experience and social analysis. My past involvement
with development efforts had been at a local level; here was a chance of

engaging in meaningful macro-level work. More important, this time the problem of the job would not be about where the money came from, but how to spend the considerable resources judiciously.

But I had underestimated the scale and the nature of the problems. In spite of enormous energy and careful planning by the executive directors of the IDT, a key problem remained: how to create capacity among the poorest people to enable them to participate meaningfully in major development efforts. The IDT had set itself the task of promoting the development of the poorest people of South Africa, the victims of apartheid. It had four main areas of focus: housing, education, rural development, and health.

The capacity of poor people to engage effectively in the development process and to use substantial resources had been found to be extremely limited. The most devastating impact of apartheid on poor black South Africans was the destruction of people's faith in themselves as agents of history. Their life experiences were scarred by survival strategies which destroyed trust and faith in their fellow human beings. Moreover, their dealings with development agencies had in many cases merely reinforced their mistrust of systems and their fellow human beings. They had been taken advantage of for so long that they had become apathetic.

The writer Colin Turnbull could be accused of lack of empathy with his subjects in his book *The Mountain People*. And there might well be justification for this criticism. Unfortunately, some communities in South Africa showed patterns of behaviour which were not dissimilar to those Turnbull described in his book on an African community living on the edge of survival in the mountains between Uganda and Kenya.[35] Their desperate poverty had led to the development of extremely utilitarian behavioural patterns: parents were even prepared to abandon

---

35 C. Turnbull, *The Mountain People* (New York, 1972).

their children to ensure their own survival. Mistrust was the guiding principle in their human relations. This extreme poverty almost made them unreachable for development purposes.

Phola Park, a squatter camp on the East Rand, presented similar features. It had deteriorated from being a model of resilience and creative self-governance to a wasteland ravaged by war in which criminals and opposing political tendencies fought for control. Ironically it was their extreme need for development which made the people of Phola Park unreachable. Because of their focus on today's battles they had become losers in the war on poverty and the possibility of a future they could believe in. What made for good oppositional politics in the late 1980s constrained these people's ability to take a long-term view.

The IDT had to learn to negotiate directly with communities. It was a laborious task, but it had long-term benefits. Its annual reports told the story of an organisation that was an important model for sustainable development. The model was indigenous to South Africa but shaped by experiences in other countries. The IDT had chosen to work with community-based groups and nongovernmental organisations in relationships that were mutually empowering and promoted public accountability. It commissioned studies to explore alternative policy approaches to the problem areas in the country: education, housing and rural development. It forged partnerships with Kagiso Trust, the Development Bank of Southern Africa and the private sector, to maximise development resources. It also made many mistakes, but acknowledged them and hopefully learned from them.

It was through my involvement with the IDT that I came into contact with then President F W de Klerk. At the time the Codesa talks that would determine the future of the country had broken down. During this period violence flared in KwaZulu/Natal and in the townships on the Reef. It was a tense, awful period yet De Klerk chose this moment to appear on television with Chief Mangosuthu Buthelezi who had refused to participate in the talks. And the date De Klerk chose for this appearance was 16 June (1992), the sixteenth anniversary of the Soweto uprising. I was bitterly disappointed at the president's crass disregard for political sensitivities.

Distraught and angry, I voiced my anguish to Judge Jan Steyn, chief executive at the IDT. 'Phone him and tell him,' he said, and duly produced De Klerk's private number. I phoned. If De Klerk was taken aback by my call he hid it and was nothing but courteous, listening carefully to my point of view. I told him I was worried about the future of the country and the future of my children and I did not want to see this conflict undermining our future. When I'd finished he said, 'You know, Dr Ramphele, you may not understand but as a political leader whatever your own thoughts are and whatever your own way of doings things, you have a constituency that sometimes drags you into doing things that you may not think you should be doing if you had all the cards on your side.' That was all he said but it made a deep impression.

(As a coda I should add that since then we have remained on good terms and when I decided to establish Agang, I met with him to lay out my plans. I think of him as a man who did what he thought was the best he could under the circumstances.)

---◇◇◇---

Apart from my duties on the IDT and at the university, in the first half of the 1990s I became increasingly involved in the corporate world in South Africa. In South African political parlance, the corporate world sat at the extreme end of the profane. The Big Five or Six, who had major control over the Johannesburg Stock Exchange, were the 'untouchables': Anglo American Corporation & De Beers, Rembrandt, Sanlam, Old Mutual, Liberty Life. The antipathy of political activists towards the big corporations was understandable. Not only did they remain silent at crucial points in the history of South Africa, but they benefited from the political environment provided by racial discrimination.

The iniquitous migrant-labour system enabled the mining industry to make high profits without the added problem of social responsibility for the families of black workers. It was true that the sending countries of these migrant workers also benefited from the system, and that it cost the mining industry lost opportunities in not being able to have a stable workforce. But the system of migrant labour, and with it the despicable hostel compound system, were introduced into South Africa by the mining industry. It was not a system imposed on the industry by the government of the day.

Nor did big business play the creative role in the development of human resources it could have played. It followed the policy of job reservation for white workers with little effective protest. It did not invest in the education of its own workers, let alone that of other underprivileged people. The money that trickled down for social responsibility projects was too little and unfocused to make any real impact. Even when the Sullivan Code obtained in the 1970s and 1980s little progress was made because most institutions played the game of tokenism. Those that did not, failed to understand the importance of the need to tackle access, human development and institutional culture. Thus the few blacks who found their way into managerial positions became frustrated and angry.

It is understandable that my former activist colleagues and some friends were dismayed at my decision to accept invitations to sit on the boards of Anglo American and Old Mutual.[36] Why should I step into such profanity? If in the late 1980s it had been suggested that I would find myself sitting in the boardrooms of these corporations, I would have

---

36 I resigned from the Old Mutual board at the end of 1994 because I felt my input was not making the impact I had hoped for.

dismissed the suggestion as fantasy. But history is full of ironies. I made the decision to engage with the large institutions because they had to be harnessed for the good of the entire population. They could not be wished away. I had no illusions about their conservative history and their likely resistance to change. But I also had faith that at some stage their proven economic prowess could be made to serve the majority. This would happen when they realised that their long-term interests would be best served only if they intersected with the developmental interests of the majority of South Africans.

My part in the 1990-91 scenario exercise sponsored by the Old Mutual-Nedcor group of companies to examine future options for a changing South Africa was crucial in my decision to become involved in the world of big business. The major conclusion of our study was that a successful transition from authoritarian rule to a prosperous democratic order would only be possible if political and socioeconomic transformation received equal attention. The study also concluded that the complexities of the problems were such that no single sector of society could meet the challenges ahead. Social compacts between the government, organs of civil society, including trade unions, and the private sector were the only sensible approach for South Africa.[37] I believed that my role in the major corporations would make some contribution towards that end.

Thus it was that in 1990 I was invited through Judge Jan Steyn and our involvement with the Independent Development Trust to sit on the board of Anglo, where Julian Ogilvy Thompson was chairman. At first I was reluctant but, as I have said, Anglo exercised a huge influence on the South African economy and if you wanted to have an impact on the economy then you had to engage with Anglo. Joining that board was

---

37 Bob Tucker and Bruce Scott, *South Africa: Prospects for Successful Transition* (Kenwyn, 1992).

like going back in time. I was the only woman – the only black woman. There was an elderly black man on the board but I cannot even recall his name. Our discussions were strange and unreal. Two days before a board meeting a large pack of documents would arrive. There was no possibility of reading everything and it was clear that this was not the intention. They were there so that boxes could be ticked. I soon realised that the only way to get the board involved in a discussion was to raise an issue. At the time I was completing my doctorate on the migrant-labour hostels, so I raised my concerns. I argued that these hostels were a disaster as they were adversely affecting the lives of the men who lived in them, and they would have an impact on future generations. How could men who were treated as boys become responsible husbands and fathers? And when a master-servant pidgin language such as Fanagolo was used as the means of communication, how could a collegial relationship be established between mine management and the workers? I remember one of the board members harrumphing at my concerns and muttering, 'It's never going to happen. You can't change this. Don't even think about it.'

Despite the long miners' strike of the 1980s, and the changes in the political climate, the Anglo board was not ready for change. They sat and listened to my arguments but that generation of white liberals would politely go through the motions of being attentive yet make no changes to how they ran their institutions. It was only after a disaster at Vaal Reef, when Bobby Godsell was placed in charge of the gold mining operations, that I had someone on the board with whom I could discuss matters. I remained on the board throughout my time as a deputy vice-chancellor at UCT and only resigned when I became vice-chancellor in 1996. Anglo was one of our major funders and I did not want a clash of interests.

As mentioned, I had also joined the board of Old Mutual. My time there was brief as I found this board stifling, with nothing more than a rubber-stamp function. These two boards were my introduction to corporate South Africa and it would be ten years before I would venture back into that pond.

Chapter 28

A woman in a hurry

MY ACCEPTANCE OF THE DEPUTY VICE-CHANCELLOR POSI-tion also brought with it another change of address, this time from Mowbray to a house on the university's middle campus on Wood-mead Rd. Dr Saunders had suggested that it would be more convenient given the frequent meetings that ran on after dark, and I was only too happy to make the move. For one thing it meant I could walk to work and the boys could cycle or walk to their schools, SACS and Westerford. We lived there until early in 1993, when I bought a house in Newlands. This was all part of a careful plan to extricate myself from the univer-sity executive.

I sold the Mowbray house as well as the cottage I had bought in Muizenberg which we used for weekends at the coast, but that combined amount still left me unable to meet the price of the Newlands property. Fortunately Mr Harry Oppenheimer came to my assistance and pro-vided the shortfall finance. This assistance came about in a curious way. I happened to mention to then President Nelson Mandela that I was battling to find finance to cover the bond and he took it upon himself to approach Mr Oppenheimer. He told him what the situation was and that I had no savings, and, generously, Mr Oppenheimer agreed to fund most of the balance. But not all of it. I was able to raise a bond against what was owing and paid this off out of my salary.

Although this house was further from the university and I could no longer walk to work, Hlumelo and Malusi could still cycle to their schools, or I could drop them off. For the rest of the year I continued with my various duties as deputy vice-chancellor and as an executive on the Independent Development Trust. Work was as demanding as ever, but I had applied for a sabbatical at Harvard in 1994 and I looked forward to returning to a quieter life.

In December 1993 the three of us flew to the United States to watch from afar as South Africa prepared for its first democratic elections in April 1994. On the first day of voting, Wednesday 27 April, I went to State House in Boston along with two or three hundred other South Africans who were in that city on contract or in exile. I remember sitting there, waiting to make my cross. My heart was racing and I could not believe that this was happening. I came out of the building weeping. I was forty-six years old and I had voted for the first time.

I thought then of all the people who had died, all the people who could have been there to share this moment. I remembered that as activists people had said we were up against a brutal regime. They had warned that we would be killed. And we would reply that we would rather be killed fighting for freedom than live as slaves. Now here I was enjoying the first fruits of freedom and my friends who had died fighting for this freedom were only there because I carried their memories.

I went home to the house we had on the edge of Cambridge and sat in front of the television and watched the voting process. I wept and I laughed and I wept some more. I did not regret that I was in the United States rather than experiencing the election in South Africa. It was the emotion that counted; that and the remembrance of those who had died.

At the end of May my sabbatical ended and we returned home via London. My brother Sethiba had recently died in 1993 and my sister-in-law and my nephew needed time to grieve and heal away from the demands of daily life. Also, I wanted my mother to experience something of the outside world, and cosmopolitan London with its museums, art galleries, sights and historical sites was an ideal place. We even spent an afternoon watching tennis at Wimbledon, courtesy of an invitation by a friend from Boston to his suite at the tennis spectacular. I had rented accommodation for us in Piccadilly near the Ritz Hotel and for two weeks we existed in a bubble of happiness. Late in June we flew back to Cape Town and reality.

My immediate task was to establish the Public Information Centre with Dr Wilmot James under the auspices of Idasa (the Institute for Democracy in South Africa). This centre became a mini think tank that was meant to enable the transformation from an unaccountable authoritarian political culture to one that was open and democratic. We believed that to achieve this the dissemination of information was critical. Consequently the Public Information Centre was founded on three programmes. Firstly we instituted a Parliamentary Information Service that alerted people to what was being discussed in Parliament and the key issues in these discussions. We supplied interpretations of what had transpired and what decisions had been taken. There was also a Budget Information Service that presented what was in the national budget and how it affected taxpayers, and explained how people could influence the budgetary process. The third programme involved a Poverty Research Service: it analysed the situation and looked at government policies in this regard and how these policies were being implemented. Our intention was to create something similar to the Brooklyn Institute for Social Research in the US by providing material and intellectual support to citizens. We saw the Public Information Centre as a resource that society could use to test the principles of democracy. To meet this ideal we also held workshops and seminars, and published papers and articles.

As an aside it needs to be recorded that despite this highly active agenda, the life of the Public Information Centre was, unfortunately, a short three years. The reasons for the demise of the centre were various, but a major contribution was my resignation and return to UCT as vice-chancellor. It was absorbed into Idasa, where it continued until Idasa's end in early 2013. However, the centre's budgetary programme run by Warren Krafchik went on to provide a template for similar programmes which he operates in various countries. Many of the other ideas have been implemented by Richard Calland in his position as director of the Democratic Governance and Rights Unit and associate professor in the public law department at UCT. He specialises in the law and practice of the right to access to information and whistle-blowing protection, ideas which were part and parcel of the Public Information Centre.

In mid-1994, the Public Information Centre was the focus of my political and social concerns. It was an extremely exciting time and one during which the demands of providing good foundations for the young democracy were pressing. As had been my intention since the start of my sabbatical, I now told Dr Saunders that I was going to resign from being deputy vice-chancellor. 'No,' he said immediately. 'You can't do that.' But I felt I had instituted a culture of transformation at the university that could continue within the systems that had been set up. I was keen to engage fully with the new challenge of the Public Information Centre, which was also more in keeping with my desire to be out of the front line.

During this time I was meeting with then President Nelson Mandela and mentioned to him my decision to resign from the university's executive. I also had a suspicion that Dr Saunders was grooming me for the position of vice-chancellor, a position I did not want. At that stage he had not made an outright approach but he had dropped hints that this was the direction of his thinking. When we met, President Mandela listened to my justifications and excuses for resigning and at a point in our discussion, raised himself up and said, 'I'm sick and tired of your headstrong approach. What is this Idasa? What is this Public Information Centre? You are going to take this position.' I responded, 'But Tata, let's go beyond the job and look at the Public Information Centre. This centre is laying stronger foundations for democracy. It will help people understand democracy.' To which he replied, firmly, 'No, you will take this position of vice-chancellor at the university. We need models of transformation in our key institutions and UCT is key.'

Now I have never been instructed to do something and then meekly obliged. I do not take kindly to being told what to do. More specifically, I felt that I could make a significant contribution through the Public Information Centre. I can talk to ordinary people. What I had done through my research and through my public projects was to break down the walls that separated us as a nation. I knew what it was to talk with people whose only address was a bed. This, I believed, was where my duties lay, not sitting in an institution of higher learning. However, both Mr Mandela and Dr Saunders were hard men to gainsay. Dr Saunders particularly had various tricks up his sleeve. One of them was to convince me that I only needed to give them two days of my time each week. As I was already feeling guilty about leaving an unfinished agenda, I agreed to his terms but let it be known that my focus would be the Public Information Centre.

Having consented to being considered for the position of vice-chancellor, I was required to meet with various constituencies at the university. The first of these was a public address to the university community. And so, in late 1995, I arrived at one of the most dramatic afternoons of my life. The meeting was held in the Jameson Hall and I knew that many issues were at stake, not least that I had to redeem my reputation as an agent for transformation. The previous afternoon I spent time imagining how the students would approach this meeting, but I did not anticipate the rudeness and anger. During the two hours not one academic and not one woman, either student or academic, made a comment or asked a question. It was just me and young male students. As far as they were concerned, I had aggrieved them with my stern approach to sexual harassment. I had aggrieved them with the boundaries I set for transformation. I had aggrieved them with my insistence that they excel. They felt I lacked empathy, that I was a sell-out, that I was siding with the enemy and did not care for black people. As far as they were concerned, I was only interested in my own career and the future of white people. To be blunt, and they were, I was using the position to board the gravy train.

For those two hours I absorbed the anger, the sense of betrayal, their loss of dignity, their humiliation, their rude insinuations and steadfastly refrained from entering the fray. They were not a threat to me. They were projecting the wounds and pain of their lives and the fear that they would never really be good enough. Many of them were perspiring with anxiety. This was not an easy time for them or for me. At one point they even stated that a white vice-chancellor would be preferable as they would then know with whom they were dealing. Their attitude saddened me. However, during my days as an activist I had first encountered the psychology of the oppressed who feel that every encounter with authority contains the possibility of humiliation and the threat of loss of dignity. My actions in expelling those involved in rape or my outsmarting them during the Bremner protest had served to reinforce their vulnerability. I was supposed to be their mother, yet of the university's executive I was the harshest. Eventually on that testing afternoon I saw their anger diminishing and they became calmer. In the end I was carried out on their shoulders and we continued our discussion in the SRC offices. Now I was their champion and they were celebrating their success.

In the days that followed I did presentations before the workers and the council. Each night I went home thinking, you might not have wanted this but you made a decision and you will stick to that decision. This has always been the shape of my life: once I make a decision I stay with it. The following week the senate sat to evaluate the candidates. Later I would learn that there were strong voices against me. Professor

Brian Kantor went so far as to proclaim that I would ruin the university. Despite these voices of dissent, the majority voted in my favour.

I remember Dr Saunders coming out of the session and hugging me. I was humbled. I was pleased. My thoughts were, right, now the work begins.

Chapter 29

The VC years

ONE OF THE ADVANTAGES OF MY YEARS AS A DEPUTY VICE-chancellor was that I knew what was working and what was moribund. With the help of Senior Deputy Vice-Chancellor Wieland Gevers, we instituted a university-wide consultation on the vision, mission and the way forward for UCT's transformation. My intention was to complete a single term in the position. With the half-a-year overlap before Dr Saunders stepped down, we set in place the preparatory work.

My first days were devoted to forming a group of people, a team that could develop, share and enact my vision for the university. These had to be people who could dismember the octopus that the university had become and replace it with a sleek and healthy creation. To do this I had to win hearts and minds. I did not view anyone as an enemy but rather I saw council as stuck in an old boys' network that had paid more attention to continuing traditions than to management and maintenance. In turn many of them saw me as a foreigner, an outsider. There was not only Professor Kantor's outrage that I would ruin the university but Professor Cliff Moran, the dean of the faculty of science, told me personally that he believed we had nothing in common, no shared values, and that it was a gross error having me as a vice-chancellor. In short he was saying I was an outsider. I was not an academic, I was black, and heaven forbid, I was a woman. Men such as Moran and Kantor had never met black women like me. Their experience was with their domestic helpers and perhaps junior black colleagues. For them I could have come from outer space. But these were the people I had to work with and get to become positive contributors to the transformation of UCT.

Much to his surprise, one of the first people I approached was Professor Brian Kantor. He knew that his proclamation that I would ruin the university had reached my ears so it was a somewhat baffled man who accepted my request to lead and improve the Commerce Faculty. That faculty was in a mess. It had been badly run and desperately needed an injection of order. Who better to do this than a man of Professor Kantor's experience and skills? In the coming years he would make of that faculty a world-class facility. Much the same process happened in the Medical Faculty, although I met with considerable resistance at first. The school had been run as a series of fiefdoms but once the dean relinquished his position to allow new blood, it became again the crown jewel of the university. However, I should say that it took many months of tea and scones, many sherries, the consumption of many of my prized wines with the barons of the Medical School before the situation was resolved. In both these instances, and in all the others, my approach was not to make enemies. The transformation was not about me; it was about the university. As I repeatedly explained to them, I was not there to maintain standards, I was there to raise them. Or rather, I was there to create an environment where they could raise the standards.

As the days unfolded I realised that I was pleased to be in a place where I could establish a model that could be used as an example of transformation elsewhere in the country. I enjoyed the challenge. I have always enjoyed challenges, and now that I had taken on this challenge I wanted it to work. We were in the business of making history. Every day was an opportunity to do something as there was so much to do.

I would meet with the team – as I liked to think of them – every Friday morning. It was a tradition I had inherited from Dr Saunders but whereas he had tended to use the occasion informally, I insisted on an agenda so that there was coherence and direction. This agenda was drawn up two days before the meeting and if people wanted to speak to a topic they were required to refine their thoughts to a maximum of two pages. Not every meeting was about business; sometimes they were an opportunity for chats and laughter.

As I had made a point of studying the administration of American universities during my sabbaticals in the United States, there seemed to be many of their attributes that could be incorporated into the new UCT. For one thing, I knew that the financial administration of the university had to change. For another, I knew that the registrar, Hugh Amoore, was of vital importance to me in correcting the university's administration. Yet he was a man who had such a huge workload that his desk was forever awash beneath a sea of papers, files and documents, a sea that had no low tide. His job needed to be split and a separate position needed to be created for a financial director. Mr Amoore was unhappy about this decision and threatened to resign and take a position at Rhodes, but I had the backing of Dr Saunders and the new dispensation came about during our overlap period. Never once did I panic at these threats and once Mr Amoore realised he was not irreplaceable he remained to become a valuable part of my team. Indeed, the new arrangement introduced financial management and allowed Mr Amoore to concentrate on areas of the administration where he had invaluable expertise and experience.

Other important members of my team were Professor John Martin who was the research deputy vice-chancellor and Helen Zille whose portfolio was communications. She became a sounding board and an advisor especially through the difficult period when the number of faculties were collapsed from ten to six. There was much resistance to this especially from the arts, humanities and education faculties. Helen Zille would always advise patience and a willing ear. As vice-chancellor you need to be a real listener especially when you are dealing with constituencies that are not used to being told what to do and how things should be done. Let alone that there are budgetary constraints to what they would like to do.

While there were concrete tasks ahead, there was a primary need to develop a mission and vision for the university. The essence of my vice-chancellor's address was that there could be no equity without excellence and no excellence without equity. This I wanted to percolate through the mission and vision statement. We needed to position ourselves as a world-class university although there were many at the university who believed that world-class and African were contradictory terms. Besides, who was this foreigner to have the temerity to believe she could do this? I came to realise that the tragedy of many English-speaking South Africans was that they viewed the English liberal way as the standard that everyone should be ruled by. Post 1994 they believed this was the standard we should adopt. What other form of existence was there? However, despite this prejudice my ideas of equity and excellence as inextricably linked went into the mission statement. I should stress that this statement was produced from a process that included input from representatives from the workers, the students, Professor Andre Brink and Professor Gevers. It came to form the foundations on which UCT has built successive mission statements.

In many ways creating a mission and vision statement was an easy process. The more daunting task was that of reshaping the university's faculties. The pillar on which so much of this transformation rested was Professor Gevers. He was the one who designed and drove this massive undertaking and without him I would not have met my targets within the three-year time frame. I recall how on Thursday afternoons we would walk on the mountain to discuss what lay ahead and strategic ways to achieve it. I had the broad strokes but it took the mind of a polymath to get into the detail. One afternoon I saw Professor Gevers 'read' – digest might be a better word – a huge tome then present summaries of the central points. Without this man the massive job of transforming the university would have been a painful and lengthy affair.

It was an advantage that he had been at the University of Chicago and that we both believed that we could learn from the structures and processes of American universities. In the English system academics were more or less free-floating radicals who taught what they liked when they liked. I believed that we needed coherent programmes. For instance, take my son Hlumelo in his student years. He was bright but lazy. He soon realised that he could get away with doing the minimum amount of work and still pass. But what good was this? It was not right. We needed to produce young people who were literate, numerate and well rounded in their social behaviour. And it was in this respect that the American college system was superior to the English one. The American system encouraged young people to set high goals and with their semester-away programmes and their drive to get students involved in community development they produced well-rounded people. Programmes like these were my ideal, but first the faculties needed transforming.

That it was necessary to consolidate the various faculties was axiomatic. Many of them were headed by failed researchers who had risen through age into positions where they had no abilities or skills relevant for equity and excellence. They had been allowed to tarry in these jobs because the university could hide behind the international reputations of its science, engineering, legal and medical faculties. My opinion was that for a university to be world class it had to be world class throughout the disciplines. Equally important, if we were to set an example to our students then we needed the faculty deans to be people who would inspire excellence. As I have mentioned there was resistance to these changes, and I would continue to suffer from migraines.

One of the biggest and most testing challenges I faced over a number of years was outsourcing the auxiliary services of cleaning and grounds maintenance. When I first joined the university's anthropology department in the mid-1980s I was horrified at the dust on the shelves and tables. When I complained my white colleagues, stricken with guilt, would explain that the cleaners had low wages and therefore could not be forced to work. I found this attitude difficult to accept. The cleaning staff were also a disruptive influence on campus. They would deliberately strike during exams and disturb the examination process. UCT was not a factory. It was an educational institution and this sort of behaviour was detrimental to the future of the country. When a cleaner was caught banging on an exam room window during a strike I had him arrested and fired. This action did not endear me to the workers or the students, who frequently sided with the workers in these disputes. However, I maintained my decision to outsource the cleaning services.

A little research established that these workers were earning more than junior nurses and teachers. Their salary package included a loan account and on the strength of this many of them had acquired houses and bonds that they could not service. As a result they borrowed from the university, treating UCT as their private bank. Far from being underpaid and under-appreciated, these workers enjoyed fair wages and excellent conditions of service. When they next went on strike in an attempt to make the university ungovernable, I published this remuneration information in the weekly Monday Paper and this ended the alliance between the students and the workers. In fact the students went so far as to pelt the workers with tomatoes, angered at how they had been misled.

At about this time the universities were changing their statutes and these had to be passed through Parliament. Blade Nzimande was chair of the parliamentary portfolio committee that handled this matter and obstinately took the side of the workers by obfuscating issues and causing unnecessary delays in the procedures. Our new statutes made a clear distinction between academic and governance matters because although students and workers could comment on academic matters they could not be part of any decision-making process. As far as governance was concerned, we were a transparent organisation, and they had a say there. In the end it took eighteen months and the assistance of consultants to not only get these statutes through Parliament but to get the cleaning staff off our payroll. We were then free to obtain proper gardening services and cleaning contractors. Today, with the current labour laws, managing and changing this process would have been a nightmare. Even then it was undoubtedly the hardest task I faced. The more radical students and academics never forgave me, labelling me a right-winger, a Margaret Thatcher. I am happy to be labelled anything provided the job gets done.

Funding the changes

ANOTHER TASK THAT WAS DEMANDING IN A DIFFERENT way was the matter of fundraising. The university was in a parlous state. Not maintaining infrastructure is a false economy but one that had prevailed at UCT. Partly this attitude stemmed from the lack of awareness displayed by people who had grown up in a system and accepted their environment. I was a newcomer and I thought the campus needed serious attention. For instance, the vice-chancellor's residence, Glenara, had exposed electrical wires nailed to the walls. The house was in dire need of maintenance and renewal. It was a Victorian-era university asset and I insisted that it be attended to before I moved in. Once that process was finished it was a home fit to host the king and queen of Sweden.

Much the same dereliction applied elsewhere. The main administration building, Bremner, was a beautiful old building but it had been allowed to go to wrack and ruin in many places. A process of renovation was needed. Indeed, it was necessary to initiate the upper campus renewal project if the university was to be a world-class institution. The library, for example, was antiquated. When I visited the University of Southern California and saw their library I knew that this was what we needed. My belief was that spaces should not only be functional but inspirational. How could we send young people into the world when the environment where they studied was decaying? Many came from poor backgrounds and we needed to show them that they could aspire to better living possibilities.

My fundraising activities for the university had started during the cross-over period towards the end of Dr Saunders's term as vice-chancellor, and it was from him that I learnt the tricks of the trade. He was well connected in the United Kingdom and we would set off to raise funds there. Yet these ventures were somewhat haphazard in that we went with no clear goals and no plan. We would arrive at a 'give or take' figure and after we had made our pitch this was the number that would be put on the table. The pitch itself was a Tom and Jerry act. Dr Saunders would give the background to what was required, I would elaborate with our vision for a future South Africa and spice up the project into something essential and vital. If the truth be told, this was how we raised the money from the Rhodes Trust in Oxford to build Africa House on the middle campus.

Once I was vice-chancellor, fundraising required monthly travel to the United States and the United Kingdom. I had inherited a huge debt at the Graduate School of Business (GSB) and no clear idea from the previous administration of how to fund it. My first approach was Allan Gray in London, who said he would provide finance if the GSB was renamed after Nelson Mandela. I knew Mandela would do this for me but I also knew that the ANC would not allow it. Allan Gray was forth-right. He would not finance the debt but he would donate R20 million for scholarships and bursaries, which would free up the existing budget to finance the debt. This R20 million came as a relief but it did not solve a greater problem: the management of the GSB. To sort out this problem Nick Segal was appointed. He had extensive experience in business and in major corporations and he understood how the world worked. He introduced programmes that were targeted at specific businesses and soon the problem that had been the GSB receded.

What I had learnt from Dr Saunders about fundraising was that a team approach was better than a single-handed pitch. Together with Helen Zille and Andrew Sillen, the director of development, we devised a different strategy: we would put together a professional outline that detailed what we wanted to achieve, how we would achieve it, how much it would cost (and these costings were measurable), and what the outcomes would be. In providing this sort of information, Andy Sillen with his knowledge and experience of the funding process in the United States was a past master. The university had fundraising offices in both New York and London and the people there worked hard to make UCT an attractive proposition for people and organisations interested in financing education in Africa.

Every month end for most months of the year I would attend the Wednesday council meeting and then catch that evening's flight to Miami or Atlanta. On the Thursday I would be in New York for meetings then and on Friday and Saturday morning. I took the Saturday evening flight back home. Fortunately I am a good sleeper and with the help of some muscle relaxants I was able to sleep on both legs of the round trip. But this schedule took its toll. My migraines continued and there was only one way to treat them: with my doctor's prescription and a handy syringe for self-injection.

I recall one occasion when we were to approach Anglo Plats (Anglo American Platinum) for funding for a new chemical engineering build- ing. With projects such as this we would target local funders for the simple reason that our students would be vital to their future growth and prosperity. When you can confidently tell a funder such as Anglo Plats that UCT was (in those days) producing more black engineers than another university and then explain how research in that department can benefit the industry, the people you approach are inclined to take you seriously.

On the day we were to fly to Johannesburg to see Anglo Plats I awoke with a migraine. I had a severe and splitting headache. I was throwing up. I injected myself and caught the plane with Andy Sillen and Profes- sor Cyril O'Connor, the dean of the engineering faculty. In Johannes-

burg we performed what was becoming for me a well-rehearsed routine. I would set the scene and the context, O'Connor would add the
technical details and Andy Sillen would reveal the plans for the building and the costings.

Barry Davidson, the CEO of Anglo Plats, was a compulsive smoker
and literally did the sums on the back of his cigarette pack. We needed
R50 million in total and although platinum was recording record com-
modity prices he was reluctant to be the sole sponsor. He suggested we
approach Sasol for the rest, which we did, and achieved our objective.

The upper campus project gave the university not only a facelift but
seemed to rejuvenate the spirit. Much of the finance for this project
had been raised from local companies and it is in this respect that Harry
Oppenheimer proved a true and generous patron of the university, of
which he was then ex-chancellor. My contact with the Oppenheimers
stretched back to my student days in the 1970s at the University of Natal
when I had been the recipient of an Ernest Oppenheimer bursary. Later,
as head of the Zanempilo Clinic, I could appeal to Anglo for assistance
when the funds ran dry, and they were always forthcoming. Harry
Oppenheimer knew how my life had unfolded, my relationship with
Steve Biko, my banning and banishment orders, but it was not until the
mid-1980s that we met officially at a UCT function. In 1990 he asked
me to sit on the Anglo board and although he was off the board at that
time we got on well and would often meet to talk about the country,
politics, global issues, my family. The thing about Harry Oppenheimer
was that he was engaged with his world, he took an interest in what was
happening.

Often I would contact him simply to talk. He was a good sounding
board. He would say diffidently, 'Well, I have no idea what I would do
in your situation but you might want to think of this or that.' He had a
way of making suggestions that was not prescriptive and hardly seemed
like a suggestion at all. Always his advice was helpful. Given this back-

‚round, when the upper campus project hit a shortfall, the first person I called was Harry Oppenheimer. He was reliable. To this day I am loyal to Harry Oppenheimer, the person, and still sit on the board of the Oppenheimer Memorial Trust.

———◇◈◇———

I always felt during my term as vice-chancellor that each day history was being made. When history is made it occurs without the benefit of precedent and therefore there can be mistakes. Knowing this did not make the job any easier. Also, I am a perfectionist and an impatient person and can be demanding as a leader. For some I might have come across as lacking in empathy and uncaring but there was a job to do. There was a demanding task to be achieved and a strict timeline in which to meet the deadlines.

Looking back, I think that possibly the thing I am most proud of is changing the institutional culture of UCT. It was not easily done but it was necessary and I have no regrets in this regard. When I first stepped onto that campus in the mid-1980s it was a university unconscious of its responsibilities towards the wider society, unconscious of a need to educate in a way that would make a contribution to the transformation of South Africa. By this I do not mean simply the numbers game, although the student demographics had to change as well, but I mean educating young people to be democrats.

For example, in the matter of gender equity you could not take the attitude towards sexual harassment that 'boys will be boys'. Because, unlike at UCT, this attitude has persisted across the broader society. We are today paying for this in the high levels of violence by men towards women and children. Had other institutions and businesses taken the approach adopted by UCT, we would not be in the position we are today where daily the rights of women and children are horrifically violated. You cannot be a democrat and slap your wife. Had I neglected to deal with sexual harassment on campus, UCT would have suffered in the longer term. Harsh and frequently unpopular decisions had to be taken and policies to change the institutional culture were vital.

But not only was it a matter of changing societal attitudes; there had to be a change in the relationship of the vice-chancellor with the deans and the academics and the students. The university had to become more strategic in its academic programmes. And here I have to thank Professor John Martin, an engineer who understood the value of performance based programmes and led the team who instituted this new approach at the university.

I also witnessed a major change in the attitudes of black students. In the 1980s I saw black students who had excelled in the examinations crossing out their marks on the results lists pinned up on notice boards. To achieve high percentages was seen as making yourself white, and so to excel was an invitation to ridicule and embarrassment. Gradually during my years on the executive I saw this change to a point where students wanted to be better, they wanted to be on the deans' lists. A culture of excellence became a matter of pride. It is axiomatic that young people will rise to the level of expectation. Conversely they can be hampered and shackled by low expectations. It is a bitter irony that today the government has chosen not a culture of excellence but one of mediocrity and decreed that matric pupils who receive 30% in three subjects and 40% in three others have achieved a pass mark. They are crushing the potential with which children are born. They are diminishing our future.

It is not for me to measure the success of my time as vice-chancellor – only history can do that. Suffice to say that many of the changes and transformations made by my executive team would only achieve their full potential in the coming years. However, as a measure of the transformation of the university I have been pleased to note not only the change in culture but a change in the university's demographics. In the early 1990s a third of the student body was black and during my term this increased to the point where nearly half were black. Equally encouraging, by 2006, the female component of the student body stood at 51%.

Without doubt, though, the high point of the last days of my term was the completion of the new library. It was literally finished on the day I left and could not have come at a more opportune moment. In a metaphoric sense the past had been remade as the present and this archive of knowledge was now housed in an environment that was not only functional but an inspiration. I could leave the university knowing that there had been changes and, equally important, that solid foundations had been laid for future generations.

Moving on

IF MY YEARS AS VICE-CHANCELLOR WERE DEMANDING, THEN those demands were also felt by my family. It was tough on my sons and I am grateful for their fortitude and good humour. When my term as vice-chancellor started Hlumelo was eighteen years old. He had just left school and was about to enter UCT as a student, while Malusi was still in high school. Of course we went through our fair share of teenage issues and of course there were injuries, and mishaps, and a number of girlfriends. But nothing was ever untoward or beyond a reasonable discussion.

I remember refusing to buy Malusi something he wanted but that I felt he did not need. He snapped back at me, 'You're just jealous because you grew up poor.' This caught me by surprise but I had to laugh. You need a large dose of humour when it comes to parenting. On another occasion I gave in to his requests and bought him a scooter even though I was against the idea. Unfortunately he was knocked down by a car, but he escaped the accident with only minor scrapes and bruises. Such are the hazards of bringing up children and I give thanks that it was never any worse than this.

Raising Hlumelo and Malusi as a single parent was difficult. My mother came to stay for long periods and Makgatla Mangena, who has been with me for 37 years, has been the anchor in the home. Raising sons without a father is far from ideal. Boys need the presence of a man or they have nothing on which to model themselves.

ın this regard, Malusi's father had a strange relationship with his son.
Je kept his distance, preferring not to be a part of his son's life. I
could not understand this, but it was not my place to intervene. However, when Malusi was preparing to leave for initiation it seemed only
right that his father should oversee the process. Not only did I feel this
was important but so did Hlumelo. He was adamant that we should
respect Sipo's right to direct matters. Eventually Hlumelo contacted Sipo
but to no avail. Sipo did not want to become involved because the rituals
would be conducted at Steve Biko's home in King Williamstown. He
imagined that Hlumelo's grandmother, who had in fact already passed
on, did not like him, and he believed the Biko family would be hostile
towards him. Nothing could have been further from the truth, yet this,
unfortunately, was how matters rested.

Not long afterwards Sipo developed pancreatic cancer, a particularly
destructive and agonising illness. On his deathbed he requested that
Thami, his daughter from his first marriage, make contact with Malusi
and establish a relationship. When Sipo died, Malusi was at college in
Los Angeles. It was only right and proper that he return home to bury
his father, which he did. The rituals were performed in Port Elizabeth
and it was during this sad time that he and Thami met. Since then they
have developed the close relationship that was their father's dying wish.

However, Sipo's death lay in the future while towards the end of the
1990s other events were beginning to form in my life.

Often I have looked back over my life and felt that although I am my
own agent and have made my own decisions, frequently I have been
presented with opportunities. For instance, I was drawn into establishing a clinic in the Eastern Cape and then another one in Limpopo during
my banishment there. The deputy vice-chancellor position I did not
want, just as I did not want the position of vice-chancellor. And the same
can be said for my next appointment, as an executive at the World Bank.

The World Bank position came about in a strange way and Hlumelo played an indirect role in influencing events. Towards the end of th 1990s he was staying with a friend of mine in Washington while completing an internship at the World Bank. It so happened that Jim Wolfensohn, then president of the World Bank, mentioned to my friend in Hlumelo's company that he was struggling to find someone to champion a human development portfolio at the bank. Mr Wolfensohn had been appointed president in 1995 and been influenced in the intervening years by two people, the economist Dr Amartya Sen, and the diplomat and legal expert Professor Hisashi Owada. Dr Sen's book *Development as Freedom* set out the proposition that in a world where the increase of wealth had occurred in amounts unknown before, there were millions of people in the developing world still bound by the chains of poverty. These people were literally enslaved. They might not be called slaves but they were denied the most basic human rights and remained suppressed by economic poverty, social poverty and political tyrannies. He believed that the major reason for development was to spread freedom to these 'enslaved' millions. Professor Owada was Mr Wolfensohn's senior advisor during the years 1999 and 2000, and went on to be president of the International Court of Justice where he is still a judge. The thinking of these two men convinced Mr Wolfensohn that you could not consider development without thinking of education, health and nutrition.

He had heard of my interests in health and education as essential components to the promotion of development and mentioned to Hlumelo that he was considering such a portfolio at the World Bank, which might interest me. Hlumelo got the word back to me and suggested that I needed time out and that such a job would be interesting and challenging. At that point I expected staying on for a second term as vice-chancellor, although as far as I was concerned the major changes had been made and what remained was maintenance work. The impatient part of me is not good with maintenance, so Mr Wolfensohn's approach in 1999 was intriguing and timely. I accepted.

My acceptance was on the grounds that I would serve a single five-year term. I certainly had no intention of moving to the United States for a longer period. Upping and leaving the country before its first democratic decade was over was not an easy decision, especially as it went with considerable upheaval for Malusi. He was in his matric year and needed to finish his schooling without this sort of traumatic uprooting. Fortunately good friends agreed to accommodate him for that year.

Having accepted the position, I now needed to inform not only Nelson Mandela but also President Thabo Mbeki and various other people I used as confidants, including Harry Oppenheimer, of my decision. This was not easy. Mr Mandela particularly was not impressed. 'I've never seen you scared,' he said to me, 'but this time you look scared.'

'Tata,' I responded, 'I've done what I needed to do at the university.'

He could see that it had not been an easy decision for me and said he would not make it any harder, but he was not pleased. However, I had somewhat softened the blow by recruiting his wife, Graça Machel, as chancellor at UCT.

Thabo Mbeki was likewise uncomfortable with my decision. To show his disapproval he declined to meet me at his office in the Union Buildings and summoned me to Luthuli House, the ANC headquarters. I was not intimidated by him and he knew this. Our meeting was awkward, strained. Harry Oppenheimer was likewise displeased but respected my view when I told him I had fought so many battles and needed a break.

If becoming vice-chancellor at UCT had brought with it challenges, then the tasks facing me at the World Bank were of an infinitely different order. The bank was a post-Second World War creation ostensibly for the reconstruction of Germany. What I found when I got there was an archaic institution with a full-time board, a president and five managing directors. Inevitably with this sort of situation there was role confusion and as my portfolio was new, it was not easy to define in the bank's traditional field of operations. Because I required some struc-ture, in other words, a platform from which to work, I gathered the elements that had been neglected by the bank, particularly the World Bank Institute. This had been intended as an entity to educate the bank's clients about development issues. The first question I asked was: Should we not use this institution to not only direct education outwards to the clients but also to retrain and enable the bank's staff to under-stand and deal with developmental issues? Although this made sense, there were many in the bank who were opposed to any new approaches. It was to be the first of many battles.

I need to take a step back here. The year before I went to the World Bank I had compiled a report sponsored by the World Bank and the Rockefeller Foundation that reviewed the state of higher education in the developing countries. Called 'The Peril of Promise', its main finding was that policies of providing for primary education in developing coun-tries without continuing this through to higher education were self-de-feating. Indeed, it was perilous thinking of development in developing countries without investing in education beyond primary education. The report had been released early in 2000 and was doing the rounds of the World Bank portfolios when I arrived there.

One of my first confrontations was with the executive director repre-senting the United States, who informed me that she had a mandate to stop any investment in higher education in developing countries. The prevailing political climate at the time was conservative and the wisdom was that developing countries should be grateful for whatever handouts came their way. Education beyond primary education was a luxury.

I could not believe what I was being told. Where was the logic? Where was the foresight? Yet to her the rationale was simple. To her and her cohorts only the elite would benefit from higher education and the United States was not in the business of financing the elites.

So what are you going to do? I challenged them. How are you going break the cycle of poverty by walking away from higher education? How are you going to sustain primary education if you are not training teachers through higher education? Who is going to write the textbooks? Who is going to set policy? Have you recruited me from Africa because of my primary school credentials? I asked. They had not thought through these issues. And now they were caught on the back foot because, clearly, without higher education, primary education would wither and collapse.

Also, the Africa portfolio was under-resourced, yet Africa was the very region where development was most needed. Fortunately the bank's vice-president for the region was supportive, but it was equally clear that as I was the first director for sustainable development issues, there was an expectation that I would solve these problems and effect changes within the organisation.

Thus began my period at the World Bank. Everything was a battle. I had to be tough-minded and stick to my points and my beliefs, and this did not endear me to some people. In many ways the challenges I faced here were much tougher than the tasks that had faced me as vice-chancellor of UCT. At UCT I was dealing with an institution. I had worked there and understood the place. I knew the higher education sector and I knew the country. But here I was in foreign hostile territory. I was not an economist. I did not fit in with the scheme of things. I had not gone through the ranks. Many people at the World Bank spent decades patiently climbing the organisation's management ladder. Yet I had come from the failed continent (a report by *The Economist* declaring Africa a failed continent had just been published) and gone straight to the top. To make matters worse, I was a woman.

Ironically, at the time, the World Bank was focusing on women in development. But here too I thought their approach was misguided. There was nothing wrong with women, I said, what was wrong was the relationship men had with women. You needed a gender-based approach, and one that started at the bank itself, where there was disparity between payment levels for men and women. Women with the same qualifications and experience had lagged behind their male colleagues as a matter of custom. How could the World Bank preach gender equality in development policy to its members when it did not practise it on the home front? To a degree I was able to influence a positive change when it came to the selection, promotion and treatment of staff, but it took internal inquiries to bring these changes about.

I can only imagine that the Ivy-League trained economists took one look at this woman from Africa and wished she would go away. Fortunately I had the advantage of being supported by Jim Wolfensohn, at least in the beginning, but as the years wore on he came under increasing pressure from members of the board and senior staff members to downplay these matters. As he wanted to renew his contract with the bank for a further term, his support for me became hesitant. We clashed on some issues. His main criticism of me, and it was probably valid, was that I would not compromise. Compromise was a major tenet of World Bank negotiations but I was an uncompromising activist. Which did not make for an easy life.

Perhaps changing the way people at the bank viewed the world was one of the most important challenges I faced. For instance, each year the bank offered a summer internship as a way of getting young people into the institution. Yet no one in management ever questioned which summer – it was automatically assumed to be the northern summer even though, at the time, Jim Wolfensohn, an Australian, was president. I raised the issue and the old guard capitulated and allowed internships that took account of the southern hemisphere's summer as well. It was a small victory but it illustrated the bank's frame of reference which was determined by the northern countries, yet it was a development institution and most of the development needs were in the south.

Chapter 32

An exit strategy

IN MANY RESPECTS THE WORLD BANK WAS A TOXIC ENVI-
ronment – for a number of reasons that had as much to do with its
organisational structure as the stressful demands of the job.

Typically the working day started at seven a.m. and would frequently
end with a cocktail party for some visiting delegation. It would be gone
ten p.m. before I crawled into bed. And then it would be up for a four a.m.
flight to Bangkok with the change in time zones and a rigorous schedule of meetings. Two days later it would be London with a similar schedule and then back to Washington. Within a year I had broken my back.
Medically, my condition was known as a herniated disc and it was
stress-related. Small consolation then that I was having fewer migraines;
now the stress had found a new vulnerability.

Those with high-stress careers who spend long hours in aeroplanes
are particularly at risk of this condition. I was also exercising frequently
in a gym and may have hurt my back there. Whichever way it occurred, it was an accident waiting to happen.

A herniated disc meant a lot of pain. When I stood or sat the sciatic
nerves were pinched, so travelling was hell. When I lay down there was
no pain but once I stood up there were shooting pains down my leg that
were pure agony. Jim Wolfensohn had also fallen victim to a herniated
disc and assured me that only an operation would cure the problem.
Initially I tried physiotherapy and then cortisone injections until, in
January 2002, I checked myself into Johns Hopkins for the operation.

It was successful and although I have to look after my back these days, the pain had gone. As a footnote it is worth mentioning that when I first approached a doctor about my back problem he remarked that I was another one of the casualties of the World Bank. It was known as a sick institution. Sometimes the sickness manifested itself physically; more usually priests or psychologists had to deal with staff breakdowns. It was an unhappy place and part of the problem was that it was a diverse institution that brought together people from more than a hundred and forty countries. Diversity is a good thing, but too much of it can be difficult to handle. There were too many people fighting their own corners without the guidance of an overall strategy.

Also, the directors were continually policed by the full-time non-executive board members. They would second-guess the president, and they were continually pressing me to explain why I was underplaying economic development in favour of human development. When I reversed this question and asked how they could develop a country in a sustainable way without paying attention to health and education, I received belligerent emails accusing me of disrespect. From Jim Wolfensohn I heard there was considerable animosity towards me, but I was there to perform a function and so I simply ignored these emails.

The way the bank was structured had much to do with its own toxicity. A full-time board meant that the staff were under constant scrutiny; in fact, they were policed. Minor disputes could end up with a board member when disgruntled staff bypassed the management structures designed to handle their problems. This resulted in confused lines of reporting, and unhappiness. Moreover, the manner of the shareholding was such that the major contributors held the greatest sway. To this end the United States had veto powers over any policy with which they disagreed – as I have demonstrated regarding higher education.

It soon became clear to me that instead of the focus being on world development, it was on the individual countries. With more than a hundred and forty countries represented, each country was lobbying for their slice of the pie. The appointment of vice-presidents, for instance, was supposedly done on merit, but each vice-president would come with a constituency – the region they represented. And their focus would be on that region rather than keeping a global perspective. For an idealist like me with a world vision, this was disillusioning. I discovered I was ill prepared for. an environment geared to constant tension. I remember that Jim Wolfensohn would go to each board meeting prepared for a fight. Often he would lose his temper. Most of the time he was trying to paper over the cracks and keep disparate units together. It was a difficult process to manage.

One of my fellow directors, who saw how I was struggling with the internal politics, suggested I contact an executive management coach he knew and to whom he referred colleagues. Her name was Katherine Strickland and she had experience in various organisations, including JP Morgan. She was a gem. She helped me understand that the issues were not about me, nor about the nature of the decisions I took or the actions I embarked on. At issue was how I managed the structure. She taught me to manage those above me, those colleagues on an equal footing, and my staff.

This was the first real personal development process I had undergone in the latter part of my life. It helped me get much into perspective and helped me play to my strengths. I am a street fighter and would rely on my intellectual prowess to deal with confrontations. The result was that I might win the battle but lose the war. Katherine Strickland taught me not to undermine my strongest suit but to empathise with the other person and to win them over through collaboration. Initially I saw her once a fortnight but then less frequently until our consultations dropped to a need-to basis.

Despite the perspective and helpful strategies provided by Katherine, the continual infighting eventually began to wear on my nerves. By 2003

I had had enough. Fortunately an exit strategy appeared in the form of an inquiry into international patterns of migration. Migration was an issue that the world was not dealing with very well; in fact, it lurched from crisis to crisis. What was needed was an analysis of migration as a ongoing phenomenon in an interconnected world where you could track and detail the impact on financial flows or the distribution of talent. One crucial question, for example: which countries were losing their intellectual capital and which countries were benefiting from this? I was co-chair on this commission and it took me back to the kind of research I loved and with which I was most comfortable.

I approached Mr Wolfensohn and suggested that this would be my last project with the bank. At the time there was intense lobbying for reversals of some of the things that he had stood for and he was an embattled president. We agreed that this commission was an appropriate way out.

Once the report was prepared, it was presented to the United Nations. Like so many things that drift about in the United Nations, it circulated for a while, but no action was taken. However, I now started travelling throughout Africa, Asia and Latin America presenting the report and was spending less and less time in the United States. Eventually I suggested to Mr Wolfensohn that I base myself in Cape Town as it was easier travelling in the continent from there than making trans-Atlantic hops. Again he could see the advantages, and I was partly released from the toxic institution.

I have to admit that I left Washington – the city – with very mixed feelings. When my term started I had rented a house in a gated complex in Georgetown, the most beautiful part of the city. Not long afterwards I bought a small semi-detached house in the Cloisters. The Cloisters had been part of Georgetown University, a university started by Catholic monks and built to resemble a monastery. Eventually the church hived off this quarter and it was redeveloped into modest but comfortable accommodation. From my home there it was only a short walk, and one I frequently undertook, to the Potomac River or into the forest, and, oh, in spring, Washington was buoyant with new life and vitality. It was good to be alive in that place. At the time Malusi was staying with me and Hlumelo would often visit from the west coast. Consequently I have fond family memories of those years.

Contrary to my sentiments about Washington, I did not leave the World Bank with mixed feelings. Being there was like living in a pro-verbial pressure cooker where everything was constantly on the boil. It was an attractive proposition to be going home. Not that home had been far from my activities for the last four years. In fact, I had found that I could not escape South Africa. For instance while I had been advocating the World Bank's progressive HIV policies everywhere in the developing world I was constantly confronted with President Mbeki's HIV denialism. It was an embarrassing situation. I have come to realise that South Africa has a way of not letting go of its citizens even when they live in distant lands.

It was a relief to return to the country. I came home equipped with the report on migration and as South Africa did not have a migration policy – and still does not, for that matter – I motivated for a discussion on migration in the hopes that it would move government towards initiating such a policy. I had the support of Dr Wilmot James – then head of Idasa and head of their migration policy – and I told the min-ister, Nosiviwe Mapisa-Nqakula, that I would give her my full support to push this matter. It was not to happen. Inertia, ennui, the obfusca-tions of bureaucracy, call it what you will but when we had a chance to formulate policy about this important international issue, we missed it. And since then migration has fallen off the agenda.

Despite this local setback I was still travelling throughout the conti-nent and meeting with the respective heads of government. It helped me get to know the continent better. I realised that one of our weaknesses in South Africa was that we knew more about Europe and North America than we did about Africa. One thing was clear: many African countries had got their education systems right whereas we had failed miserably. Also noticeable was the relationship between good governance and development. In countries where there was transparency in this matter and where there was no corruption, development occurred for the benefit of the most vulnerable in society. At the time even Zimbabwe was still working, but in the intervening years I have watched with sadness as things fell apart there. That country is a lesson in how beneficiation can be derailed. It is also indicative of Africa's underperformance which diminishes the entire continent in the eyes of many elsewhere in the world. Until President Mbeki's HIV policies, South Africa was regarded as a country apart from the continent. Until then we were highly regarded. And this would have continued especially with the New Partnership for Africa's Development (Nepad) campaign, but when that was set against the denial of a disease that had the potential to destroy our country's future, we lost momentum. We lost respect. It was a more sombre country to which I returned, one certainly less buoyant than the one I had left at the end of the previous millennium.

◈◈◈

New beginnings require new outlooks. From the moment I had first visited Cape Town I had dreamed of a house that was close to the sea. I wanted to be able to see the ocean, smell its ozone and the headiness of drying seaweed, hear the crash of its breakers. The stretch of coastline that appealed to me most was the Atlantic seaboard, and it was up and down this stretch of coast that I dragged Malusi for two weeks. It was winter. It was cold and wet. It was the worst time to be house hunting. But towards the end of the search we came to a house that was badly in need of renovation. I stood on the lawn. I could see the sea, hear it, smell it.

It was the view that convinced me, since the house itself was a disaster zone. It had been built in the 1930s, then turned into a pleasure palace in the 1970s by a British fun lover who put in a sauna and a pool room and painted the outside walls a sick orange colour. It needed what estate agents call TLC – tender loving care. I sold the house in Newlands and put the proceeds into this one. An architect drew up plans for the renovation and the work was overseen by my financial advisors. In typical builders' tradition the deadline was extended and I spent the first two weeks of my return to the country in the Twelve Apostles Hotel, a short way down the coast, while the paint dried.

When I finally moved in I decided this was the house that I would leave feet first. This was my dream home. I had always had in mind a house situated like this; I did not realise it would be so perfect.

Chapter 33

Being an active citizen

I CAME BACK TO SOUTH AFRICA TO RETIRE. I HAD MY DREAM house, I now wanted to fulfil another dream: use my time to write and read and travel. In 2004 I was fifty-seven years old and I felt that I had done what I needed to do in my life. So throughout 2005 I wrote and read and stood in my lounge and looked at the sea: I was now doing what I most wanted to do. During this time I wrote *Laying Ghosts to Rest: Dilemmas of the transformation in South Africa*. I had the time for reflection and each day the freedom to write.

But then slowly South Africa came knocking. There were invitations to sit on various boards. My son Hlumelo, an entrepreneur, asked for my support. I became chair of his Circle Capital Ventures, a venture capital company that had invested in Medi-Clinic and Eduloan. This was preceded by an invitation to be a director on the Medi-Clinic board, and after that came approaches from Standard Bank and Anglo. I agreed to both these but decided that would be my quota. I did not want to overburden myself as I still had this notion of having space to read and write and travel.

I had returned from the World Bank with a much better idea of how the world economy worked – and failed to work – and I had experience of other countries and how they tackled problems similar to our own. With this background I had no intention of getting involved in government but I did feel that it gave me a platform as an active citizen. Being an active citizen had been a constant refrain throughout my life and just because I wanted to retire did not mean that I would still that voice. I felt that if I was to contribute to transformation in the country then one way was through the private sector and another was to support government wherever there were good people doing good work. Hence my support of Naledi Pandor as Minister of Education and later Science and Technology, and Mosibudi Mangena, a friend and compatriot, as Minister of Science and Technology.

It is axiomatic that the economic might of every country is in the hands of the private sector. Government is an enabler of a country's business, but for transformation to be meaningful it had to occur where the country was shaped. Hence my engagement with the likes of Medi-Clinic, Standard Bank and Anglo. If I could use my skills to change their domains then I could help contribute to the sustainable development of the country.

Then, in 2007, I was approached by Old Mutual and Nedbank to chair another scenario planning exercise. We had been through this before in the early 1990s but we needed new visions. I saw here an opportunity to explore systematically ways to get the government, the private sector and the nongovernmental (NGO) sector to work together. I also saw it as a way possibly to mend some things that had broken. For instance, the NGO sector particularly had been damaged by a government critical of their role; they needed to be reintegrated. One way of mobilising people for active citizenship was through the NGOs, so revitalising this sector appealed to me.

My return to South Africa occurred during a time when President Mbeki was at his strongest. His belligerent attitude had struck terror into the hearts of many academics and commentators who were labelled as counter-revolutionaries the moment their public comment did not toe the party line. They were frowned upon as disloyal and many were cowed into silence. I felt strongly that this clampdown on freedom of speech had to be broken and as I had nothing to lose, I felt it imperative to speak out. Part of being an active citizen was about speaking up when the need arose. If something good had occurred you acknowledged it. But if something was wrong – and most of the time things were going in the wrong direction – then I believed it was important to say so. I felt it was important to set the tone so that citizens believed they were entitled to comment on government failings. I did so. But I did so from the sidelines. At the time I still had no intentions of going into the rough and tumble of politics.

Hlumelo decided to marry his Georgetown School mate Leila Akahloun in 2005. It was a fairy-tale wedding celebrated both in Washington DC, Leila's home-town, and in King Williamstown, Hlumelo's father's home. White wedding trappings mixed happily with Xhosa traditional marriage rites. It was a great milestone for me to have a beautiful daughter-in-law with whom to share the responsibility of gluing the family together.

Sadly, their marriage later hit the rocks and despite my attempts to keep them together, it ended in divorce. I retain a mother-daughter relationship with Leila whom I love very much.

Hlumelo went his own way and struggled to re-root himself until he was catapulted into the role of a father when his son Luthando Bantu Biko was born in January 2009. Luthando has given me more joy than I had known with my own sons. He is very much his father's son but has some of my personality. We just love each other – Khulu (from Makhulu – Grandmother) is a source of treats and attention, and he is a bundle of joy to me. Lewatle also joined the single-father family almost a year ago. She is a quiet child who has yet to show her personality. Hlumelo has turned out to be an attentive and caring father who took responsibility from day one. He is engaged to Chuma Noyo, Luthando's mother, and they plan to marry in 2014. I am very proud of him, also of his success as an entrepreneur.

Malusi has chosen to remain a bachelor, having come back home after his studies at the University of Southern California and training as a consultant with Deloitte & Touche. He is an entrepreneur in the Information Technology environment and loves what he does. Hlumelo plays a supportive role as big brother but gives Malusi his space. It is rewarding to watch them together.

◈◈◈

Life continued in much this way until in 2008 I was asked by Minister of Science and Technology Mosibudi Mangena to chair the board of the Technology Innovation Agency (TIA). The agency had been established in terms of a government act and now needed to fulfil its role. He knew that I had a keen interest in technology and innovation and that during my World Bank days I had seen technologies very effectively used in the approach to development. With my experience there and my overview of what other countries were doing he persuaded me that my input would be appreciated. Once again I was venturing into a position I had not sought out. But it sounded interesting, and what possible problems could there be?

It turned out that there were some major ones. Mangena had 'neglected' to tell me that there was no board and that the agency did not exist in anything but name. However, there were seven entities dealing with various technologies and promoting innovation that had functioned under the department and were now pulled into the agency's ambit. These seven entities – the Innovation Fund, Tshumisano Trust, Cape Biotech Trust, PlantBio Trust, LIFElab, BioPAD Trust, and the Advanced Manufacturing Technology Strategy – were seven different empires run to all intents and purposes by demigods. One of the projects receiving funding through one of these entities concerned an electric car which had absorbed R600 million before someone decided the project was not working. What Mangena was asking me and the other people appointed to the board to do, was to build the agency from scratch.

When I was appointed vice-chancellor at UCT I went in with my eyes open. With TIA I went in blind. As board members we were non-executive appointments receiving a typical board fee. Yet we had to make sense of these entities, establish what they were doing, and bring them together in the agency to support the government's mandate to advance technology and innovation. There was no overlapping structure which bound the entities, there were no governance guidelines, there were tardy financial records when there were any records at all. Most of them had never been audited. To use that wonderful Afrikaans word: it was a gemors. A monumental mess.

What was supposed to have been an oversight job with five board meetings a year became a full-time job. The agency did not have a CEO so we had to appoint one. And then we had to consolidate the entities in terms of staffing and projects. Inevitably, when you consolidate there will be fallout. People were retrenched. Projects that had been funded without accountability and transparency were spiked. Systematically we cleaned house. This meant flying all over the country to perform executive duties, the sort of duties that are not usually required of non-executive board members. Equally importantly we had to establish a paper trail to find out what had happened to all the money that had been pumped into these entities when they were under the auspices of the Department of Science and Technology. Although this was a major undertaking and revealed bureaucratic ineptitude in a vital area for our development as a country, very little of this found its way into the press. But then, sadly, there is a lack of science reporting in the press and so a major story and the real history of the agency remains untold.

Finally we were able to track back some financial documents to 2002 and in the 2008/2009 financial year a partial audit was undertaken. By 2010 we had consolidated the accounts of the entities and a new CEO was appointed. Simphiwe Duma had been the CE and Chief Engineer at Psidot Technology Holdings (Pty) Ltd (Psidot Technologies), and also

Chief Engineering Consultant at Lebone Engineering (Pty) Ltd. He was trained at MIT with a string of qualifications from the UK and South Africa, and I was pleased that he decided to do his national service with the agency. That year, the 2010/2011 financial year, we inevitably received a qualified audit. We were assisted by Treasury and the Accountant General to work through a long list of procedural matters which ensured that in the 2011/2012 and 2012/2013 reporting periods the agency received two clean audits. However, it has to be pointed out that the strict criteria of the Public Finance Management Act were ill suited to the work done by the agency. For an institution concerned with investing in innovative projects where there was no way of knowing the outcome, financial reporting mechanisms should allow greater flexibility. It was important to upgrade the agency to a status where it was free to pursue innovative projects – innovative technology cannot thrive in a rigid accounting structure.

As I expected, the housekeeping undertaken at the agency was to have repercussions. Among those retrenched there were bound to be many disgruntled by this outcome. Among some of those were a few who considered themselves whistleblowers and when my term on the board ended in March 2013, they agitated for the new board to institute a forensic audit. Despite two clean audits I had apparently acted in ways that undermined good governance. Also I had apparently not monitored Duma's foreign trips, many of which were undertaken to establish partnerships with similar agencies that resulted in internships for young people at technology institutions in Europe and North America.

Yet when I left the agency's board I was optimistic about the future of that institution, and I still am.

Chapter 34

Mobilising against the fear

THERE WAS NO ALTERNATIVE BUT TO VIEW THE CALL FOR a forensic audit by the TIA board as harassment. In February 2013 I had announced the formation of Agang as a political party which brought a new dimension to the political landscape. As new as it was, Agang was a threat because here was an alternative for those thirteen million people who had failed to go to the polls in the last election, let alone the five million who had gained voting age in the interim. Among those eighteen million were huge numbers of the disenchanted and the disillusioned who were tired of the prevailing vacillations and corruption of the ruling party. Agang, it seemed to me, was the product of my campaign for active citizens come full circle. And although I had carefully avoided the cut and thrust of party politics all my life, I had reached a point where I felt I had no alternative but to step into that bruising space. I was after all a street fighter. Besides, I was invested in this country, both in its present and its future. I had grandchildren and I wanted them to live here.

The movement towards Agang can be seen in my engagement with the corporate world, with government – particularly my involvement in establishing TIA – and with various NGOs. A significant development here had been the formation of Letsema Circle Trust in 2010. This was a practical attempt at guiding people towards becoming active citizens. I had long believed that South Africans were so passive and accepting of unaccountability, non-transparency and sheer bad behaviour by their leaders because they had no experience of being citizens of a democracy. Under apartheid white people had been as fearful as black people and now both groups had gone back into the same defeatist mood. Letsema Circle planned to show people what they could do to change the circumstances of their lives through collective action and healing and by building trust through conversations.

The circle is an indigenous idea. People sit in a circle and get to know one another and explore the nature of their issues and what expertise they have to solve their problems. In short, it is collective action. There was nothing new here. We had used this tactic during the struggle and there were plenty of models internationally where similar procedures had worked effectively. Crucial to the process is to acknowledge the state of woundedness of the participants and to move them from this to a position of self-worth and dignity.

We started a Letsema Circle project in the Eastern Cape and mobilised people in four districts – Intsika Yethu, Mqanduli, Buffalo City, Duncan Village and Uitenhage. Initially it was very exciting. Finance was raised from various foundations and we even had a memo of understanding with the Department of Health in the Eastern Cape. I had this strong belief that if you could mobilise people to feel good about who they were and how they could take the future into their own hands, then they became less of a burden on the health system. One of the practical problems of the Eastern Cape was that there were no jobs. Consequently there was no money to buy food, so people had to create sustainable agricultural practices in order to feed themselves and their children.

During the time when Matanzima was in power in the then Transkei under the 'Bantu homeland policy', massive irrigation systems were initiated in some districts in the Eastern Cape. It was said to be the largest irrigation attempt in the southern hemisphere. The systems were in some cases never completed, and in other cases had broken down over the years. Whatever the situation they had been spewing forth water, wasting a precious resource. If these systems could be repaired and used as originally intended, vast areas could be irrigated and agriculture would be stimulated. To achieve this end we talked to the people in these areas. We talked to the chiefs. We talked to the Department of Rural Development. Everybody was determined to make these systems work.

Yet sadly, in the end the money that had been promised never materialised. In fact, R10 million was given to Bulelani Ngcuka and his partners to help them build a dairy farm in Ncora supplying milk to the privately owned Sunningdale Diary. The disappointment among those who hoped to benefit from the irrigation scheme was devastating to witness.

It was then that I realised that what I was confronting was bigger than I had anticipated. You could mobilise ordinary poor people, but ultimately they could not prevail against what I saw as a culture of patronage and impunity. This required national mobilisation.

The realisation led me to our next step: to form the Citizens Movement for Social Change. We had the moral backing of people such as Archbishop Emeritus Desmond Tutu, former Science and Technology minister Mosibudi Mangena, former UCT vice-chancellor Professor Njabulo Ndebele and businessman Bobby Godsell. I felt that we had to acknowledge the mistakes made in the past eighteen years of democracy. I felt that we had made an unwise political decision to avoid addressing the wounds caused by socioeconomic and human rights violations. Nor were we paying any attention to the ongoing humiliation of poor people in our unequal and status-conscious society. Many of us had turned our attention away from public life and occupied ourselves with material and other personal interests. We had become a nation preoccupied with accumulating wealth as a status symbol. Worse, we were in a vicious cycle of self-loathing, dependency, supplication, apathy and self-sabotaging behaviours including suicidal lifestyle choices, looting of public resources by those meant to be public servants, the destruction of public property in the name of protest, and brutal violence at home, at work and in public spaces. It was time to make a change.

In April 2012 we set up offices in Rondebosch. It was my intention that the younger generation would drive the movement. My days of this kind of activism were over – or so I thought. Unfortunately the governing of the country was deteriorating rapidly. Nationally, things were going from bad to worse. I remember Hlumelo coming to me and saying, 'I can see what you are doing but until the political system changes you are just whistling in the wind.' This gave me pause. Here was my son saying to his 65-year-old mother, 'Go back into battle because my generation is not battle-ready. Too many of us are stuck in situations where we have a lot to lose. You have the credibility and the profile which we lack.'

Ironically, I was at a point where I was anticipating stepping back from public life. My dream of writing, reading and travelling loomed large in my plans for my next five years. After a period where my sons had been involved in their own lives, we had in recent years revived old family traditions of travelling together. We had holidayed in Greece and Turkey in 2011 and in Spain in 2012. My five-year plan was to do more of this and to play with my grandchildren as they came along. What Hlumelo was now asking of me changed everything.

Taking the decision to move from active citizen to a party politician was difficult. It was so counter to how I imagined myself. I was not a public figure. Even in the Black Consciousness days, although I was part of the inner core, I was not in the front line. I worked behind the scenes. I worked at a practical level of establishing models for mobilisation, of encouraging people to take charge of their lives. So for me this was a jump into an area I had always avoided. It was a leap of faith.

But when I look back on the decision, I wonder what choice there was. I knew that nothing would change until the political dispensation changed. And this was a frightening realisation. We, as a people, were paralysed with fear. We have always had too much respect for authority. From precolonial times through the centuries of colonialism, through apartheid and into the present, we have been too subservient. Even today, with a constitution for protection, we are not active citizens. As I discussed the political situation with people what alarmed me was their reluctance to get involved. People were afraid of losing or damaging their businesses if they were seen to be politically involved. They worried about their private lives. NGOs were afraid of losing funding. The icy hand of the tripartite alliance (the ANC, COSATU and the SACP) meant that even nurses and teachers, who bore the brunt of poor governance, were intimidated into defending the ruling party's position.

Thus, what choice?

As Hlumelo put it, 'You have five more active years. When you're in your 70s you won't have the energy.'

What choice?

I had to take the leap of faith.

Agang

M Y DECISION TO LEAP WAS NOT A SPUR OF THE MOMENT decision but more a gradual shift in my thinking. There were times when I said yes, and then times when I thought, no, you're not ready. Since my return from the World Bank, Helen Zille had been trying to persuade me to join the Democratic Alliance. In the middle of 2012 I started talking seriously to the DA but I was wary of simply slipping into the position of leader of the DA, a position they were offering. At first I thought the prize was an agreement with the DA on a way of transforming politics in South Africa, an idea which Helen Zille had already spoken about.

We came very close to attaining this position but in the end I felt the DA people failed to understand the extent to which the country needed to change. A prime example was the situation with Cape Town. For seven years the DA had been running the city yet there were still squatter camps. I could not understand why. I believed that we were capable of more than accepting the inevitability of squatter camps. Why did we accept the adage that the poor would always be with us? Was this not admitting defeat? Was this not saying that we were trapped in a mindset that reflected the worst of apartheid and colonialism?

My book *Conversations with My Sons and Daughters* had gone through five prints in its publication year, 2012, and another reprinting in 2013. This told me something. There were a number of people interested in exploring alternatives that were not offered by the current political parties. As I met with young people I heard a refrain: we want to take up the challenge confronting us, we want to be more active and engaged but we do not have the platform. We will not vote for the ANC because of their corrupt, autocratic ways, nor will we vote for the DA because we know they do not understand the transformational challenges facing the country.

With these comments foremost in my mind I went back to the DA. I did not believe that the English-speaking white supporters of the DA understood the inequities visited on the majority in the country and the consequences of their perpetuation for the quality of our democracy. Some, including Hlumelo, would argue that the political settlement of 1993 allowed white privilege to remain unchallenged. Hlumelo calls it the 'Great Fraud' that let white people escape redressing the socio-economic consequences of apartheid. I felt the DA was complacent, trapped in their inability to realise that poverty could be eradicated.

Eventually my discussions with the DA reached a point where we agreed on the principles: most importantly, that the economy needed to be restructured. We agreed we needed to work together. The DA was an established machine but it needed to be repositioned. And repositioning meant more than rebranding the DA. This problem would not be solved by my presence as leader of that party. My presence would not obliterate the misgivings of the majority of black people.

Take Malusi as an example. He grew up playing with Helen Zille's children. He was always welcome in their household. He did not doubt for a moment that Helen Zille was committed to a better South Africa. Yet he told me that he would rather die than vote DA. How often would this sentiment not be repeated across the country? So what would be achieved by my joining the DA or even joining a rebranded DA? Nothing.

Clearly what was needed was a new platform. If the DA were to be part of that platform they had to agree to undertaking a complete re-alignment of South African politics. It would involve the smaller parties, but it was more than simply a matter of absorbing them. The DA were dismissive of the smaller parties – for good reason, as many of them were dying parties – but the element they did not understand was the power of symbolism. Just because a voter was disillusioned with Cope, for example, it did not mean that this person would believe in the DA. I suggested that if we were to launch a new initiative that included the DA then I should do it alone. This way the DA would be seen as part of the initiative rather than the manipulating power behind a black figurehead. If Helen Zille and I did it in tandem people would see the new initiative as the DA in drag and that would not solve the fundamental issue of a people's psyche that had long been wounded by white racism. They were afraid of white racism. Polling statistics showed that 60% of black people believed that if the DA won an election they would reinstitute apartheid. The DA dismissed this as nonsense but my experience was that this was what most people believed. Either you denied those beliefs or you created an initiative that made those beliefs irrelevant.

We moved from this position to one where I would launch Agang and woo the smaller parties until they felt comfortable in the new party. After that the DA would join and we would then announce this powerful new party. That was the theory, but there is a wide gap between theory and practice, especially in politics. It was not to be. However, Agang went ahead and approached the other parties.

While this strategy was important we realised our biggest opportunity lay in the disenchanted and the young. As I've mentioned, thirteen million did not vote in the 2009 election and since then a further five million young people had reached voting age. The disenchanted and the disillusioned were everywhere. I had talked with them in areas around Cape Town, in KwaZulu-Natal, in Gauteng, in Limpopo. Wherever we had gone, we had sought out – and found many – who had been further marginalised over the last two decades.

Perhaps one of the most telling meetings I had was with a group of women living in the bush beside a squatter settlement in KZN. They had nothing, the told me. They had no hope. They were waiting for death. But you have children, I replied. What about your children? They told me that they had to hire a taxi to get their children to a school many kilometres away. Often they did not have the taxi fare which meant the children missed school. They said their children's safety when travelling was in the hands of God.

This conversation haunted me. I sensed that the mood among most poor people was despairing. There were some who still had hope but they were the minority.

When I launched Agang in February 2013, I said that I saw a great future for our country. One in which we finally realised true freedom for all. Freedom from poverty, crime and corruption. A job, a home, a life of dignity. I said that I was inspired by a passion for freedom and a burning ambition to aim higher. To expect excellence in education, in healthcare, and in policing. To restore integrity to public life and pride to public service. To restore the trust between citizens and their leaders. When I said this I was many months away from meeting those women in the bush but I was talking about them, about returning them to the life of our nation.

What was most rewarding in the months that I toured the country talking about Agang and our vision was how groups of people that we had not even thought to approach came to us. We met with leaders of the Greek community, of the Chinese community, of the Indian community where, in Chatsworth, there was so much anger and despair. We met with groups of farmers, groups of business people who called us to meetings they had arranged. I recall one such breakfast meeting in Kloof where some seventy business people had gathered. These were middle-class people whose children were all in local private schools. Many of those children had been brought along to the breakfast. They were traditional DA voters but they no longer believed that the DA was equal to the tasks facing the country. At the end of the meeting they told me that this was the first time that they had been given any hope that the country could change. The term they used was a flicker of hope. I realised it was Agang's challenge to turn that flicker into a flame.

This, of course, placed a responsibility on the Agang leadership to mobilise the resources to keep that hope alive. Fortunately these responsibilities, which could also be seen as burdens, were not considerations that kept me awake at night. Once I set myself on a course I proceed without wavering. And so it was with Agang. But what was different now from my experience at UCT and in the World Bank was how others came forward to help. People left senior jobs to work for Agang. Where I had started out with just three people when Agang was launched, within five months we had a team of thirty that included volunteer fundraisers, brand marketers offering their services for free, people willing to canvass wherever there was an opportunity. There was enormous goodwill.

But while Agang would quickly form itself into a political party, much is owed to the help I received from two people in particular. One was Zohra Dawood, a lawyer and historian, who had been with me when I formed the citizens movement. We had met when she was with the Open Society Foundation where she was executive director from 2001 to 2012, responsible for the development of policies and a strategic vision for the foundation. She had joined the foundation in 1999 after working in President Nelson Mandela's government as an advisor.

The other was Mills Soko, who had had a distinguished career through academe and government, culminating in his position as Associate Professor of International Political Economy at the University of Cape Town's Graduate School of Business. He was also the founding director of Mthente Research and Consulting Services, deputy chairperson of the editorial board of *New Agenda*, and a research associate of both the South African Institute of International Affairs and the Institute for

Global Dialogue. I had known Mills Soko from my days with Idasa, and then we reconnected through the citizens movement. When Agang moved from an idea to a reality he was one of the first I recruited.

As 2013 wore on we would daily have ANC members entering our offices to assure us of their support. The fear factor was still present; it was an element that would not vanish overnight, but I could tell that the more we succeeded in establishing our public profile the more it encouraged people to take a stand. A consequence of this was that I declared my financial net worth. My intention was to demonstrate my accountability. I wished to show that I had nothing to hide, especially as accountability and transparency were the foundation pillars of Agang. Agang stands for clean, competent governance as the key to restoring the promise of freedom. Corruption is a betrayal of that promise. It was soon obvious that this had been a good move. People were not interested in my financial affairs but they did want to know that I would not lie to them or hide matters from them.

Imagine if corruption could be stamped out. Each year it was estimated that some thirty billion rand was lost through corrupt practices. With clean and accountable government this money could go to provide schools, books for schools, it could improve the health system, provide more funds for policing, build houses, it could free up a stagnant economy. It was clear that the state had been captured by corrupt people and become a mafia state.

Some of the voices that were loud and insistent during the struggle years were those of our spiritual leaders. Yet with a few notable exceptions, my spiritual father Desmond Tutu being the most prominent among them, the spiritual leaders were quiet in the face of this corruption. To a degree they had been silenced by the blustering of the Mbeki government but what I could not understand was why they were ignoring the moral degeneration before their eyes. There were people walking the streets, or should I say strutting along the streets, who owed large amounts of tax. Why were these people not arrested? Why were these people not taken to court? This laxity showed the sort of government we had.

What was also worrying, and a factor that said something about political life here – although this practice was not uncommon else-where in the world – was the sudden necessity for me to have body-guards. Never before had this been a consideration. When soon after the founding of Agang I was advised to undertake a risk assessment, the finding was that I was now in a game with high stakes and therefore physically at risk. How convenient would it be if I had a little accident in my car? As the mysterious car accident was a factor of South African life under apartheid and was still a factor, my personal security had to be taken seriously. This was a sad reality of our political life.

Now I stand in my Camps Bay house and I gaze out at the sea. I can smell it. I can hear it. I am where I want to be. I am doing what I know is the right thing even if my dream of writing and reading and travel-ling has been, shall I say, deferred. In the coming years I want to watch my grandchildren grow up in this country. I want to play with them down there on that beach or in the red soil of our Limpopo home. I want them to continue living and thriving in a country where many have sacrificed so much so that they, and their generation, may have a better life.

I have seen much of the world and this is a country unmatched. It would be very sad if we were to lose it. I think now, too, of those women in the bush in KZN; they might have said they were waiting for death but they still scrimped and saved to get their children to school. In this, despite their despair, they saw a future. We cannot fail them.

All my life I have fought for this country. It has been and it remains a fight worth the fighting.

By the same author:

Ramphele, M. 2012. *Conversations with my sons and daughters.* Johannesburg: Penguin.

Ramphele, M. 2008. *Laying ghosts to rest: Dilemmas of the transformation in South Africa.* Cape Town: Tafelberg.

Ramphele, M. 2002. *Steering by the stars: Being young in South Africa.* Cape Town: Tafelberg.

Ramphele, M., Lock, M., Das, V., Kleinman, A., & Reynolds, P. (Eds.). 2001. *Remaking a world: Violence, social suffering and recovery.* Berkeley: University of California Press.

Ramphele, M. & Hawke, B. 2000. *Human rights and human development: Third annual Hawke lecture.* Adelaide: Bob Hawke Ministerial Library, University of South Australia.

Ramphele, M. & Council on Higher Education (South Africa). 2000. *Towards a new higher education landscape: Meeting the equity, quality and social development imperatives of South Africa in the 21st century.* Pretoria: Council on Higher Education.

Ramphele, M., Crush, J.S., McDonald, D., & Southern African Migration Project. 1999. *Immigration and education: International students at South African universities and technikons.* Cape Town: IDASA.

Ramphele, M. 1996. *Across boundaries: The journey of a South African woman leader.* New York: Feminist Press.

Ramphele, M. 1996. *Embracing the future: Address by Dr Mamphela Ramphele on the occasion of her installation as the 7th vice-chancellor of the University of Cape Town, 11 October 1996.* Cape Town: University of Cape Town.

Ramphele, M. 1995. *Mamphela Ramphele: A life.* Cape Town: David Philip.

Ramphele, M. 1995. *The affirmative action book: Towards an equity environment.* Cape Town: IDASA.

Ramphele, M., Antrobus, P., & Randall, J.S. 1994. *Women transforming societies: Sub-Saharan Africa and Caribbean perspectives.* Cambridge, Mass.: Radcliffe College,

Ramphele, M. 1993. *A bed called home: Life in the migrant labour hostels of Cape Town*. Cape Town: David Philip.

Ramphele, M. 1993. *Standards, The loaded term*. Cape Town: University of Cape Town.

Ramphele, M., Pityana, N.B., Mpumlwana, M., & Wilson, L. (Eds.). 1991. *Bounds of possibility: The legacy of Steve Biko and Black Consciousness*. Cape Town: David Philip.

Ramphele, M., Molteno, F., Simons, M., & Sutherland, M. 1991. *Committee of enquiry into sexual harassment, final report*. Cape Town: University of Cape Town.

Ramphele, M. 1991. *Education for non-racial democracy*. National Lecturers' Conference held at Hewat Training College, Athlone, 9-11 May 1991.

Ramphele, M. & McDowell, C. (Eds.). 1991. *Restoring the land: Environment and change in post-apartheid South Africa*. London: Pharos.

Ramphele, M., Okeke, E., Anderson-Manley, E., Eshete, A., & Obeng, L. (Eds.). 1991. *Women transforming societies: Sub-Saharan Africa and Caribbean perspectives*. Cambridge, Mass: Radcliffe College.

Ramphele, M. & Wilson, F. 1989. *Uprooting poverty: The South African challenge: Report for the second Carnegie inquiry into poverty and development in Southern Africa*. Cape Town: David Philip.

Ramphele, M. & Boonzaier, E. 1988. The position of African women: Race and gender in South Africa. In: Boonzaier, E. & Sharp, J. (Eds). *South African keywords: The uses and abuses of political concepts*. Cape Town: David Philip.

Ramphele, M. & Wilson, F. 1987. *Children on the frontline: A report for Unicef on the status of children in South Africa*. New York: Unicef.

Ramphele, M. 1986. *Zimbabwe, the lessons for us here in South Africa*. Cape Town: Southern Africa Labour and Development Research Unit.

Ramphele, M. & Ramalepe, R. 1984. *Rural health care: The tears and joy*. Cape Town: Southern Africa Labour and Development Research Unit.

Index

Abe Bailey Institute 86, 108
Abram, Goolam 79, 88, 118
Abramowitz, Carol 247
Adams, E.B. 99–100
African National Congress *see* ANC
Agang 283, 329, 334–340
Akahloun, Leila 325
Alexander, Neville 253
Amoore, Hugh 297
ANC (African National Congress)
  anti-pass
    campaign 46
  in exile 191, 224, 241, 245
  issue of traditional leadership 267
  unbanning 246
Anglo American Corporation 222, 283, 284, 285–286, 305, 323, 324
Anglo America Platinum 304–305
anti-pass campaign 46, 49
ASSECA (Association for the Educational and Cultural Advancement of Africans) 118
Australia 253–256
AZAPO (Azanian People's Organisation) 265

banning orders
  Mamphela Ramphele 162–166, 167–169, 172, 173, 175–176, 177–180, 204, 212
  restrictions 116–117
  Steve Biko 97, 115, 117, 127, 129, 130, 140, 141
  Winnie Mandela 128
Bantu Education 37, 67, 96
Bantu World 118
Baragwanath Hospital 67, 72, 123
BCC (Border Council of Churches) 148–149
BCM (Black Consciousness Movement) *see also* BCP
  banning orders on members 115–118
  banning of organisation 185
  emergence 82
  importance 240–242, 264–265
  maturation 86–88, 89, 90–91
  philosopy 58–9, 136, 137, 274
BCP (Black Community Programmes) 95–98, 115, 117, 129–130, 138, 181
  see also Zanempilo Community Health Centre

*A Bed Called Home: Life in the Migrant
   Labour Hostels of Cape Town* 230
Bekker, Philip 49, 73
Bermuda 251–253
Bethesda Normal College 15, 55–65
Biko, Bukelwa 113–114, 139–140
Biko, Hlumelo (son)
   childhood 203, 213, 214–215, 247,
      249, 288, 299, 309
   children 325
   knowledge of father 201–202
   marriage and divorce 325
   MR's pregnancy and his birth 174–
      175, 180, 181–183, 185, 186
   political views 332, 333, 335
   relationship with MR 271, 272, 310,
      310–311, 323
   in United States 320
   visit to Mandela 266
Biko, Khaya 125, 126
Biko, Lerato (daughter) 121–122, 123,
   124–126, 202
Biko, Lewatle (granddaughter) 325
Biko, Luthando Bantu (grandson) 325
Biko, Mamcete 143–144, 156, 180
Biko, Nkosinathi 115
Biko, Ntsiki 113, 115, 160, 184–185
Biko, Steve
   see also Biko, Hlumelo; Biko, Lerato
   banning (1973) 97, 115, 117, 127,
      129, 130, 140, 141
   critic of white liberals 80–81
   detention 154, 158, 159
   detention and death 182, 183–185
   leadership 149–151

marriage 113, 115, 160
   MR's support as activist 87, 98–99,
      180–181
   relationship with MR 79, 107–108,
      109, 110, 113, 114, 117–118,
      120–123, 125, 132–133, 150, 151,
      159–161
   role in BCM 82, 86–88, 90, 91, 136,
      137, 265
   role in BCP 95–98, 115, 117,
      129–130, 138
   role in SASO 82, 88, 89, 110
Black Community Programmes *see* BCP
Black Consciousness Movement
   see BCM
Black Review 97
Border Council of Churches (BCC)
   148–149
*Bounds of Possibility: The Legacy of Steve
   Biko and Black Consciousness* 265
Brink, Chris 298
Bunting Institute 228–230, 243, 269
Buthelezi, Mangosuthu 137, 282–283

Calland, Richard 291
Carnegie Inquiry into Poverty and
   Development (Second) 209, 213,
   217–218
Carolus, Cheryl 241
Chikane, Frank 241
*Children on the Frontline: A Report for
   Unicef on the Status of Children in South
   Africa* 218–219
Christian Institute 95, 96, 115, 130,
   185

Circle Capital Ventures 323

Citizens' Movement for Social Change 331–332

Codesa (Convention for a Democratic South Africa) 276, 282

Coloured Labour Preference Policy 221

community life 127, 128, 143–149

Contralesa (Congress of Traditional Leaders of South Africa) 266, 267

Convention for a Democratic South Africa (Codesa) 276, 282

Conversations with My Sons and Daughters 334

Cooper, Jane 229

Cope 336

corruption 321, 339–340

Cry Freedom 184–185

cultural traditions 18–20, 22–26, 27–30, 42, 43–45

DA (Democratic Alliance) 334, 335–336, 337–338

Daily Dispatch 136, 137, 174, 179

Davidson, Barry 305

Dawood, Zohra 338

De Beers 222, 283

Defiance Campaign 49

De Klerk, F.W. 246, 282–283

Democratic Alliance *see* DA

Development as Freedom 311

Duane, Thomas 169, 181, 183–184, 187, 195–196

Duba, Langa 88

Duma, Simphiwe 327–328

Dutch Reformed Church 12, 15, 17, 25, 47–50, 60, 64

Eglin, Colin 252

Elberts, Liz 199–200, 200–201

Equal Opportunity Research Project 274–275, 276

Federal Theological Seminary 130, 138

Ford Foundation 222

Fortune, Hester 98

Gandhi, Ela 90

gender equity 224, 225–226, 229, 267, 275, 306–307, 314–315

gender roles
domestic 27–30, 207–208, 210–211, 230–237
professional 238–240, 242

Gevers, Wieland 295, 298–299

Godsell, Bobby 286, 331

Gordimer, Nadine 241

Graduate School of Business 303

Gray, Allan 303

Guguletu 214–216, 220, 221, 226–227, 269

Haigh, Bruce 198, 210, 253, 255

Happy Valley Clinic 89

Hartzenberg, Ferdie 253

Harvard University 228–230, 289

Haya, Nohle *see* Mohapi, Nohle

HDA (Western Cape Men's Hostel Dwellers' Association) 221–222, 224–226

Helen Frantz Hospital 11, 20

Hope, Anne 94

Horwood, Owen 82

ICCO (Interchurch Organisation for Development Cooperation) 139, 175, 187
Idasa (Institute for Democracy in South Africa) 290–291, 320
IDT (Independent Development Trust) 280–283, 285, 289
Institute for Democracy in South Africa *see* Idasa
Institute of Race Relations 97
Interchurch Organisation for Development Cooperation *see* ICCO
Ithuseng Community Health Centre 190, 191–192, 196, 204

James, Wilmot 290, 320
Jordan, Baba 171
Jwili, Patrick 76

Kagiso Trust 280
Kantor, Brian 293–294, 295, 296
Kente, Gibson 155
Khoapa, Bennie 96, 97, 98, 129, 135, 138, 140, 181
King Edward VIII Hospital 110–111, 115, 118, 119
King, Martin Luther, Jr 85, 148, 150
King, Ted 248, 271, 272
Kliptown Congress of the People 49
Kraai, Nomsisi 95
Krafchik, Warren 291
Kranspoort Mission Station 17, 21, 31, 32–33, 39–40, 47–50, 60, 68
see also Dutch Reformed Church
Krantzplaas 21, 51
Kruger, Jimmy 172, 197

Kussell, David 221
Kutumela, Miriam Mokgadi 53

Laka, Moloko 64
Langa 213–214, 221
Laying Ghosts to Rest: Dilemmas of the transformation in South Africa 323
Lekota, Terror 241
Lenyenye 177–180, 185–186, 187–189, 193–195, 196, 199, 204–205
Letsema Circle Trust 329–331
liberal politics (white) 79, 80, 81, 241
Livingstone Hospital 118, 119–120, 204, 207

Mabaso, Mamotšatši (aunt) 123
Machel, Graca 312
Mafole, Tomeka 97
Mafuna, Bokwe 99, 115
Mafuna, Leah 187
Mafungu, Victor 107–108
Magele, Malusi (son)
  birth 202–204
  childhood 208, 213, 216, 249, 288, 320
  education and career 312, 325–326
  political views 335
  relationship with father 310
  relationship with MR 309, 321
  visit to Mandela 266
Magele, Sipo (husband) 202, 204, 206–207, 208, 209–211, 212–213, 310
Magele, Thami 310
Mahlaela, Malesela Thomas (uncle) 14, 260

Mahlaela, Matlala Aletta (Mamphela)
(maternal grandmother) 12–13, 14,
17, 20, 74
Mahlaela, Moseto Moses (uncle) 14
Mahlaela, Ramadimetsa Salphy see
Mogomotsi, Ramadimetsa
Mahlaela, Sethiba Michael (maternal
grandfather) 12, 25
Mai, Angela 130–131
Mamorobela, Nkabati 178
Mandela, Nelson
MR's move to World Bank 312
release from prison 244, 250
support for MR 263–265, 265–267,
288, 291–292, 303
Mandela, Winnie 128, 172, 219
Mangena, Makgatla 178, 185, 207, 309
Mangena, Mosibudi 324, 326, 331
Mapisa-Nqakula, Nosiviwe 320
Martin, John 297, 307
Mashalaba, Ntsiki see Biko, Ntsiki
Mashalaba, Vuyelwa 79, 84, 95, 113, 114
Matshoba, Deborah 95
Matsipa, Joel 108
Mbanjwa, Thoko 138, 154, 159, 198
Mbeki, Govan 241–242
Mbeki, Thabo 224, 312, 320, 321, 324
Mediclinic 323, 324
Meetse-a-Bophelo Hospital 165–167,
169–170
Mgulwa, Ben 79
migrant labour
from Kranspoort 49, 50
hostels 213, 214, 221–222, 224–226,
229–230, 286

role of mining industry 284
support for families 40–41, 43
migration analysis 319, 320
The Mind of South Africa 236
Mkhatshwa, Smangaliso 170
Mmabane, Dick (husband) 70, 72–73,
75, 103–110, 111–113, 114
Mmabane, Ellen (sister-in-law) 111
Mmabane, Machipi (mother-in-law)
103–104, 107
Moerane, M.T. 118
Mogomotsi, Ramadimetsa (aunt) 15, 46,
75, 106
Mogomotsi, Rosemary (cousin) 109
Mogomotsi, Solly (uncle) 46
Mogooane, Greta 65
Mogotlane, Klaas 88
Mohapi, Mapetla 118, 130, 137, 148,
152–153
Mohapi, Nohle 118, 132, 152, 191
Mohuba, Lelau 204
Mokgashi, Mapula 178
Mokgashi, Matthews 178
Mokoape, Aubrey 79, 87, 88
Mokoape, Keith 85
Mokoka, Clement 91
Molaba, Khoadi 76
Moletsane, Nontobeko 133, 213
Moletsane, Thami 213, 214
Molobi, Eric 280
Molokoane, Mphika 64–65
Moodley, Jayshree 118
Moodley, Strini 88
Mooney, Fr 168, 169–170, 172, 175,
178

Moran, Cliff 295
Morobe, Murphy 241
Moseneke, Dikgang 252
Moshakga, Pauline 33, 53
Motau, Helen 66
Mpukumpa, Johnson 222
Mpumlwana, Malusi
  activist 85, 118, 125
  detention 153, 198–199
  marriage 159
  naming of Hlumelo 186
  role in BCM and BCP 97, 130, 138,
    141–142, 148, 265
Msauli, Dubs 144, 150, 153
Mt Coke Mission Hospital 123–124,
  130, 131–132, 132–133, 139
Mtintso, Thenjiwe
  activist 95, 150, 241
  detention and banning 154, 158–159,
    171
  employee at *Daily Dispatch* 137
  support for MR 180, 183
Mvovo, Mxolisi 121, 138, 153, 168
Mvovo, Nobandile (Bandie) 121, 122,
  123, 154, 156, 186, 191–192
Mxenge, Griffiths 153

Naidoo, Jay 241
National Union of South African Stu-
  dents *see* NUSAS
Naudé, Beyers 95, 130, 212, 241
Ndamse, Nobantu 138, 141
Ndebele, Njabulo 331
Ndzengu, Mziwoxolo 133, 171, 175
necklace murders 146, 216, 219

Nedbank 324
Nengwekhulu, Harry 92, 115, 265
Nepad (New Partnership for Africa's
  Development) 321
New Farm community 89–90, 91
Ngcuka, Bulelani 331
NGO sector 324
Ngubane, Ben 79, 81
Nhlapo, Welile 97
Njwaxa Home Industry 138–139
Nkathazo, Super 222, 225
Nongauza, Beauty 133
NUSAS (National Union of South Afri-
  can Students) 79, 80, 81, 115, 136
Nyanga 221
Nzimande, Blade 300

O'Connor, Cyril 304–305
Ofcolaco Mission 168, 170–171, 175–
  176, 195
Ogilvie Thompson, Julian 285
Old Mutual 283, 284, 285, 286–287,
  324
Open Society Foundation 338
Oppenheimer, Harry 288, 305–306, 312
Owada, Hisashi 311

PAC (Pan Africanist Congress) 46, 87,
  246, 252
Palweni, Chapman 79
Pan Africanist Congress *see* PAC
Pandor, Naledi 324
Paton, Alan 241
Pemba, Xola 119
Peteni, Lester 214

Pityana, Barney
  activist in SASO and BCM 86, 88–89,
    94, 245n32, 265
  detention and banning 115, 116, 121,
    122, 128
Pityana, Dimza 121
Pityana, Loyiso 115
police *see* security police
Public Information Centre 290–291,
  291–292
Puka, Morongwa 181, 187

Radebe, Nomangisi 121
Rakgale, Leo 173
Ramalepe, Lazarus Lekgolo 193, 196
Ramalepe, Mankuba 187–188, 193
Ramaphosa, Cyril 241, 251–252
Ramgobin, Mewa 90
Ramphele, Letladi (nephew) 259, 261
Ramphele, Mamakiri (sister-in-law) 259,
  261
Ramphele, Mamphela Aletta
  see also Biko, Hlumelo; Biko, Lerato;
    Magele, Malusi
  Agang 283, 329, 334–340
  birth and childhood 11–12, 18, 21–
    22, 26, 30–31, 32–54
  detention and banning 153–159,
    162–166, 167–169, 172, 173, 175–
    176, 177–180, 204, 212
  education 33, 37, 55–71, 158
  health 243–244, 247–250, 304, 316–
    317
  identification with Steve Biko 235–
    237

marriage to Dick Mmabane 70, 72–
  73, 75, 103–110, 111–113, 114
marriage to Sipo Magele 202, 204,
  206–207, 208, 209–211, 212–213
medical career 115, 118, 119–120,
  131–132, 133–136, 137, 139–140,
  144–145, 187–189, 191–192, 209,
  220, 268–269
medical studies 75–78, 89–90, 98,
  99–101, 110–111, 199
political activism 79–85, 87, 89–90,
  91–95, 98–99, 111, 118, 130–132,
  136–137, 140–141
relationship with Steve Biko 79, 107–
  108, 109, 110, 113, 114, 117–118,
  120–123, 132–133, 150, 151, 159–
  161
Steve Biko's death 183–185, 198,
  199–201
UCT anthropology department 220–
  226
UCT at SALDRU 216–220
UCT deputy vice-chancellor 236, 239,
  240, 270–279, 288, 289, 291, 295–
  301, 310
UCT vice-chancellor 290, 291–294,
  303–308, 310, 312
work at Harvard 228–230
work at TIA 326–329
work in Lenyenye 187–189, 191,
  193–196
World Bank executive 311–316, 317–
  320
writings 91n14, 217–220, 230, 243,
  265, 323, 334

Ramphele, Mashadi Ramaesela Ruth (sister) 18, 20, 46, 47, 51, 62, 67, 104, 109, 122–123, 157, 185, 261

Ramphele, Mathabatha Alfred (brother) 18, 51, 61, 72

Ramphele, Matlala (niece) 261–262

Ramphele, Mbatha (cousin) 51, 109

Ramphele, Molepo (brother) 17, 74, 156–157, 162, 175, 185, 196

Ramphele, Oupa Phoshiwa (cousin) 22

Ramphele, Phoshiwa (brother) 17, 33, 34, 51, 260

Ramphele, Phoshiwa Nicodemus (paternal grandfather) 15, 17, 25, 26–27, 30, 51, 52, 109, 259

Ramphele, Pitsi Eliphaz (father)
background 15, 25
illness and death 67, 68, 72, 73–74
member of Dutch Reformed Church 47–49, 50–51, 60
relationship with MR 34–35, 36, 259
teacher and principal 15, 17, 25–26, 36–37, 41, 47
visits to Uitkyk 21–22, 26, 27

Ramphele, Ramaesela Christina (paternal grandmother) 9, 15, 23–25, 26, 27, 29–30, 51, 52, 259

Ramphele, Ramaesela Ruth Tsheola (paternal great-grandmother) 15–16, 17–18, 25, 26, 33, 34, 36

Ramphele, Rangoato Rehab (nee Mahlaela)(mother)
background 11–12, 13–15, 25
care of Lerato 123, 125

challenging of rigid rules 27, 28, 29–30
domestic competence 30, 34, 35, 35–36
family home in Krantzplaas 21, 51
husband's death 73–75
supportive mother to MR 179, 185, 186, 195, 205, 207, 260, 262

Ramphele, Sethiba Michael (brother) 18, 34, 51, 52, 188, 207, 211, 259–262, 289

Ramphele, Thomas (brother) 73, 172–173

Rees, John 95, 135

Russell, David 117

SACC (South African Council of Churches) 95, 96, 135, 148, 191

SACP (South African Communist Party) 46, 241–242, 246

SALDRU (Southern Africa Labour and Development Research Unit) 216–217, 220

Samela, Voti 138

Sangotsha, Pumla 154

SASO (South African Students' Organisation) 81, 82, 86, 88–89, 91, 92, 93, 94, 110, 111, 115, 130

Satchwell, Kathy 212

Saunders, Stuart 271, 272, 273, 276, 277, 288, 291, 292, 294, 295, 296–297, 297, 303

Schlebusch Commission 115, 117

Sebe, Charles 129

security police

attitude 127–129, 154, 174, 175, 177, 179, 189–191
treatment by 50, 121, 130, 152, 153, 157, 158, 162–166, 215
Segal, Nick 303
Seipei, Stompie 219
Seko, Matsela 166, 170
Sen, Amartya 311
Serote, Mongane 241
Setotolwane High School 60, 65, 68, 73, 260
Sibeko, Temba 148–149
Sibisi, Charles 79
Sillen, Andrew 303–304, 304–305
Soko, Mills 338–339
Solombela, Seolo 85, 145, 154, 159
Sotomela, Nomvume 227
South African Communist Party see SACP
South African Council of Churches see SACC
South African Students' Organisation see SASO
Southern Africa Labour and Development Research Unit see SALDRU
Soweto riots (1976) 152, 214
Sparks, Allister 236
SPROCAS 2 (Study Project on Christianity in Apartheid Society) 95–96
Standard Bank 323, 324
Stanton, Timothy 138, 198
Stephanus Hofmeyer School 17, 47
Steyn, Jan 283, 285
Stofberg Bible School 15, 16, 17
Strickland, Katherine 318

Stubbs, Aelred 156, 172, 173–174, 187, 207–208
Suppression of Communism Act (1950) 116, 122
Sutherland, Carla 275
Suzman, Helen 196–197, 197–198

Technology Innovation Agency see TIA
Terrorism Act 152, 153, 154
TIA (Technology Innovation Agency) 326–329
Tickeyline Village 169, 170–171, 172–173, 176, 178
Touborg, Margaret 228
traditional leaders 266–267
Tucker, Raymond 171–172, 197, 212
Turner, Rick 90, 91, 95–96
Tutu, Desmond 148, 191, 192, 208, 219, 248, 331

UDF (United Democratic Front) 244
Uitkyk 17, 21–22, 26, 30–31, 51, 73
United Democratic Front (UDF) 244
University of Cape Town
deputy vice-chancellor 236, 239, 240, 270–279, 288, 289, 291, 295–301
fundraising and Upper Campus Project 302–308
student seminar (Dec 1969) 86, 108
vice-chancellor 290, 291–294, 303–308, 312
work in Department of Anthroplogy 220–226, 300
work in SALDRU 216–220
University of Fort Hare 76, 88, 97, 130

University of Natal 69, 70, 71, 75–78, 81–82, 82–83, 84, 89, 305
University of the North 69, 70, 72, 73, 77, 83, 104–105, 110
Uprooting Poverty:The South African Challenge 217–218, 224, 243
Urban Foundation 214

Van den Bergh, Lein 175, 187
Van den Ende, Dr 182, 183, 186, 202–203
Van der Merwe, Koos 252–253
Van der Merwe, Lukas 47–50, 60, 68, 74
Verwoerd, Hendrik 66–67
Vorster, John 82

Walton, Tracy 228
Western Cape Men's Hostel Dwellers' Association *see* HDA
West, Martin 220, 277–278
Williamson, Craig 190, 191

Williamson, Lisa 190
Wilson, Francis 192, 209, 216–220, 222, 227, 232, 244
Wilson, Lindy 227
Wilson, Monica 220, 220–221, 223, 232
Wilson, Tim 192
Winterveld 91–93
Wolfensohn, Jim 311, 315, 316, 317, 318, 319
Woods, Donald 136–137, 174, 179
World 185
World Bank 311–316, 317–320
World University Service (WUS) 191

Zanempilo Community Health Centre 131, 133–136, 139–141, 143, 144, 305
Zenzile, Welcome 222
Zille, Helen 297, 303–304, 334, 335, 336
Zimele Trust 148